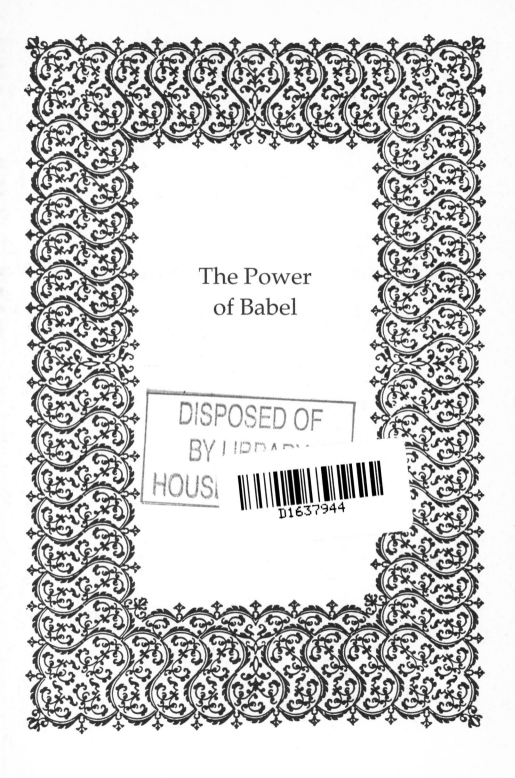

The Power
of Babel

Reviews of

Ali A. Mazrui

Cultural Forces in World Politics

'Mazrui delights in dualism and dichotomy, in pairs and parallels, and the paradoxes thereof. Bringing the south's point of view to the north, the east's to the west, and in return showing how the north and west's standpoint and behaviour have been culturally conditioned may begin to loosen hidebound beliefs. A book that makes one think...' Bob Marshall in *The Bookseller*, London

'... presents an alternative view of the world that does not see Europe or America as the only players in world affairs.' Rosalinde Yarde in *The Times Higher Education Supplement*, London

'... probably his most controversial yet...' *BBC World Service*, London

'What Ali Mazrui is best at is flying kites' David Maugham Brown in *Social Dynamics*, Durban

'... commands attention and merits respect simply for attempting to construct a full-blown thesis that might illuminate today's politics.' Kevin J. Kelly in *The Daily Nation*, Nairobi

'Many of the arguments which Mazrui advances will infuriate and offend principally because they are so manifestly true...' Guy Arnold in *The Journal of Southern African Studies*, Oxford

'Himself a cultural mongrel (he is an Afro-Asiatic westerner) Mazrui is, perhaps, better placed than any of us to use Afro-Islamic and Judeo-western prisms to discern the cultural forces that are at work in world politics.' William R. Ochieng' in the *Weekly Review*, Nairobi

'This is an erudite, encyclopedic and provocative essay.' Andrew J. Pierre in *Foreign Affairs*, New York

'Of all the academics writing on the Third World and particularly on Africa, Professor Ali Mazrui alone seems to have mastered the art of effortlessly picking out the gems from cavernous mines of history...' Anver Versi in *The New African* and *Al Qalam*, London

'The book will be controversial and will even give offence to some – notably in the comparison between apartheid and Zionism – but it will not and should not be ignored.' Keith Somerville in *International Affairs*, London

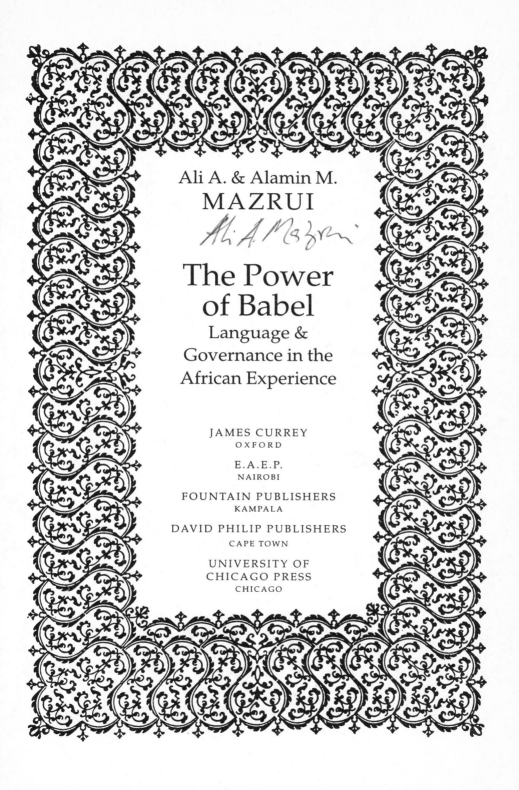

Ali A. & Alamin M.
MAZRUI

Ali A Mazrui

The Power
of Babel

Language &
Governance in the
African Experience

JAMES CURREY
OXFORD

E.A.E.P.
NAIROBI

FOUNTAIN PUBLISHERS
KAMPALA

DAVID PHILIP PUBLISHERS
CAPE TOWN

UNIVERSITY OF
CHICAGO PRESS
CHICAGO

James Currey Ltd
73 Botley Road
Oxford OX2 0BS, England

The University of Chicago Press
Chicago 60637
USA

in association with
The Institute of Global Studies
State University of New York
Binghamton, New York, USA

East African Educational Publishers
PO Box 45314
Nairobi

Fountain Publishers
PO Box 488
Kampala

David Philip Publishers (Pty) Ltd
PO Box 23408
Claremont 7735
Cape Town, South Africa

1 2 3 4 5 02 01 00 99 98

British Cataloguing in Publication Data
Mazrui, Ali A. (Ali Alamin),
   The power of Babel : language and governance in the African
   experience
   1. Communication policy – Africa 2. Africa – Languages
   3. Africa – politics and government
   I. Title II. Mazrui, Alamin, M. III. Institute of Global
   Cultural Studies
   306.4'4'096

   ISBN 0-85255-808-2
   ISBN 0-85255-807-4 Pbk

Library of Congress Cataloging-in-Publication Data
Mazrui, Ali Al'Amin.
   The power of Babel : Language and governance in the African experience / Ali
   A. Mazrui. Alamin M. Mazrui
      p.   cm.
   Includes bibliographical references and index.
   ISBN 0–226–51428–5 (alk. paper). -- ISBN 0–226–51429–3 (pbk. :
   alk paper)
      1. Africa--languages.   2. Sociolinguistics--Africa.   I. Mazrui:,
   Alamin M.   II. Title.
   P381.A35M39   1998
   409'.6--dc21   97-32844
                                                              CIP

The Arabesque border of fleurons used on the title page and the part titles
      was designed and assembled by Bruce Rogers for an edition of
      Sir Thomas More's *Utopia* (New York, Limited Editions Club, 1934).
   The Monotype designs were based on Arab tooling for book bindings.

Set in 9½/11 Palatino
by Long House Publishing Services
and printed in Britain by
Villiers Publications, London N3

To the memory of
Omari H.Kokole
with affection and gratitude

Contents

vii

Contents

PART III
Regional Studies

Contents

Alamin M. Mazrui & Ali A. Mazrui

About the Authors

Ali A. Mazrui has taught at universities in Great Britain, Uganda, Nigeria, Ghana, Malaysia, Egypt, Australia and the United States. In addition to his current position as Director of the Institute of Global Cultural Studies & Albert Schweitzer Professor in the Humanities, State University of New York at Binghamton, he holds the appointments of Albert Luthuli Professor-at-Large, University of Jos, Nigeria, Andrew D. White Professor at-Large Emeritus and Senior Scholar in Africana Studies, Cornell University, Ithaca, New York, Ibn Khaldun Professor-at-Large, School of Islamic and Social Sciences, Leesburg Virginia, and Walter Rodney Professor at the University of Guyana, Georgetown, Guyana. He is the author of over twenty books, including *Towards a Pax Africana* (1967), *The Trial of Christopher Okigbo* (1971), *Africa's International Relations* (1977), *The African Condition* (1980) and *Cultural Forces in World Politics* (1990). He has also been a BBC Reith lecturer and presenter of the acclaimed nine-part BBC/PBS television series, 'The Africans: A Triple Heritage'.

Alamin M. Mazrui, Associate Professor of Black Studies at Ohio State University, has a doctorate in linguistics from Stanford University where he began his teaching career. He has taught at universities in Kenya and Nigeria and has served as a consultant to non-government organizations in Africa on such subjects as language and urbanization and language and law. He has a special interest in human rights and civil liberties and has written policy reports on those subjects. He is also the author of five books, including a play and an anthology of poetry in Swahili, and *Swahili State and Society* (1995) with Ali A. Mazrui.

xi

Acknowledgements

This volume is greatly indebted to the late Omari H. Kokole, who was himself a gifted linguist who spoke several African languages. Dr. Kokole helped in editing all the chapters written by Ali Mazrui, and also made broader suggestions about the structure of the volume.

Dr. Parvis Morewedge, the publishing coordinator of the Institute of Global Cultural Studies, State University of New York at Binghamton, was instrumental in getting the language project off the ground. Dr. Thomas Utpuh, who was once at the same Institute and is now at Syracuse University, helped in the research for updating Ali Mazrui's chapters.

Most of the chapters in this volume are based on papers once presented at conferences or published in scholarly journals (See first page of the section on References for details about the sources). But by revising these articles and assembling them together as chapters in a single book, the authors hoped to bring the complex issues of language and governance in Africa into sharper relief.

INTRODUCTION
Africa's
Linguistic Legacy

Between
Expansionism & Nationalism

The linguistic balance sheet on the interplay between the indigenous and Western legacies in Africa so far has been decidedly in favour of European languages that came to the continent as part of the colonial cultural package. This linguistic state of affairs, we contend, has evolved as a result of two interrelated factors: originally, the failure of African societies to be expansionist enough in territorial terms, and later, the failure of African people to be nationalist enough in linguistic terms. Let us look at each of these factors in turn.

Words, numbers and nations

The literature about Africa is replete with references to the artificiality of its colonial borders. But what makes those borders particularly artificial is neither the multi-ethnic societies they have created nor the 'tribes' they have divided, regrettable as the consequences may seem. Even more artificial is the very concept of precise borders in Africa's 'traditional' cultures – and how the new culture of borders has related to the oral tradition, to African languages, to ethnicity and to the nature of conflict.

The culture of precise national borders presupposes a culture of precise measurements. And measurements of this kind normally presuppose numeracy which, in turn, is usually connected with literacy. Cultures of the oral tradition have tended to score low in numeracy as a rule.

Both illiteracy and innumeracy, of course, are partly a reflection of the pre-capitalist conditions that characterized much of the continent in pre-Islamic and precolonial times. The majority of sub-Saharan African societies before Islamization and Westernization did not engage in elaborate mathematical calculations. Many indigenous languages do not seem to have had native words for numbers beyond a hundred.

There were exceptions, of course, such as the Nile Valley from Ethiopia to the Mediterranean. Indeed, Beatrice Lumpkin has argued that Africa was the birthplace of mathematics:

1

Introduction

Wherever there are humans, there is mathematics because every language has number words and concepts of logic needed for mathematics – the words 'and' and 'or'. Since Africa is widely believed to be the birthplace of the human race, it follows that Africa was the birthplace of mathematics and science. (Lumpkin, 1985:103)

She denies too close a connection between numeracy and literacy, citing prehistoric evidence in the interlacustrine region of Eastern Africa:

> Before the beginning of time, people did record numbers. A fossil bone found near Lake Edwards, Zayre [sic] was carved in the year 8000[BC] to make a very early record of numbers that may be a multiplication table, a record of the phases of the moon, or even a game score. The tally marks carved in the Ishango bone show numbers 3, 6, a space, 4, 8, then, 10, 5, 5, 7 on one side. On the other side are 11, 21, 19, 9,11, 13, 17, 19. (Lumpkin, 1985:103)

While it is indeed true that basic counting of one's children, or cattle, or the number of trees on one's farm, has been widespread in preliterate societies, elaborate mathematical calculation outside literate cultures has been virtually unknown. By implication the oral tradition diminished the culture of calculation and measurement.

This preliterate culture which, at the same time, lacked an elaborate mathematical orientation may have sustained societies with a relatively limited surplus drive and an underdeveloped urge to accumulate. In other words, precapitalist Africans were simply not 'greedy' enough to be expansionist. There were, of course, a few empires scattered in precolonial African history. But most of these expansionist societies – builders of ancient Mali, Ghana and Songhay, for example – had been initiated into capital accumulation and the culture of writing and elaborate calculation through the process of Islamization.

Bertrand Russell once argued that civilization was born out of the pursuit of luxury. Adam Smith before him had argued that the wealth of nations was born out of the pursuit of profit. And Karl Marx was convinced that the march of history was activated by the pursuit of surplus. Was quantification a precondition in each case? Whether one pursued civilization, wealth or surplus, some minimum level of human greed was necessary. The question has arisen whether the majority of pre–colonial African societies were simply below that level of greed. Was Africa insufficiently calculating?

Among the consequences on the positive side was greater egalitarianism, especially in those African societies which did not become states. But underdeveloped acquisitiveness and greed can have 'negative' consequences as well – including a slower pace of innovation, a slower utilization of nature to meet society's economic needs, and less sophisticated forms of mathematical engineering and architecture. Outside Ethiopia and North Africa there are no precolonial African equivalents of the Taj Mahal, or the Forbidden City of China, or the Palace of Versailles. Precolonial Africa did not have adequate surplus drive to be able to leave such monuments to ancient luxury. No mathematics, no monuments!

It is true that climatic abundance and fertility of the soil might have contributed to this relative cultural complacency. If necessity is the mother of invention, abundance can be the mother of inertia. But is the relatively weak culture of calculation and measurement part of the explanation for the continuance of the weak surplus drive? If the oral tradition weakened Africa's numeracy and capacity to calculate, is the oral tradition one of the reasons why most precolonial cultures were inadequately greedy?

Once again we have to study culture as an intricate miracle of interdependent variables. Nomadic lovers of animals who pay no attention to juridical frontiers between political jurisdictions; cultivating lovers of land who are inadequately territorial; the absence of the written word weakening the culture of calculations; and a weak surplus drive with the oral tradition.

The colonial impact, and the culture of writing and mathematics that it fostered, have had wide-ranging consequences, of course. Into cultures inadequately driven by surplus, colonialism introduced capitalist greed without capitalist discipline, and helped to promote Western consumption patterns without Western productive techniques. By the time the colonial powers departed to return to Europe, what had started as inadequate African greed exploded into a frenzy of postcolonial African acquisitiveness. Western tastes had indeed taken root in Africa – but not Western skills. Was Africa experiencing calculation – or a culture of *miscalculation*?

Even if Russell was right that without the pursuit of luxury, elaborate civilization would have been impossible, it does not follow that *any* pursuit of luxury leads on to civilization. Post-colonial pursuit of luxury among African élites has been negative by both the African and Western criteria of civilization.

But there is one area of political life where African governments have kept national greed in check – the domain of territorial appetite. With one or two exceptions, territorial expansionism has not been a feature of post-colonial African behaviour. Such border disputes as those between Libya and Chad, or between Somalia and her neighbours, have had special circumstances.

One of the reasons for this continued restraint in territorial expansionism in Africa is related to the fact that independent African states were born at a time when the world was already bound by a new international ethos of 'respecting the territorial integrity' of other states. Well before the emergence of this new principle in inter-state relations, capitalist Europe had acquired other people's territories across the seas with insatiable appetite, introducing in the process its cultures, languages and political and economic systems. In this same period, however, much of Africa lacked the territorial greed to extend its influence even beyond the boundaries of ethnicity. Linguistically and otherwise, then, Africa not only became an easy prey of expansionist Europe, but its non-expansionism reduced the capacity of its own languages and cultures to resist the European linguistic penetration as well as to counter-penetrate other regions of the world.

Reduced political space for the exercise of territorial greed in the twentieth century, however, has also had certain consequences for the politics of nationhood in post-colonial Africa. And it is to the nature of these politics that we must now turn.

Nationhood: the tragedy of peaceful borders

It is one of Africa's glories that in spite of artificial borders which have split ethnic and linguistic groups, there have been very few border clashes or military confrontations between African countries. But it is also a terrible fact to acknowledge that one of the tragedies of the African state is that there has not been enough tension and conflict between states. The balance between external conflicts and internal conflicts has tilted too far on the side of the internal. The external borders have been too friendly. And as human history has repeated time and time again, civil wars often leave deeper scars, are often more indiscriminate and more ruthless, than are inter-state conflicts short of either a world war or a nuclear war (Licklider, 1993). The United States, for example, lost more people in its own civil war in the 1860s than in any other single war in its 200-year history, including Vietnam and the two world wars.

Moreover, the history of the nation-state in Europe reveals a persistent tendency of the European state to externalize conflict and thus help promote greater unity at home. A sense of nationhood within each European country was partly fostered by a sense of rivalry and occasional conflict with its neighbours. And the consolidation of the sovereignty of European states, too, was forged partly in the fire of inter-European conflicts. The Peace of Westphalia of 1648, often credited with the formal launching of the nation-state system, was signed after thirty years of European inter-state conflict (Lee, 1991).

What ought to be remembered, therefore, is that the state system which Africa has inherited from Europe was nurtured in the bosom of calculation, conflict and war. It can even be argued that, just as one cannot make an omelette without breaking eggs, one cannot build and strengthen statehood and nationhood without the stimulus of calculation and conflict. The only question is whether the conflict is with outsiders or with the state's own citizens. Post-colonial Africa is burdened disproportionately with internalized conflict – which is, at least in the short run, detrimental both to the consolidation of statehood and to the promotion of a shared sense of nationhood in the population.

One of Africa's post-colonial tragedies continues to be, paradoxically, that there have been no external wars for which to plan and calculate, and for which to invoke a sense of national purpose. And where there was a semblance of inter-African state conflict – as in the case of Ethiopia and Somalia in the 1970s and early 1980s – the regional conflict was almost overshadowed by the wider superpower rivalry between the Soviet Union and the United States. Excessive external participation in the conflict between Ethiopia and Somalia deprived the regional confrontation of any compensating value as a unifying force for either Ethiopia or Somalia. On the contrary, Somalia's defeat in the Ogaden struggle was the *coup de grâce* which helped to precipitate that country's descent into anarchy – without saving the Ethiopian government of Mengistu Haile-Mariam from military and political collapse (Ottaway, 1982).

In other words, when an inter-state African conflict is excessively a reflection of some wider rivalry between big powers, the inter-state conflict loses the compensating advantages of either consolidating local statehood or unifying a local sense of nationhood. Neither Ethiopia nor Somalia gained from their own conflicts of the 1970s and 1980s.

On the other hand, the politico-military disagreements between Nigeria and Cameroon in the 1990s about disputed islands are potentially unifying for both Nigeria and Cameroon. On the Nigerian side, the unifying potential would have increased if French troops were more visible in apparent defence of Cameroonian interests. Here were the beginnings of a culture of calculation and numbers.

Linguistic frontiers and national boundaries

Having lacked the impetus of external conflict, statewide nationalism in Africa is made more difficult by the weakness of loyalty to indigenous languages – a factor that in turn has facilitated Euro-linguistic penetration. The less nationalistic a society is, the more vulnerable it becomes to penetration from outside. The fact that most African languages south of the Sahara were unwritten before European colonization is one of the reasons for Africa's diluted commitment to their preservation. The national boundaries of most African states lack the underpinning of any national linguistic identity.

Linguistic nationalism is that version of nationalism which is concerned about the value of its own language, seeks to defend it against other languages, and encourages its use and enrichment (See Williams, 1994). Africans south of the Sahara are nationalistic about their race, and often about their land; and of course many are nationalistic about their particular 'tribe'. But nationalism about African languages is relatively weak as compared with India, the Middle East or France. In this generalization we include Africans in South Africa, a case to which we will return. If we are right, what are the reasons? We pursue the implications more fully below.

It is indeed relevant, but not adequate, to point out that most sub-Saharan national boundaries have created multilingual countries. Deciding which indigenous language to promote as the national language within those boundaries carries the danger of ethnic rivalry. This is perfectly true. Any move to make Hausa the national language of Nigeria could precipitate a national crisis in Yorubaland and Igboland.

But India too is a multilingual country. And language policies have sometimes provoked riots. The original constitutional ambition to make Hindi (a northern language) the language of all India understandably has met stiff resistance in the South. Compromises have had to be made. In spite of the presence of so many languages in India – and sometimes because of it – linguistic nationalism is one of the political forces in the land (Rao, 1979).[1]

Where African languages differ from India's is partly a matter of scale. While the three major Nigerian languages (Hausa, Yoruba, and Igbo) are spoken by some 20 million people each (Hausa more, others less), most African languages are spoken by far smaller numbers. In contrast, some Indian languages are spoken by up to a hundred million people. Hindi is spoken by several hundred million.[2] In a multilingual society, does the scale of the linguistic constituency contribute to nationalistic sensitivity in defence of the language? Let us look at this more closely later.

In addition to linguistic diversity and linguistic scale, there is the distinction between the oral tradition and the written. The overwhelming majority of sub-Saharan African languages belonged to the oral tradition until the late nineteenth and early twentieth centuries. There is no ancient written literature outside Ethiopia and the Islamized city states of East and West Africa. Without substantial written tradition, linguistic nationalism is slow to emerge, although there are exceptions, such as the linguistic nationalism of the Somali based mainly on the oral tradition (Laitin, 1977). The Somali culture is based on a genius of words but not of numbers.

The main Indian languages have a long written tradition, with ancient poets and many written philosophical treatises. Works of literature, written when most of Europe was still in the Dark Ages and maintained and transmitted over the generations by priests and scholars, are invaluable in promoting linguistic pride among the speakers of the language. These help to deepen a propensity for linguistic nationalism.

But the written tradition can include one additional element – *sacred* literature. Because most African languages were unwritten until relatively recently, those oral languages do not have sacred scripture. Sacred scripture is itself an additional fertilizer for linguistic nationalism. Linguistic nationalism among the Arabs has been influenced greatly by the Holy Book, the Qur'an, as well as by great Arab poets of the past.[3]

Finally, we must bear in mind that the humiliation of black people has been much more on the basis of their race than on the basis of their language. African nationalism is therefore much more inspired by a quest for racial dignity than by a desire to defend African languages.

All these are massive generalizations with a lot of exceptions. Some Ethiopians were literate and sophisticated long before the written word was common currency among the Anglo-Saxons in the British Isles (Bender, 1976). Large sections of the Tanzanian population today have shown nationalistic attachment to the Swahili language. They write not just letters to the editor but poems to the editor as a matter of course. Again, we shall explore the implications later in this book.

And yet Africans describe their countries as being 'English-speaking' and 'French-speaking' in spite of the fact that the proportion of speakers of these imperial languages is so small, and in a manner never encountered in ex-colonial Asia. One of the gross linguistic anomalies of post-colonial Africa, in fact, is that whole classes of countries are named after the imperial language they have adopted as their official language. We do constantly refer to 'Francophone Africa,' 'English-speaking Africa,' 'Lusophone Africa' and the like. Asia, too, was colonized; and yet nobody refers to 'Anglophone Asia' or 'French-speaking Asian countries'.

What, then, is the difference between Africa and Asia? It lies in the scale of political dependence on the imperial languages, linking them much more firmly to the African countries, and their very identities, than to the former Asian colonies of European powers. Business in government offices, in legislatures and judiciaries in much of sub-Saharan Africa is conducted primarily in European languages. Not only is the fundamental law still based on European principles, but the laws are expressed entirely in European languages. And in countries like Nigeria, Ghana, Mozambique, Zambia, Zimbabwe, Angola, Uganda, Senegal and Gabon all speeches addressed to the nation have to be given in the relevant European language. This is quite apart from the educational systems of sub-Saharan Africa, almost all of which are predicated on the supremacy of European languages as media of instruction, and some of which completely ignore indigenous languages as worthy topics of educational study.

It is in this sense that terms like 'Anglophone' and 'Francophone' Africa are appropriate – not because they describe how many people in those countries speak those languages, but because they describe the degree and perhaps nature of the lingo-cultural dependence in the societies concerned.

In any case, what is the alternative terminology? We know that there are real differences between countries previously ruled by Britain, countries previously ruled by France, and countries previously ruled by Portugal. When we are referring to them in the aggregate we could refer to them as 'former British' or 'former French' colonies – but, given a choice, Anglophone and Francophone Africa are likely to be preferred to 'former British Africa' and 'former French Africa'.

Of course, not all Francophone African countries are in reality former French colonies. On the contrary, the largest Francophone African country – the Democratic Republic of Congo (formerly Zaire) – is a former Belgian rather than former French dependency. And if in the course of the twenty-first century Congo (Kinshasa) is described as the largest French-speaking country in the world (larger than even

France), it would mean, in our sense of the term, that the population of Congo had by then outstripped that of France; that the political system of the Congo (in spite of the intrusion of English and Kiswahili) was still basically Francophone; that the French language was indeed finding a new world to conquer in equatorial Africa. In mineral wealth in the twenty-first century Congo (Kinshasa) may also be the richest French-speaking African country in the world – provided we do not simplistically reduce the concept of 'Francophone' to the numerical domain of number of speakers at a given moment in time.

What is significant for our purposes, then, is the idea that because sub-Saharan Africans are rarely strong *linguistic* nationalists, they are seldom resentful of their massive dependence on the imported imperial languages. And as long as this linguistic dependence continues to be a pervasive feature of the African condition, it would not be inappropriate to use the vocabulary of 'Anglophone', 'Francophone' and 'Lusophone' to describe different regions of the continent.

An African politician may speak six or more indigenous languages fluently. Yet, if he or she does not speak the relevant European language, he or she cannot be a Member of Parliament in the great majority of sub-Saharan African countries. We shall address this issue in greater detail in Chapter 9. As we indicate in that chapter, the official language of constitutions all over sub-Saharan Africa is European. Constitutions are therefore unintelligible to the majority of the population. In the great majority of African countries not a single African constitution has been translated into an African language. We shall explore the implications.

It is difficult to build a culture of constitutionalism in Africa if concepts like 'civil liberties', 'due process', 'independence of the judiciary', and 'habeas corpus' are never translated into indigenous languages accessible to ordinary citizens. Constitutionalism becomes foreign as a system partly because it is completely alien linguistically. Indigenous languages are treated as if they were still purely oral – 'unworthy' of the written heritage of constitutions. Dr. Hastings Banda spoke only English and could become president of Malawi. There is no example in sub-Saharan Africa of a president who is elected to the presidency without a European language.

Yes, linguistic nationalism is weak in Africa south of the Sahara. Surprisingly, the two greatest exceptions are two peoples who are otherwise vastly different from each other – the Somali and the Afrikaners. It is arguable that they are the only ones who are true linguistic nationalists in sub-Saharan Africa. They are very possessive, defensive and proud of their languages, and have regarded their languages as central to their cultural identity.

Do the similarities end there? The Somali are pre-eminently a people of the oral tradition, who did not even have an official orthography for the Somali language until 1972 when Siad Barre finally chose the Roman alphabet.[4] Some would argue that the Afrikaners have had only one hundred years of a written tradition. Afrikaans is widely regarded as a language which was largely oral until the nineteenth century.

The Somali have never attempted to impose their language on anybody else over the centuries. Afrikaans, on the other hand, is widely perceived by many South Africans not only as the language of the former oppressor but the actual instrument of oppression. Many South Africans believe that Afrikaans was forced not only on millions of school children but also on rural workers, peasants, broadcasting media, domestic employees, and simple neighbours in Afrikaans-speaking areas. Unlike the Somali language, Afrikaans was not simply defended against outsiders – it was imposed upon them. Did Afrikaners carry linguistic nationalism too far? Was the downgrading of the 'other' languages of South Africa unique?[5]

Afrikaners might argue that this was not different from the behaviour of other Europeans elsewhere in Africa. All Europeans had cultural arrogance towards indigenous African peoples for much of the twentieth century. On this issue the Afrikaners would be correct. But Europeans also differed in degree of their own linguistic nationalism. The French and Portuguese policies of assimilation – while in some respects radically different from apartheid's Bantu education philosophy – did converge with Afrikaner nationalism on the issue of *language*. They all put pressure on their subjects to learn their respective languages. The British imperialists were somewhat different. We hope to demonstrate that their policies of indirect rule allowed for considerable cultural and linguistic relativism. Indeed, British administrators and settlers within Africa sometimes distrusted the influence of the English language upon the natives.

If the Somali and the Afrikaners are the only genuine linguistic nationalists south of the Sahara, where does that leave those Black South Africans who are championing greater recognition of indigenous languages? If Black South Africans are like other Blacks on the continent, they are really defending racial dignity rather than linguistic purity or linguistic autonomy. Language becomes just another aspect of the defence of the race – and a valid aspect. The defence of the Black race requires a multi-faceted agenda, including language. This kind of 'race nationalism' also explains the quest for African languages among African Americans. But the focus for Blacks is racial dignity rather than linguistic aspirations (Mzala and Hoffman, 1990/91: 408–26).

But if African languages in South Africa are being defended for racial rather than linguistic reasons, does that make their defence less valid? The answer is 'No'. African languages do *demand* and *deserve* a much fairer deal on the African continent than they have so far received. One solution is to have Afrikaans declared an African language, with all the consequences. The resources in universities allocated to Afrikaans would go to Departments of African languages which from now on would include the heritage of Afrikaans.[6] The immense resources allocated to Afrikaans in the state-owned media would now go to African languages more generally, including Afrikaans. This would include current resources for publishing in Afrikaans and for the promotion of education in Afrikaans.[7]

The other solution would be to declare Afrikaans a non-African language. The question would then arise whether the country needed two official languages which were not African. Zaire was ruled by Belgium which had two European languages – French and Flemish. But Zaire adopted only one of them as its official language – French. Is Afrikaans the equivalent of Flemish in Zaire? Should Afrikaans be phased out as an official language – not tomorrow, but in the year 2008, a decade from now?

The third solution is to insist that Afrikaners are *sui generis* and unique; their language is neither African nor non-African, but a bridge between the two. The French claimed that *EurAfrica* was the association of African states with the European Union.[8] Afrikaners might claim that the real EurAfricans are Afrikaners. There was a time when they identified with *Africa* as a place but not with *Africans* as a people. They loved the land but not the people. Today the Afrikaners' love of Africa as a place is probably undiminished; but are they also learning to love Africans as people?

If they are, sooner or later the Afrikaans language has to decide whether it is indeed an African language – whatever the material consequences. After all, Somali linguistic nationalists are destitute and even desolate – but still love their language. Afrikaners may one day make the final transition from being *EurAfrican* to being bona fide *Africans* , accepting the consequences.

The struggle continues all over sub-Saharan Africa to lend linguistic coherence to artificial national boundaries. Somalia had found such coherence between nationality and language – but had no statehood to support them. South Africa has statehood but no linguistically coherent nationhood. The political gaps continue to yawn tragically.

Apart from the case of Somalia and the Afrikaners in South Africa, however, linguistic nationalism in much of Africa has continued to be relatively weak. And, as we pointed out at the beginning of this introduction, it is the combination of this weak linguistic nationalism and the non-expansionist history of much of Africa that made the continent vulnerable to increasing linguistic penetration by the more expansionist Western world. The result over the decades has been an imbalance in the global flow of languages, creating in Africa a complex and dynamic linguistic constellation. Aspects of this complexity and dynamism inspired the following chapters.

Notes

1. In the Indian case, for all practical reasons, the compromise has resulted in a situation in which English and/or Hindi coexist, at least for inter-province communication.
2. For the distribution and quantity of speakers of languages in our comparison, consult Bernard Comrie (1990).
3. Islam has effectively promoted Arabic far beyond its original home, and has had tremendous influence on the Arabic language. Consult Moshe Piamenta (1979).
4. A fascinating account of the development of the written Somali language may be found in Denis Herbstein (1991).
5. For a treatment of the whole issue of the different languages employed by the 'nations' of South Africa, consult Nxumalo Mzala and John Hoffman (1990/91).
6. We are greatly indebted to Dr. Peter Thuynsma for stimulation and guidance about the politics of language in post-apartheid South Africa.
7. Of course, during the apartheid regime, it is well known that both legally and financially the majority was systematically discriminated against.
8. France has had a unique relationship, both politically and culturally, with African countries. Consult, for instance, André Andereggen (1994).

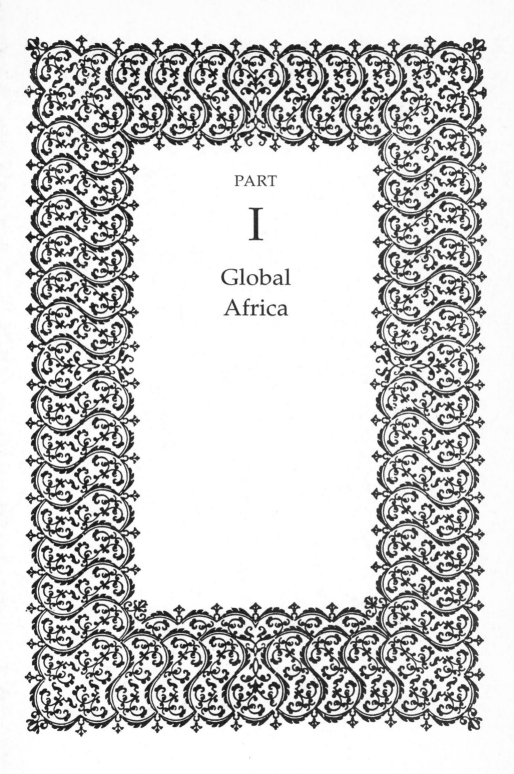

PART

I

Global
Africa

1
Language & Race
in the Black Experience

An African Perspective

One out of every five black people on earth has a European language for a mother tongue. The dominant European languages in the black world are English, French, Portuguese and Spanish. Dutch trails behind as the fifth Eurafrican language. It is found among people of mixed race in South Africa and in places like Surinam. The largest black nation outside Africa is in Portuguese-speaking Brazil.

French is more dependent upon the black world for its global status than English. While the majority of French-speaking people are white, the majority of French-speaking countries are black. Over twenty African countries have adopted French as the main language of national business. Italian has not been adopted as a national language in any African country, but it is widely understood among élites in Somalia, Ethiopia and Libya. As for the German language, it has a residual role in Namibia.

Although in Africa itself European languages are seldom mother tongues, it is one of the ironies of literary history that the first black winner of the Nobel Prize for Literature has not been an African-American or a Jamaican for whom English is the mother tongue, but a Yoruba-speaking Nigerian, Wole Soyinka, in 1986. Similarly, the most honoured black user of the French language in France has not been a black Frenchwoman or man (from, say, Martinique) for whom French is the mother tongue, but Leopold Senghor, the philosopher-poet and former president of Senegal.

Much more common than linguistic accolades for blacks from Europeans, however, is the link between languages and white domination over blacks. Our emphasis in this analysis will be especially on the African part of the black experience, though aspects of the conclusions are of much wider relevance.

The history of language in Africa in the twentieth century reflects closely the fact of continuity and change in African political, social, cultural, psychological, and economic realities. The period characterizes the consolidation of colonialism and racism with their far-reaching linguistic and cultural policies, the struggle for independence, the emergence of neo-colonialist trends and the rise of African self-consciousness in matters relating to the preservation and promotion of African national institutions.

In many ways the half-century before independence constituted a period of maximum threat to indigenous languages in Africa; and yet at the same time they were the years of codification, new orthographies, and literary output for some languages which were previously unwritten. African languages were threatened by colonial policies which gave a new emphasis to European languages in education and administration. And yet some of the major indigenous tongues acquired new orthographies based on the colonially imported Latin alphabet and were consequently better preserved in writing than had been possible in their days as purely oral tongues. Colonialism threatened the indigenous heritage by the promotion of European languages. And yet colonialism inadvertently helped the preservation of African oral legacies by the miracle of the written word. This chapter is partly about this interplay between the tongue and the pen, between the indigenous and the imported in the field of language in cultural transition.

Language policy and racial attitudes

European arrogance during the colonial period had two major components: the premise of a superior race and the premise of a superior culture. The balance betweeen racial arrogance and cultural arrogance varied from one imperial power to another. On the whole, the French were more culturally arrogant than the British, refusing to mix cultures in colonial schools and insisting on the supremacy of French civilization. The British, on the other hand, were more racially arrogant than the French, insisting on the segregation of the races between schools but permitting the mixture of cultures in the curriculum. It has been said that the French did not mind who made love with whom provided the preliminaries were conducted in impeccable French. The British did mind who made love with whom. Sometimes they minded who made love at all. It would therefore be a mistake to assume that these differing imperial powers, so distinct in their racial attitudes, would evolve the same language policies in their colonies. Different forms of imperial arrogance had different implications for language planning in the colonies.

Because the British were less culturally arrogant than the French (though more racist), African languages fared better under the British raj. Indeed, a distinction can be drawn between Germanic-speaking Europeans generally (the Germans, the British, the Flemish, the Afrikaners) and the Latin-speaking Europeans (the French, the Portuguese, the Italians and the Spaniards). The Germanic Europeans were more likely to insist on the segregation of the races. The Latin Europeans were more likely to dismiss 'native cultures'. Sometimes for purely racist reasons (as in the case of the Afrikaners in South Africa) Germanic-speaking Europeans insisted on the greater use of indigenous languages in education and a greater recognition of African cultures.

In contrast, Latin Europeans were more mesmerized by ideas of assimilation (or Portuguese *assimilado*) and showed less tolerance toward indigenous languages than did the Germanic-speaking (or Teutonic) powers. As a result one was far more likely to see newspapers in indigenous languages in schools in British colonies than in French, Portuguese or Italian colonies in this late colonial period. We shall spell out these policies more fully later.

At their most extreme French colonialists believed that no African was good enough unless he or she spoke French. On the other hand, there are German whites in Namibia even today who believe that no African is good enough to speak German. There were certainly white settlers in colonial Kenya who forbade their

14

servants from speaking English to the master's family, even if the servant's English was much better than the master's Kiswahili. The social distance between the servant and the white mistress especially was often maintained by ensuring that the servant did not address 'the Memsab' (East Africa's equivalent of *Mem-Sahib*) in the English language. When the Germans promoted Kiswahili in colonial Tanganyika and the British did the same in colonial East Africa as a whole, the reasons were sometimes purely racial, sometimes due to missionary zeal or colonial convenience, and sometimes scholarly.

Two cases of European domination in this period happened to be internally bilingual: Belgian domination of the Congo (French and Flemish) and the Anglo-Afrikaner domination of South Africa. There were dilemmas to be resolved by the white oppressors themselves in these subjugated countries. In the case of Belgian domination of the Congo, the dilemma was indeed between the Latin legacy of the French language (intolerant of indigenous languages elsewhere in Africa) and the Germanic legacy of Flemish (in the tradition of greater accommodation with local languages elsewhere). The power of Francophone Belgians in the metropole in this period ensured that the French language was the one which was bequeathed to the Congo. The power of the Flemish missionaries and educators 'on the ground' in the Congo ensured some tactical tolerance for indigenous languages and avoidance of French 'assimilation' as a policy in the Congo. Francophone power in Belgium resulted in the exclusion of Flemish in the colonies. Flemish power locally in the Congo resulted in the minimization of the French impact and the promotion of indigenous languages.

The other European dilemma in Africa concerned South Africa. The competition between Afrikaans and English was more purely inter-Germanic rivalry in our sense. Two versions of the Teutonic paradigm had clashed. For reasons which were designed to protect the white man rather than preserve African culture, the Afrikaners preferred to slow down 'the Westernization of the native' in this period. Language policy was part of this deceleration of the Westernizing process. Afrikaners preferred 'Bantu Education' as a device for keeping Africa 'African' and white power supreme!

But unfortunately for the Afrikaners, this was a period of pan-African identification among their 'natives'. More and more black South Africans felt that if they had to choose between English and Afrikaans, the former was of greater pan-African relevance. On one hand, Afrikaans was a symbol of white oppression; on the other, the English language was a means of communication with much of the rest of Africa. Two Germanic languages had widely differing implications. Afrikaans was a language of racial claustrophobia. English, on the other hand, was a language of pan-African communication. The Soweto riots of 1976 – the use of Afrikaans as a medium of education in African schools was a major and precipitating grievance – were part of that linguistic dialectic.

What of the role of Arabic in Africa during this period? In the Maghreb, the French tried to strengthen two rivals to Arabic: the French language itself and the indigenous Berber. French language policy tried to foster a triple heritage of verbal communication in the Maghreb — Arabic, Berber, and French. It was part of France's policy of divide and rule, which had more success than it deserved, at least until the 1940s and 1950s when North African nationalism tried at last to transcend ethnic and linguistic differentiation.

Along the Nile Valley (mainly under the 'Germanic' British), Arabic had an easier time. The supremacy of Arabic in Egypt was challenged far less strongly than it was in the Maghreb. Indeed, Egypt was a fountain for the spread of Arabic elsewhere. Northern Sudan was increasingly Arabized partly as a result of the impact of Egypt. Many Sudanese resented Egypt's political influence. Paradoxically, most of them nevertheless embraced Egypt's cultural, linguistic and religious leadership.

What about Southern Sudan? Although this period experienced some of the worst confrontations between Sudan's North and South, especially from the mid-1950s onwards, it also witnessed the most rapid linguistic Arabization of the South ever. In most other parts of Africa, the spread of the Islamic religion has usually been faster than the spread of the Arabic language. This is true of the Islamization of Hausa-speaking, Wolof-speaking or Swahili-speaking regions of Africa. By contrast, Southern Sudan has experienced a faster spread of the Arabic language than of the Islamic religion. Southern Sudanese are less likely to go to the mosque than to pronounce with sophistication the Arabic words *Insha' Allah* (If God wills).

Language situation and language policy

The spread of Arabic along the Nile Valley is only one instance. In the period since 1935 there have been other languages which have spread geographically far beyond the areas where they were spoken in the preceding years. Some languages have become languages of contact, inter-ethnic communication and lingua francas.

Four forces have been particularly important in the spread of languages: religion, economics, politics, and war. The spread of Arabic in Africa historically has been mainly under the momentum of the spread of Islam. But, as we have indicated, Arabic is spreading in Southern Sudan today because of political and economic considerations rather than as a response to religious conversion. The role of war in the spread of Arabic in the South is more complicated.

Christian missionaries all over Africa have also played a part in the spread of languages. The use of indigenous languages for the spread of the gospel has sometimes favoured particular African tongues as against others. Proselytism has once again disseminated not just 'the Word' in the sense of religion, but 'words' in the more literal sense of language.

The economy has also played a part in the spread of languages. Migrant labour, urbanization and the expansion of markets in this period have all brought people of different linguistic backgrounds together. The dramatic growth of mining industries since 1935 has served as a magnet for attracting linguistically diverse workers with a resulting need for languages of contact.

The years from 1935 also happen to be the period of expanding involvement of the masses in politics, initially in the struggle against colonial rule. The political mobilization of the masses, especially after the Second World War, increased the political use of both the imperial languages and some of the African ones as well.

The Second World War itself had linguistic as well as other consequences for Africa. The multilingual Africans enlisted into the armed forces created a need for a common language of command. Sometimes the imperial language of the particular European power was simplified for military needs. In British Africa the use of an indigenous lingua franca sometimes seemed to make better sense. In East Africa, Kiswahili developed into a military lingua franca for the King's African Rifles. Later on, the importance of Kiswahili within Uganda's armed forces created a surprising linguistic bond among men from otherwise diverse cultural backgrounds. When in power in the 1970s Ugandan soldiers even gave Kiswahili the status of a national language in the country, and expanded its use in the mass media.

Both in relation to the armed forces and for other reasons, the gender question has also been a factor in the spread of languages in Africa. About half of the men in Uganda speak some kind of Kiswahili but a far smaller portion of Ugandan women do. More important than the masculinity of the security forces is the fact that migrant labour in Uganda and elsewhere is more likely to consist of men than women. Urbanization in Africa generally also involves more mobility among men than among women. As a generalization we should therefore conclude that bilingualism and multilingualism in Africa (and perhaps in most other societies) is more widespread among men than among women.

If religion, economics, politics and war have played a part in the spread of languages, they have sometimes also threatened the survival of some of the smaller languages. Many African languages have been losing speakers through assimilation to other language groups. Some are slowly disappearing as the number of their speakers dwindles. Many factors have contributed to this state of affairs since the 1930s. Among them are improved communication in the geographical and linguistic sense, colonial and post-colonial language policies, the work of language promoters including missionaries, ministries of education and broadcasting and to some extent teachers and linguists. There is also the sheer dynamism of some languages to survive, thrive and expand, while others contract in a situation of linguistic competition.

It is generally acknowledged that the African continent constitutes the most complex multilingual area in the world. The complexity results from the high numbers of languages, the way they are distributed, the relatively low numbers of speakers per language, and intensive language contact in many areas of the continent resulting in widespread multilingualism. It is thus difficult to know exactly how many languages there are in the continent, partly because of the problem of delineating languages and dialects; moreover, there is considerable variation among language names in different areas.

Then there is the role of language in deciding where one ethnic group ends and another begins. The question arises: Can there be different races with the same skin colour? Are black African groups which differ in speech a case of different 'races' or different 'tribes'? When C.G. Seligman published his classic but controversial *Races of Africa*, the first problem he had to confront was the definition of 'race.' Who are the Bantu? What constituted a Nilote? Who are the Hamites and Nilo-Hamites? Seligman admitted that language by itself was not an adequate guide to 'race'.

> Yet the study of the races of Africa has been so largely determined by the interest in speech, and it is so much easier to acquire a working knowledge of a language than of another part of a man's cultural make-up, that names based upon linguistic criteria are constantly applied to large groups of mankind and, indeed, if intelligently used, often fit quite well. Hence, in describing the great racial groups of Africa, terms such as 'Bantu', which strictly speaking have no more than a linguistic significance, are habitually employed. (Seligman, 1957: 1-2)

In general, Seligman used the term 'race' to mean a family of related 'tribes' like the Bantu, but even the definition of 'tribe', in turn, had to be overwhelmingly reliant on linguistic criteria. The Nilotes are those who speak Nilotic languages; the Bantu are those who speak Bantu languages. In this case we mean speech in terms of the mother language.

17

Even within 'tribes' we can say the Baganda are those to whom Luganda is the first language. Imagine applying the same criterion to the English language. The English are those to whom English is the first language? What would the Scots have to say about this? Imagine the response of Jamaicans and Trinidadians. The point becomes even clearer if you move from language to community. It may be defensible to say those to whom Luganda is the first language are Baganda. It is much more controversial to say that those to whom English is the first language are themselves English.

Languages: communalist and ecumenical

What we have here is a distinction between communalist languages and ecumenical languages. Communalist languages are those, like Luganda and Luo, which can be used to define a race or a tribe. Communalist languages are race-bound or 'tribe-bound', and define as communities those who speak them as mother tongues. Ecumenical languages are in fact extra-communalist. They transcend these boundaries of racial or ethnic definition.

Communalist languages could be highly absorbtive in the sense of allowing even newcomers to the language to be categorized racially or 'tribally' as natives, provided they have, in fact, succeeded in being assimilated linguistically. This phenomenon has been striking in Buganda itself, where new groups coming in during the last two or three generations, acquiring Luganda gradually as a first language, have in time become Baganda. They become Baganda once Luganda becomes their first language.

Are communalist languages only spoken by one or two million people? This, of course, is not the case. There are communalist languages that are spoken by many millions. It is indeed arguable that the language which has the most speakers in the world, Chinese, is itself a communalist language with its expanding billion speakers. The situation is still such that we can say that the Chinese are those to whom Chinese (Cantonese or Mandarin) is the mother language. If they live in Korea and are gradually assimilated into Korean language and culture, they do after a generation or two become Koreans.

In Africa the most important non-European languages are Arabic, Hausa and Kiswahili. Arabic or Hausa are communalist languages in their different senses, but Kiswahili has ceased to be that. At the moment the majority of those who speak Kiswahili speak it as a second or third language, and there is an increasing number of people who grow up bilingual in Kiswahili and their own 'tribal' language in Tanzania, Uganda, or Kenya. It will become increasingly difficult to say that whoever speaks Kiswahili as a first language is a Mswahili. Kiswahili is, therefore, less absorbtive than even Hausa, but that may also be its strength. The Waswahili, in the original sense of 'the people of the coast', were defined to some extent in terms of some degree of Arabization and Islamization. Because they are now politically marginal, their language stands a chance of being acceptable to others.

But the same cannot be said of Hausa. When, in the old Federal Parliament of Nigeria, before the first coup of January 1966, it was proposed that Hausa should be adopted as the national language of Nigeria, strong voices were heard against the proposal. Chief Anthony Enahoro, for example, said in parliament:

> As one who comes from a minority tribe, I deplore the continuing evidence in this country that people wish to impose their customs, their languages, and even

18

more, their way of life upon the smaller tribes. (Quoted by Schwarz, 1965:41)

And a Nigerian Minister visiting India in 1953, in relating his country's problems to a comparable multilingual situation in India, reaffirmed that:

> We are not keen on developing our own languages with a view to replacing English. We regard the English language as a unifying force. (Quoted by Schwarz, 1965:41)

Since then the fears of adopting one of the Nigerian languages have assumed even sharper significance. Certainly, in the wake of the Nigerian Civil War, and a suspicion in some quarters of a potential Hausa domination of the country as a whole, it has become even more rash to reactivate the campaign for the adoption of the Hausa language as a national language. For the time being then, Hausa is set to remain a communalist language.

A more startling communalist language is Arabic, 'startling' partly because of its distribution across different nations, and partly because of the great variety of colours of those who speak it. One would have expected Arabic to be as extra-communalist as the English language. Just as English has native speakers who range from Australian industrialists and English dukes to black fishermen in St. Kitts in the West Indies, so Arabic has native speakers who range from white Lebanese millionaires to black Sudanese soldiers. And yet while English is ecumenical, Arabic has retained its communalist nature in spite of the diversification of the colours and origins of its speakers.

The Arabs as a 'race' defy pigmentational classification. They also defy any attempt to place them in any particular continent. Are the Arabs Asians, Africans, both, or neither? It is not often remembered that there are more Arabic speakers within Africa than outside Africa. Arabic may have started in the Arabian peninsula, and then spread into the Fertile Crescent, and into Africa, but the balance of preponderance of speakers has changed. In some ways the situation is the equivalent of the change in relationship between England, as the birthplace of the English language, and the United States. The mother country, England, is now overshadowed by her former imperial extension and the danger now is of Britain becoming an extension of the United States rather than the other way round.

Does the analogy hold in the relationship between Arab Africa and the rest of the Arab world? It certainly holds as between the old Arabic peninsula proper, on one side, and Africa and the Fertile Crescent combined, on the other. Countries of the peninsula proper, especially Saudi Arabia from which the Arab invasion of the seventh century originated, are now overshadowed numerically even by Iraq and Syria on their own. If we put Africa on one side and the rest of the Arab world as a whole (peninsula and Fertile Crescent) on the other, the preponderance of Arabic speakers is still on the African side. As the Egyptian scholar and statesman, Boutros Boutros-Ghali, once put it, in a book published in 1963:

> It must not be forgotten that sixty percent of the Arab community and seventy-two percent of the Arab lands are in Africa. (Boutros-Ghali, 1963:328)

Although by crossing the Atlantic the English language became less communalist, by crossing the Red Sea Arabic remained as communalist as ever. Those who spoke Arabic as a first language became after a generation or so Arabs. The result was a staggering mixture of groups. As Erskine Childers once put it:

> the Arab world … comprises very many widely varying races or historical

19

ethnic groups. The short list is bewildering, and distinguishing 'racial' definitions are themselves treacherous. From west to east, the list must include Berbers, Carthaginians, Romans, Vandals, Arabians, Turcomans, Egyptians, Nubians, Haemites, Greeks, Armenians, Circassians, Assyrians, Babylonians, Hittites, Sumerians, Kurds, Persians and a small host of ancient migratory infusions who it is safer to describe simply as Semitic. (Childers, 1960: 70)

Childers goes on to say that anyone attempting to give a racial definition of 'What is an Arab' would founder hopelessly in the waves of several thousand years of migration, invasion and intermarriage.

'Arabism' has nothing to do with 'race,' but has to with language, cultural tradition and heritage…. (Childers, 1960: 70)

But Childers here is using the word 'race' as some kind of descent by blood. Muddathir Abd Al-Rahim has also used the blood definition of race, and rejected it as not meaningful when applied to Arabs.

In fact, however, Arabism … is not a racial bond which unites the members of a certain ethnic group. It is a cultural, linguistic and non-racial link that binds together numerous races – black, white and brown. Had Arabism been anything else but this, most modern Arabs, both Africans and Asians, including the entire population of Northern Sudan, would cease to be Arab at all. (Al-Rahim, 1970: 248)

But if one insists on regarding the Arabs as a nation, then the applicable criterion is linguistic. The Arabs are those who speak Arabic as a first language. Very often they are also Muslims, and have acquired other aspects of Arab culture. The central defining characteristic becomes linguistic. Arabic, in spite of the richness of pigmentation among its speakers, remains more 'race-bound' or nation-specific than the English language.

What we have here, then, is a paradox. The English people are more racially exclusive than the Arabs. But precisely because a person did not become English merely by being English-speaking, the English language became less racially exclusive than Arabic. With the Arabs, those who spoke their language became absorbed into the 'race'. With the English many of those who spoke their language were decidedly out of the 'race'. Therefore, today we identify those who speak Arabic as a native language as belonging to a particular 'race'. But those who speak English are decidedly not necessarily English. The English language is less race-bound partly because the English people have tended to be racially exclusive.

Perhaps French comes in an intermediate position between English and Arabic. The French assimilationist policy, and the colonial tendency to accord French rights to those who absorbed French culture, was strikingly reminiscent of the history of the Arabs. Perhaps if the French empire had lasted as long as the Arab empire, we might, indeed, have arrived at a situation where we could say that those who spoke French as a first language were French, be they white, brown or black. But the French language did not have enough time to become like Arabic.

We must also remember, however, that partly because the French have had low tolerance for the indigenization of their language even outside France, they may have recruited proportionally fewer speakers of French, despite their assimilationist policy, than the British have recruited speakers of English, just as much as the French policy did not foster the development of widespread pidgin varieties of French in Africa (but for reasons that are more complex).

Towards the globalization of English

There have been occasions when the racial exclusiveness of the English people has tended to make them possessive about the English language itself. This is, in fact, one of the major paradoxes of the comparative history of the English language and the French language.

French was, on the whole, intended by France to be disseminated across the globe, to become the language of high culture and high diplomacy, and to recruit to its ranks more and more creative users of the medium. There was a time when French seemed to be winning that battle. Its prestige did make it the language of the aristocracy in countries as varied as Czarist Russia and the Lebanon, Chile in Latin America and Egypt under Ottoman rule.

The English, on the other hand, were less preoccupied with the imperative of spreading their language as such. On the contrary they were sometimes arrogantly possessive about it, particularly in their colonies. Many were the Englishmen in the old colonial days who insisted on speaking Kiswahili to an African in Kenya, even if neither spoke Kiswahili well enough while both of them spoke fluent English. It became a point of honour sometimes to maintain the linguistic distance between the Englishman and his coloured subject, as a way of maintaining the social distance between them.

Colonial administrators were, on occasion, disturbed by what were regarded as the political consequences of teaching the English language to the native. Lord Lugard, the greatest of the British administrators in African history, also shared some of these reservations. To use Lugard's own words:

> the premature teaching of English ... inevitably leads to utter disrepect for British and native ideals alike and to a denationalized and disorganized population. (Quoted by Coleman, 1958: 136–7)

Yet, in spite of these influential reservations about the 'reckless' spreading of the English language, English gathered its own momentum and rapidly outstripped French both in the number of countries in the world that adopted it as a major national medium, and in the number of speakers. The British who did not want their language to become a universal language were landed with precisely that fate, while the French have had to embark on a determined attempt to stop French from receding in importance.

The major instrument for the initial spread of the English language was the British empire itself. French expansionism was also the single most important medium for the spread of French. But the British empire was bigger and more wide-spread than the French empire. Secondly, France never succeeded in producing the equivalent of a United States, that is, a linguistic child who then became bigger than the mother, and began to contribute even more than the mother in the spread of the shared language. Certainly since the disintegration of the British empire, the biggest carrier of the English language has been the American rather than the Briton. By 1966, it was estimated that there were already one-and-a-half million Americans abroad on business or technical assistance programmes, and millions more American tourists sampling the world in all its diversity.

The United States contributes large amounts of money towards the teaching of English in a large number of countries. Partly because of American leadership in important areas of science, English has become the primary language of science, aviation, sports, and increasingly even literature and the theatre. As one East African publication put it some years ago:

> When a Russian pilot seeks to land at an airfield in Athens, Cairo or New Delhi, he talks to the control tower in English. (*Reporter*, Nairobi, 30 December 1966, p. 13)

The same weekly journal drew from a recently established report estimates to the effect that by 1966 seventy per cent of the world's mail was written in English and an even bigger percentage of cable and wireless transmissions were made in that language. Sixty per cent of the world's broadcasts were already in English. And more and more countries were introducing English as a compulsory second language in schools.

Yet in spite of the phenomenal spread of the language the British at home seemed to look upon it at best as an amusing phenomenon and at worst as something which is tending to pollute and corrupt their language. On the one hand, because English is now no longer communalist or race-bound, many foreigners to the language are scrambling to bring it into their lives. But because the English people themselves continue to be relatively insular, none of the new native speakers of the language are admitted into the fold as 'English people'. Indeed, some of the new varieties of the language are not always recognized as legitimate.

An example of this scramble for possession of English was a delightful argument which broke out in the *East African Standard* (Nairobi) in 1965. A Mr M.S. Robinson, an Englishman, complained about the degeneration of the use of English in Kenya with particular reference to the impact of broadcasting on general usage. The purist response of British users of English as contrasted with the experimentalist tendencies of American users of English has asserted itself in Kenya in defence of the pristine originality of the texture of the language. Back came a reply from a non-British Kenyan, Mr S. Meghani, disputing Mr Robinson's monopolistic approach to the English language. Mr Meghani said that if Mr Robinson did not like the way African people spoke English, he should also remember that others may not like the way he did:

> English as spoken by an Englishman is not at all pleasant to listen to … let alone easy to follow.

Mr Meghani went on to challenge the claims of the English people to the English language:

> It is not at all wisdom on the part of a tiny English population in this wide world to claim that English, as presented and pronounced by Americans, Canadians, Africans, Indians and the people of Madras State is not English. It may not be the Queen's English, but then what? Has the Englishman the sole right to decide upon the form and style of a universal language?

Mr Meghani then asserted that the whole trouble lay in the name which the language continued to bear. The name, he suggested, was now a misnomer since English had far outgrown its origins.

> Strictly speaking, English cannot be called 'English' at all, since it is a universal language belonging to all. It is difficult to understand why it is still known under that horrible name; it should have another name. (*East Africa Standard*, Nairobi, 15 February 1965, p. 4)

Within a few days back came a reply from another native speaker of the language, seemingly from the British Isles. This new correspondent confessed that he held the view that civilization was bounded on the North by the Thames – and woe to those over-tolerant individuals who should substitute the Trent – on the West by the Tamar and the Severn, and on the South by the English Channel. He supported Mr Meghani's suggestion that English spoken by Mr Meghani and 'others of similar linguistic and cultural attainments, including the VOK announcers' should bear some other name. The new writer thought that was the most sensible suggestion he had heard for a long time.

> As one who holds … that the English language is an autochtonous product of the civilization (bounded on the North by the Thames and on the South by the English Channel), I feel that your correspondent's suggestion should be acted on immediately or, as he would probably prefer to put it, implemented forthwith. There is, however, no need to coin a new name for the 'universal' language. There is a time-honored one: 'Pidgin-English'. (*East Africa Standard*, Nairobi, 19 February 1965, p. 18)

This new correspondent sounded very much like a native of the British Isles. His pen name was Mr Ben Trovate. But evidently he was assimilated enough, and over a sufficiently long period of time, to have developed a strong possessive attitude to that variety of the English language spoken in the area bounded by the Thames and the English Channel.

We have had, then, the spread of English, capturing peoples and nations, and yet the rejection of those new 'converts' as linguistic equals by the originators of that language in the British Isles.

The emergence of Afro-Saxons

Before the end of this century there will be more black people who speak the English language as their native tongue than there will be inhabitants in the British Isles. Already African-Americans alone, who speak the language as a first language, are more than the equivalent of half the population of Great Britain. And then there are a few more million black speakers of the language scattered around the Caribbean and the northern fringes of South America. Within the African continent, the only black native speakers of the English language so far are the social élite of Liberia, descended from African-Americans. There are also a few black native speakers of the English language in places like Sierra Leone. But at least as important a phenomenon is the growing number of educated African families that are using English as the language of the home. A number of African children, especially in West Africa but also increasingly in East Africa, are growing bilingual in English and their own African language because their parents are highly educated and often speak English to each other.

It is these considerations which make it likely that by the end of the twentieth century there will be more black native speakers of the English language than there are speakers of it in the British Isles. An Afro-Saxon population, linguistically influential, would have come into being. But this situation has its tensions. The Ango-Saxons, liberal in some spheres, but racially exclusive in their history, have tended to create complexes among those they have ruled or dominated. And where

English conquers the black man as effectively as he was once conquered by the Anglo-Saxon race, tensions between dignity and linguistic rationality are unavoidable.

An important illustration comes from the late James Baldwin, one of the most gifted black users of the English language in this century. Baldwin once wrote an article on how he stopped hating Shakespeare. He admitted that part of his hatred of Shakespeare was originally the phenomenon of turning away from 'that monstrous achievement with a kind of sick envy'. In Baldwin's most anti-English days, he condemned Shakespeare for his chauvinism ('This England' indeed!). But his most important area of revulsion against Shakespeare was in connection with Baldwin himself being a black man condemned to being a native speaker of the English language, and in his case to writing in that language.

> It felt so bitterly anomalous that a black man should be forced to deal with the English language at all – should be forced to assault the English language in order to be able to speak ... I condemned [Shakespeare] as one of the authors and architects of my oppression. (Baldwin, 1964:14)

Some of the irritation came from the characters created by Shakespeare himself. Baldwin mentions how some Jews, at times, had been bitterly resentful of Shylock. Baldwin in turn, as a black man, was bitter about Caliban and dubious about Othello ('What did he see in Desdemona anyhow?'). Baldwin's quarrel with the English language at that stage was that it was a language which did not reflect any of his experiences. But one day he found himself in a non-English speaking situation, having to think and speak in French. Baldwin began to see Shakespeare and the English language in a new light.

> If the language was not my own, it might be the fault of the language; but it might also be my fault. Perhaps the language was not my own because I had never attempted to use it, had only learnt to imitate it. If this were so then it might be made to bear the burden of my experience if I could find the stamina to challenge it, and me, to such a test.

Baldwin found support for this possibility from two 'mighty witnesses' — his black ancestors, who had evolved the spiritual and sorrow songs, and blues and jazz, and created an entirely new idiom in an overwhelmingly hostile place; but Baldwin also found support from Shakespeare, whom he now regarded as the last bawdy writer in the English language.

> Shakespeare's bawdiness became very important to me since bawdiness was one of the elements of jazz and revealed a tremendous, loving and realistic respect for the body, and that ineffable force which the body contains, which Americans have mostly lost, which I had experienced only among Negroes, and of which I had been taught to be ashamed.

The language with which Baldwin had grown up had certainly not been the King's English. It had been the English of the black man in the New World.

> an immense experience had forged this language, it had been (and remains) one of the tools of a people's survival, and it revealed expectations which no white American could easily entertain. (Baldwin; 1964:14–15).

Black metaphor and English semantics

There is a residual racism in English metaphor, however, on matters connected with white and black colours. A few hours before I started writing this particular part of the present chapter I received in the mail an issue of the monthly magazine *Africa Report*. In the correspondence columns there was a bitter complaint, critical of President Nyerere's old regime, by a Tanzanian living in the United States. The Tanzanian complained that articles published about his country tended to 'white-wash' the regime and its failings. Personally, I have sometimes caught myself saying that one of the 'blackest stains' on Nyerere's career was his decision to let his former ambassador in Washington, Othman Sherrif, be taken to Zanzibar, probably to his death. I suppose, in such a context, one could attempt to use a different metaphor if one could stop oneself soon enough. But how much of a choice in synonyms do I have when I want to discuss blackmail? Or something sold on the black market?

It is true that most of the time when we are using these words we are not connecting them with any racist tradition which associates black with evil and white with goodness. The metaphor is so much part of the English language, beautifully integrated, ready for use unconsciously in a spontaneous flow. As metaphor, black has carried repeatedly, and in a variety of contexts, decidedly negative connotations. White has ambivalent connotations but, more often than not, favourable ones. The connotations have been so stabilized that users of the language are unconscious of those wider links with racist traditions. But does not the unconsciousness make the situation even worse?

It would not matter if English continued to be the language of the English people. But precisely because it is the most eligible candidate for universality, and also because black native speakers of the language are on their way towards becoming more numerous than the inhabitants of the British Isles, the case for a gradual diversification of English metaphor in the area of colour becomes important for African writers. They need not change the word blackmail to whitemail, or black market into white or brown market; but a new consciousness of the residual racism of the English language and new imaginative coinings of alternative metaphors, at least within African versions of the English language, would help to improve the credentials of English as an African medium. In accepting the English language as their own, black people should not accept its idiom passively and uncritically. There may be a case for the deracialization of the English language.

As a starting point in such an endeavour, we should at least be clear about the broad negative connotations which the metaphor of blackness has assumed in the English language. There is, first, the association of blackness with evil; secondly, there is the association of blackness with void and emptiness; thirdly, there is the association of blackness with death. These three areas of negative association have, in fact, multiple sub-associations. The associations with death, for example, also makes black the colour of grief. Conversely, if war is death, white becomes an alternative to green as the colour of peace. The white dove becomes the messenger of reconciliation.

But let us take each of these three broad negative connotations in turn: black is evil, black is void, black is death. That black is evil is perhaps the notion most deeply structured into the language. To some extent the difficulty has its origins in the Europeanization of Christianity. As Christianity became a religion whose chief champions were white people, angels gradually became white and the devil was black. The biblical heritage of the West profoundly influenced metaphorical usages in more popular literature. With regard to the English language, the Bible and Shakespeare might well be the greatest single contributors to the popular metaphor. From the point of view of the association of black with evil nothing has captured it more sharply than Blake's poem, 'The Little Black Boy'. The poem exclaims with a startling revelation this whole universe of metaphor: 'And I am black, but O, My soul is White.' John Bunyan and other religious writers also have made suggestions about washing a black man, or an Ethiopian, white as a way of conferring salvation upon him. John Dryden puts limitations on the degree of blackness which is admissible in heaven, as well as on the degree of whiteness which could even deserve hell. To Dryden the agony of purgatory is the predicament of him who is 'too black for heaven, and yet too white for hell' (*The Hind and the Panther*).

But, as we indicated, next to the Bible it is Shakespeare who has had the greatest single impact on the metaphorical evolution of the English language. Problems therefore arise when African literary figures, and even African heads of state, find themselves imbibing the Shakespearean idiom.

When he was president, Julius Nyerere even had to confront the ominous task of translating the Bard into Swahili. The plays which Nyerere has translated so far are *Julius Caesar* and *The Merchant of Venice*. Both include metaphors of negative association of blackness. *The Merchant of Venice* is, in any case, a play partly concerned with racial or religious consciousness. There are references in the play to black people and customs of colour. But there is also a very explicit association of the dark complexion with the devil. Portia has had to deal with earlier suitors including a French lord, an English baron, a Scottish lord and a German duke. But also among those who want her is the Prince of Morocco. In Act I, Scene 2, she notes the importance of his dark complexion, even if his entire behaviour is saintly. Blake may be satisfied that a black boy is black but has a white soul. Portia has different ideas about the black-skinned prince interested in her.

> If he have the condition of a saint and the complexion of a devil, I had rather he should shrive me than wive me. (*The Merchant of Venice*, Act 1, Scene 2, 151–3)

Mwalimu Julius Nyerere had to grapple with this racialistic insinuation, in order to render it into Swahili. He decided to translate 'complexion of a devil' more as 'face of a devil' than 'colour'.

> … kama ana hali ya malaika au sura ya
> Shetani ni heri anighofiri makosa kuliko kuniposa

Nyerere's friend, Milton Obote of Uganda, was perhaps even more consistent in his admiration of John Milton. The Satan portrayed by Milton in *Paradise Lost* had, at least in the initial phases of the rebellion, a heroic stature. Satan had rebelled against the tyrannical omnipotence of God. He had rebelled against the tradition of kneeling to pray, of flattering the Almighty with the grand epithet of singing hymns in His praise. Until he rebelled, Satan like all angels was, of course, white. Obote at school and at Makerere admired, not Satan as a symbol of evil, but Satan as a symbol of rebellion against total tyranny. Indeed, Obote adopted the name of Milton in honour of the author of *Paradise Lost*. Satan and his followers were driven out of Heaven into the great deep. They found themselves lying on the burning lake of Hell. John Milton has an epithet for Hell – it is 'Black Gehenna'. From being a white angel, Satan was becoming a black devil. We might almost say that this heroic figure portrayed by Milton, and admired by Obote, was the first black person in eternity.

And God had sentenced him from the start to a life of perpetual hell. Christian art even in Ethiopia portrays Satan as black.

Yet, what did it matter? It was precisely this issue, and the way it was formulated in *Paradise Lost*, which inspired young Apolo Obote in Uganda. What if Satan finds himself in 'Black Gehenna?'

> The mind is its own place, and in itself
> Can make a Heav'n of Hell, a Hell of Heav'n.

And then the most important poetic line in the intellectual development of Milton Obote:

> Better to reign in Hell than serve in Heav'n.

Related to the whole tradition of identifying blackness with the Devil and whiteness with the angels are the metaphors of shepherds, flocks, sheep and lambs in the figurative language of Christianity. 'The Lord is my shepherd.' But what is the Lord to do with the black sheep of Africa? We are back to the colour prejudices of Christianity and of the English language. The sheep and their wool, which is usually white. The black sheep of the family is the deviant, sometimes the wicked exception.

From blackness and its association with evil there is an easy transition to blackness and death. Sir Patrick Renison, the Governor of Kenya, defiantly resisting pressures to release Jomo Kenyatta, bracketed these two associations of darkness and death in his very denunciation of Kenyatta. He called Kenyatta 'leader unto darkness and death.' The concentration of darkness in the middle of the night carries ominous suggestions of danger and evil. The black cat is often interpreted in this tradition of metaphor as an omen of bad luck. The worse luck was death, and the worse omen, impending death. The black band round the arm at funerals, the black suit that the dead man is sometimes supposed to wear, the black dress the widow is expected to use all carry cumulative associations of blackness with death. Even in translating *Julius Caesar*, Mwalimu Julius Nyerere had to translate the phrase of Octavius, 'our black sentence'. This was the sentence of death passed by the counter-conspirators against those who might have been implicated in the assassination of Caesar (Act IV, Scene I). Nyerere's compatriot and fellow translator of Shakespeare, S. Mushi, had, in turn, to grapple with the dark recesses of Macbeth's mind. And Malcolm speaks of Macbeth as 'black Macbeth' referring to the foul nature of Macbeth's soul , as well as suggesting its orientation towards murder and death (Act IV, Scene 3).

As for the association of blackness with the void, this has given rise to a number of sub-associations, ranging from emptiness, ignorance and primitiveness, to sheer depth. The 'dark ages' are dark both because we do not know very much about them and because there is presumption of barbarism and primitivism in them. It is partly because of these preconceptions concerning emptiness and barbarity that many African nationalists, black as they were in colour, objected to Africa being described as 'the dark continent'. Why were these dark people indignant that their ancestral landmass should bear the title of 'the dark continent'? Precisely because their initiation into the connotations of the English language had sensitized them to the negative implications of such a description of Africa. Darkness as emptiness and barbarity certainly influenced Professor Hugh Trevor-Roper (now Lord) in his dismissal of the concept of African history as meaningless. In his own infamous words:

> Perhaps, in the future, there will be some African history ... but at present there

is none: there is only the history of the Europeans in Africa. The rest is darkness
… and darkness is not a subject of history. (Trevor-Roper, 1963: 87)

Conclusion

We have sought to demonstrate that the colonial period represented considerable
danger to indigenous African languages as the imperial European tongues were
promoted with greater vigour in the colonies. The threat was particularly serious in
those colonial powers of Latin expression (French, Portuguese, Italian, and Spanish)
which had a strong preference for cultural assimilation in their language policies for
the colonies. The imperial powers of Germanic expression were perhaps equally
contemptuous of indigenous languages but did not want to replace them
completely with European culture. The British policy of indirect rule, especially,
had cultural implications which resulted in greater use of African languages in
schools in the British colonies and greater promotion of African languages for
literacy under the British flag than under the French or Portugese. But languages
were affected not just by deliberate policy but also by wider social forces. Religion,
economics, politics and war played their own different roles in spreading some
languages in Africa and inhibiting others. But while colonialism threatened African
tongues by the promotion of European ones, colonialism preserved some tongues
with new orthographies.

Arabic, French and English have played a particularly important international
role within Africa. The majority of Arabic-speaking people in the world are within
Africa but the majority of Arabic-speaking states are outside. On the other hand, the
majority of French-speaking states in the world are in Africa while the majority of
French-speaking people are outside. Without Africa the French language could
never count as a global language.

Today the Democratic Republic of Congo (formerly Zaire) is, in fertile territory,
the largest French-speaking nation in the world. Congo-Kinshasa is in population
the second largest French-speaking nation after France. Fairly early in the twenty-
first century Congo-Kinshasa stands a chance of becoming the largest French-
speaking nation in the world, both territorially and in population, as Congo-
Kinshasa continues to outstrip France in demographic growth, and as Algeria
elevates Arabic above French.

Africa is less fundamental to the global status of English than it is to the universal
credentials of French. But that Africa has now entered the ranks of genius in the use
of the English language can be attested by the 1986 award of the Nobel Prize for
Literature to the Nigerian playwright, Wole Soyinka, for his work written in a form
of English which had been affected profoundly by Yoruba culture.

The continuing stigma on the African linguistic scene is the inadequate attention
given to indigenous languages by most post-colonial African policymakers.
Outside Arabic-speaking Africa, Somalia, Ethiopia, Tanzania and a few other
countries, there is still excessive African dependence upon the colonial legacy of the
European languages in both education and public life.

Since the human species itself originated in Africa, human language must have
started in this continent. It is one of the lamentations of the period since 1945 in
Africa that the African peoples have not yet shaken off the chains of linguistic
dependence on Europe, dependence on a smaller continent which is a mere recent

upstart in the long history of human communication. In most of present-day Africa, especially south of the Sahara, it is impossible to be a member of parliament without competence in a European language. It is almost unthinkable in postcolonial Africa for a head of state to be without a command of the imperial language. The resulting irony is that a continent which is the mother of human language itself has now become so dependent on imported tongues.

As for the legacies of Latin and Germanic cultures in Africa, it remains obstinately true that one is more likely to see 'vernacular newspapers' in former British than in former French colonies. Classrooms conducted in indigenous languages are more likely in African countries of Germanic expression than of Latin. While the British have indeed been more radically arrogant than the French, France has been, as we have indicated, more culturally arrogant than Britain. The history of language policy in Africa this century has been profoundly affected by this obstinate imperial dialectic, with all its wide-ranging ramifications in the process of social change.

We have also shown how darkness as a characterization of Africa's personality is still resisted by the darkest of all peoples in colour, the African nationalists south of the Sahara. The connotations of the English language, with all its accumulation of negative associations in relation to blackness and darkness, are pre-eminently to blame for these anomalies. The starting point of black aesthetics must, therefore, be not only the black power motto 'Black is Beautiful' but also the insistence that black is not evil, nor is it emptiness, nor indeed is it death. The Christian symbolism of the black soul, of the black armband at a funeral, might need to be transformed in the pursuit of new aesthetics for the black man.

Resort to symbolism from African traditions could help to provide alternative metaphors for African English. Death certainly can be portrayed as legitimately by whiteness, if African traditions of body-painting are involved, as by blackness. In the third dimension of the Islamic tradition, the dead body is covered in white cloth. And a completely white cloth could be ominously reminiscent of what the Waswahili call *sanda*, the white material that is the last apparel of man. Of course, there are occasions when African customs themselves equate blackness with negative connotations. But these anomalies are present even in the English language. The simile 'deathly white' is perfectly good English, if one remembers that a white man, when he is dead and no longer has blood flowing in his veins, becomes indeed, at last, really white. The white man only manages to live up to his name when he dies. But, on balance, the Africanization of the English language must definitely include the deracialization of English. Black aesthetics has to rescue blackness and darkness from the stifling weight of negative metaphor.

2
African Languages
in the African-American Experience[1]

Introduction:
Language, the self and the other

African societies, including those of Arab origin in the northern part of the continent, are known to have concepts of ethnic identity that are quite liberal and assimilative. 'Purity of the bloodline' is a notion that is comparatively alien to the relational universe of African peoples. To be a member of any European ethnic group, both parents normally would have to be European. But maternal or paternal parentage alone in the case of most African peoples normally would be sufficient to qualify the offspring as members of a particular African ethnic group. Ali Mazrui dramatizes this difference between Afro-Arab and European conceptions of identity in the following hypothetical terms:

> If the white citizens of the United States had, in fact, been Arab, most of the coloured citizens would have become Arab, too. It has been estimated that over seventy percent of the Negro population in the United States has some 'white' blood. And the 'white' blood was much more often than not derived from a white father. Now given the principle that if the father is Arab the child is Arab, most of the Negroes of the United States would have been Arab had the white people of the United States been Arab too. But the white Americans are Caucasian and the dominant culture is Germanic. And so if either of the parents is non-Germanic, the offspring cannot be Germanic either. (1964:22)

But the liberalism and assimilative character of the Afro-Arab concept of identity are by no means limited to the area of genetics. They also extend to the sphere of culture, and, more relevant to our present discussion, to the phenomenon of language. Anyone who speaks Hausa as a first language, for example, would under normal circumstances be regarded as ethnically Hausa. The same can be said of virtually all other African languages, to some degree or other. This stands in marked contrast to European languages which do not admit into their ethnic fold people who are not genetically European. European languages may be acquired by all and sundry; but when it comes to linguistic definitions of European ethnicity, European languages have failed to neutralize genetic boundaries. African languages, on the other hand, defy genetic boundaries in their contribution to ethnic identities.

Making another hypothetical projection, then, had the American lingua franca been Swahili, for example, instead of English, the entire African American population that for generations has been speaking English as a first and often only language, would probably have been ethnically Swahili. Likewise, if the mother tongue of African peoples throughout the world were Swahili, then the entire African diaspora might have been Swahili.

It is perhaps this assimilative tendency of Swahili and other African languages that sometimes led Julius Nyerere, the first president of Tanzania, to use the term 'Swahili' to refer to any person of African origin. Nyerere thus made Swahili, in the collective consciousness of the Tanzanian people, a local equivalent of a transcontinental, pan-African identity. It was as if Nyerere was anticipating the development of Swahili into a language of global Africa. Inadvertently, Nyerere was also pitting the liberal humanist boundaries of African languages against the narrower racial boundaries of the European languages in the stadium of international politics of human relations.

The restricted genetic (or 'racial') boundaries of the English language, a phenomenon that may have emerged with the rise of imperial capitalism in the northern hemisphere, have made it impossible for African Americans to become fully a part of the American 'mainstream'. It was natural, therefore, that language too would become a factor in the struggles for equality in the civil rights movement of the 1960s. But if the system ultimately capitulated, to some degree, in the politico-economic sphere, it was not ready to do the same in the arena of linguistics. No matter how extensively 'assimilated' African Americans were, in cultural and linguistic terms, the system ensured that they would remain 'black', that they would remain American with qualification. At the frontier of linguistics of identity, therefore, the English language simply failed to forge a nation that is truly one.

Apart from its segregative ethno-linguistic 'nature', however, the English language has sometimes been regarded as inherently racialist. With words that evoke all sorts of negative images, the English language is supposed to have served as an instrument of racism against people of colour. Thus Ossie Davis once declared that the English language was his enemy and indicted it 'as one of the prime carriers of racism from one person to another in our society' (1973:72).

In an instructional manual on racism in the English language, Robert Moore outlines some of the ways in which the English language has contributed to conditioning racial attitudes in American society. These range from the association of blackness with evil, ignorance, and death, to the employment of passive constructions to blame African victims of racial prejudice. Moore calls for what amounts to a deracialization of the English language, arguing that 'while we may not be able to change the language, we can definitely change our usage of the language' (1976:14).

Black English and African American identity

The politics of the English language in the USA came into sharp focus when, on 18 December 1996, the Oakland Unified District Board of Education in California passed a resolution recognizing the variety called Ebonics, Black English, African American Vernacular English (and a host of other names), as the language that many African American students brought to the classroom. Acknowledging this sociolinguistic reality, the board members argued, was essential in determining the appropriate instructional strategies that must be utilized to enhance proficiency in standard American English among African Americans.

Underlying this pedagogic concern, however, and behind the scenes of the national controversy generated by the statement of the Oakland School Board, was the overarching and urgent question of the relationship between language and (African American) identity in the racial context of the USA. Can black people draw from the English language in its more or less standard American form to construct an identity that is peculiarly African American? Or need such an identity be based only on a black-specific variety like Ebonics?

In his concluding keynote address at the national symposium on 'Black Studies: (Re)Defining a Discipline' – held between 22 and 24 May, 1997 at the Ramada University Hotel in Columbus, Ohio, and sponsored by the Department of Black Studies at the Ohio State University – Ali Mazrui distinguished between three possible streams of African American identity formation: mainstream Americanization; pan-Africanization; and separatist black American identity.

How do standard American English, on one hand, and Ebonics or Black English, on the other hand, relate to these identitarian categories?

If African American speech were to approximate the standard variety of American English it could conceivably be an asset in mainstream Americanization of African Americans in the socio-cultural sense of the word. While the English language may indeed be exclusivist in 'racial' terms – it precludes African Americans from acquiring an 'Anglo' identity – it has the potential of bearing the African American experience and making it part of the American national menu. This could lead ultimately to some degree of integration and provide some measure of cultural consolidation of the American leg of African American identity – a case of a shared tongue contributing to the promotion of a shared national identity. As demonstrated in Chapter 1, it is precisely this sense of linguistic Americanhood afforded by standard American English that James Baldwin came to discover while he was in France, having to think and speak in the French language. Baldwin thus came to embrace the very language, English, which previously he had hated and considered as one of the instruments of his racial oppression.

An approximation of standard American English as the African American variety may also be significant in the pan-Africanization of black people in the USA. The linguistic affinity between African Americans and élite members of some African societies during the colonial period, for example, may have been crucial to the development of trans-continental pan-Africanism. Some of the pioneers of the movement, including people like W. E. B. Du Bois from the USA, George Padmore from the Caribbean, and Kwame Nkrumah of Africa, were primarily from 'English-speaking' countries. People of African descent from the 'French-speaking' and 'Portuguese-speaking' black worlds were quite marginal in the pan-African movement in its early stages, partly because its founding figures in the Americas were English-speaking.

The intellectual dimension of pan-Africanism, in particular, must also include the Afrocentric current which, so far, has had its strongest base in the American academy. While many Afrocentrists have themselves drawn tremendous inspiration from the works of French-speaking writers like Cheik Anta Diop of Senegal, their own formulation and articulation of Afrocentric ideas has been primarily in English. If Afrocentricity were to emerge as an influential paradigm throughout the black world, therefore, it is more likely to serve as a cultural bridge between English-speaking blacks in various parts of the world, than between sections of 'Anglophone' blacks, for example, and 'Francophone' and/or 'Lusophone' blacks. It may indeed be significant that when Molefi Kete Asante, one of the leading architects of Afrocentricity, was enstooled as a chief during the summer of 1996, it was in an English-speaking African country (Ghana) rather than in Francophone or Lusophone Africa that he was so honoured.

The dual role of standard American English in African American identity formation has the potential, of course, of precipitating a certain degree of tension and even conflict between the bonds of (American) nationhood and the bonds of (black) consanguity. The national pull of mainstream Americanization engendered by the English language could be in competition with the more global pull of pan-African allegiance. The more successful standard American English may be in the integration of African Americans into the American mainstream, the more likely it will be to weaken the bonds of pan-Africanity.

The role of Ebonics in African American identity formation, on the other hand, is more complex, partly because some questions about its origins and development remain unresolved. Nonetheless, one can identify at least three Ebonics currents in the construction of black identity. The first current would favour black separatist identity within the USA. This is the current based on the idea that Ebonics is exclusively an American-grown medium of African Americans which, though essentially a form of American English, sets them apart from White America. Fay Vaughn-Cooke, the chairperson of the Department of Language and Communication Disorders at the University of the District of Columbia, for example, is among those African American linguists who seem to espouse this 'American-based' view of Ebonics and its relationship to black identity (*Black Issues in Higher Education*, 23 January 1997: 26).

Somewhat related to the above position is the hypothesis that Ebonics emerged in the USA as a creolized form of English. The bulk of the linguistic evidence, argues Adetokunbo Borishade, for example, 'supports that contention that Ebonics is a Creole language' (1994:1). This view of Ebonics can also inspire a pan-African consciousness if it can be demonstrated that the variety has some linguistic parallels with pidgin and creole forms of 'African' English. How comparable to Ebonics is Krio, the language evolved by Black repatriates in Sierra Leone? What features does Ebonics share with West African Pidgin English and, indeed, with some of the West African languages which supposedly contributed to its formation? Could such linguistic affinities constitute a basis for a pan-African identity?

A contrasting view of Ebonics, perhaps best represented by the Princeton-trained linguist and professor at Indiana State University, Carol A. Blackshire-Belay, is the one that regards it as an African-based tongue. According to Blackshire-Belay, 'Ebonics falls into the African form of languages. It is not a dialect of English, even though it uses English words'. She proceeds to point to West African languages like Igbo, Yoruba, Ewe, Wolof, Fante and Mandinka as the relatives of Ebonics (*Black Issues in Higher Education*, 23 January 1997: 26). This is a position, of course, that clearly invokes the pan-African stream of African American identity formation.

The presence alone of African linguistic items and features in Ebonics need not, of course, foster bonds of pan-Africanity. But such Africanisms do have the potential of inspiring and consolidating a pan-African consciousness among those black people who are so inclined ideologically. In general, as different positions on the presence, origins, nature and proportion of Africanisms in Ebonics continue to contend with each other, they may influence different sections of the African American population in different ways as part and parcel of the mythology of identity formation.

In this regard, the decision of the Oakland School Board to declare Ebonics an independent language of the black folk, rather than a dialect of English, is indeed a reflection of the continuing quest for an ethnolinguistic identity – in this case, one with a pan-African orientation – among African Americans under conditions of 'internal colonialism'. To some extent this situation can be compared with that of the Irish. As Deane explains with regard to Irish nationalism:

> At its most powerful, colonialism is a process of radical dispossession. A colonized people is without a specific history and even, as in Ireland and other cases, without a specific language. The recovery from the lost Irish language has taken the form of an almost vengeful virtuosity in the English language, an attempt to make Irish English a language in its own right rather than an adjunct to English itself. (1990: 10).

In the USA, African Americans are about the only minority group whose linguistic heritage has virtually been obliterated by centuries of European enslavement and racial oppression. The struggle about the 'nature' of Ebonics, therefore, must be seen as an aspect of the wider African American struggle for self-definition and (re)possession of their history. This perspective would perhaps explain why even those African Americans who do not themselves use Ebonics have found it necessary to defend its legitimacy at least as an oral tradition.

African languages and African American identity

Another dimension in the bifocal quest for ethnolinguistic identity among African Americans was the attempt to relink, in a more direct manner, with continental African languages. The demand for civil rights, therefore, sometimes came to include the right of access to the African linguistic heritage in the corridors of American academia. The existence of several African languages in American educational institutions that we now seem to take so much for granted is one of the products of those major battles for civil rights on American campuses in the 1960s.

Today African languages are taught widely in American universities and in some high schools, even though Swahili has remained by far the most popular.[2] The right of African Americans to pursue the study of African languages is now widely accepted in the United States. It is, in fact, explicitly recognized in a proposed National Language Policy, which describes one of its objectives in the following terms: To foster the teaching of languages other than English so that native speakers of English can rediscover the language of their heritage or learn a second language.[3]

The African American quest for an alternative ethnolinguistic symbol of identity rooted in the African continent, however, has not been without its detractors. In my own teaching experience in the United States since 1969, I have often been confronted with two arguments seemingly intended to deride the African American ideological motives for studying African languages. It is argued, first, that if the African American interest in African languages has been prompted by the instrumental quality of English as a language of racism and European slavery, then African languages themselves have not been completely innocent of a similar charge. It is suggested that African 'middlemen' used African languages as the media of communication with their African brethren when pursuing or mobilizing captives for the transcontinental European slave trade. How, then, it is asked, can such African languages be considered any more liberating than the European languages inherited from the 'enslavement' tradition?

There are two fundamental problems with this argument. First, it unjustifiably puts the African middlemen in the European slave trade at par with the European owners of Africans who were enslaved in the 'New World' and elsewhere. Coming from a more humane tradition of indigenous 'slavery',[4] these middlemen did not even have a sense of the multifarious horrors of the transatlantic European slavery system. They were no more than peripheral and transient 'entrepreneurs' in this new human commodity whose contact with other African peoples, except in very few instances, did not lead to linguistic dislocations of any magnitude. In essence, it is the linguistic experience in the Americas, and not the contact with African middlemen, that led to the African American loss of a continental African ethno-linguistic identity. And it is against this particular experience that African Americans now seek to establish a linguistic reconnection with the African continent.

The second problem with this argument is its ahistorical, static quality. Language is not a mass of lifeless molecules. It is, in a sense, a living organism that responds dynamically to changing politico-economic stimuli. Thus the language of Russian tsardom also became the language of Bolshevik socialism; the language of English feudalism also became the language of its liberal capitalism. So, if Swahili or Yoruba, for example, were used in the European slave trade at some point in history, they 'moved on' to become important media of struggle against, and opposition to, European imperialism. On the other hand, even after the abolition of European slavery, the English language in the United States has continued to be the language of a racialist, oppressive class that continues to articulate its legitimating ideology through this particular linguistic medium. There continues to be a cultural dimension to the legacy of European slavery, which has sometimes induced a re-emphasis on cultural continuities and a re-establishment of cultural links with continental Africa.

The second argument against the African American quest for a linguistic 'return to the source' has tended to be targeted specifically against Swahili. By the 1960s Swahili was second only to Arabic as the most widely spoken African language on the continent. It was already spoken across several national boundaries. In Kenya, Tanzania and Uganda it was beginning to acquire some national and official status. It had demonstrated its ability to serve as a common medium of communication among African people of diverse ethnic origins in their struggle against European colonial rule in eastern Africa. Later, it was increasingly to be heard on radio broadcasts throughout the world. In Tanzania, Swahili was also beginning to acquire a reputation as a counter-idiom of class oppression, as a linguistic medium of an African-based socialism or *Ujamaa*. It was also in the heartland of Swahili political culture that transcontinental pan-Africanism found its 'resurgence' with the convening in Tanzania of the Sixth Pan-African Congress. And it is the combination of these and other political reasons that rendered Swahili the most popular language among African Americans.

But as the momentum for the study of Swahili was growing, opinions reminiscent of the divide-and-rule policies of the colonial era in Africa began to emerge in the United States. Swahili, it has sometimes been pointed out, is an eastern African language, while Africans in the Americas originated from West

Africa. It is suggested, then, that their search for an ethnolinguistic identification with Africa should be directed at western African languages like Yoruba and Wolof, and not at an eastern African language like Swahili. After decades of attempts to divide peoples of continental Africa along ethnolinguistic lines, a similar rationalizing equation was brought into play at the level of global Africa.

First, it is not completely true that East Africa did not feature in the European slave trade across the Atlantic Ocean. There were Portuguese, Spanish, and French connections in eastern Africa that contributed in no small measure to the translocation of Africans. The Portuguese are known to have procured Africans to be enslaved from the East African coast from the very beginning of their encounter with the region in the fifteenth century. At first the Portuguese also supplied enslaved Africans to the French. But as a result of recurrent Swahili struggles against the Portuguese, the French turned their attention to the East African port of Kilwa and made their own arrangements for procuring slaves. The Spanish are also known to have taken thousands of enslaved Africans from the Swahili coast around the Cape to South America (Nicholls, 1971:200). Furthermore, slave raids in western Africa sometimes went deep into the Congo, where Bantu languages akin to Swahili were spoken. Following Philip Curtin's estimates, for example, Joseph Holloway and Winifred Vass argue that close to sixty per cent of enslaved Africans imported in ships known to the British Foreign Office between 1817 and 1843 came from Bantu-speaking areas of the continent (1993:xxv), and continue to demonstrate that over a third of the linguistic Africanisms in the Gullah language of South Carolina are, in fact, of Bantu origin (1994:1–77).

But to attempt to justify the promotion of Swahili or any other African language in the United States of America on the basis of these demographic features of the European slave trade is to succumb to a Eurocentric perspective. It is a line of reasoning that misconceives the nature of African American consciousness of their Africanity. The ethnolinguistic divisions in continental Africa that Eurocentric scholarship is wont to highlight do not exist, nor need they exist, in the African American collective imagination. African consciousness in the Americas has always placed emphasis on the continent's unifying qualities and not on its *divisive attributes*, and it is perhaps for this reason that transcontinental pan-Africanism, though inspired by the 'motherland', was born in the African diaspora before it established roots on the African continent. As Kariamu Welsh-Asante rightly points out:

> Perhaps it is only the diasporan African who can conceptualize and contextualize different traditions under one rubric. It is the diasporan African's privilege and position that allows her to see Africa as a concept as well as a diverse and multicultural component. (1993:1)

There is thus some sense of shared destiny among peoples of the African diaspora that seeks a common political expression which may, of course, vary in degree and form. In the process Africa has become fused to a point where any of its languages could serve as a shared source of inspiration and symbolic expression of a new consciousness among African Americans. And for reasons mentioned earlier, Swahili turned out to be one of the natural choices for this purpose.

At another level this particular African American linguistic initiative can be seen as an extension of the growing pro-Swahili sentiments within continental Africa itself. Swahili is offered as a university subject not only in eastern Africa, but in some western African universities, in places like Nigeria and Ghana. And distinguished creative writers from eastern Africa (like Ngugi wa Thiong'o) and western Africa (like Wole Soyinka) have, at different times, campaigned for its establishment as a pan-African language of the continent. There is a sense, then, in which African Americans are inadvertently responding to the silent throbbings of a continental African quest for unity whose linguistic manifestation has sometimes tended to revolve mainly around the Swahili language.

The microlinguistics of identity

We have so far discussed the question of African languages in the African American experience at a macro-linguistic political level. What, then, are some of its micro-linguistic political manifestations? There is no doubt that the micro-dimension of this issue is bound to vary a great deal from place to place, from experience to experience, from individual to individual. It is nonetheless possible to make at least two generalizations.

The first generalization has to do with naming. The demise of European colonial rule in Africa brought with it an entire naming 'revolution'. This was part and parcel of the wider movement(s) of African consciousness variously called 'African nationalism' in some places, 'Negritude' in others, 'authenticity' in places like Zaire and so forth. In clusters of domino effect, people began to drop their Euro-Christian names and 'return' to more indigenous naming systems abounding in various African languages. And since these naming systems are founded on a deep-rooted gnosis that defines relations with people, history, or the environment, their re-adoption has been, in effect, a wider cultural embrace between Africa and its sons and daughters.

The naming revolution that has been going on in Africa has also found expression among African Americans. Since the 1960s many of them have looked upon African languages as a source of symbolic affirmation of their African identity. An increasing number came to discard their baptismal names and acquire African names. In the words of Molefi Asante,

> During the 1960s and 1970s, we came to terms with our collective name and chose to be either 'African,' 'Afro-American,' or 'black' rather than 'Negro' or 'colored'. We must certainly sooner or later make the same observation on a personal level that we have made on a collective level. In the future there is no question that this will be undertaken on many occasions. It is not only logical, it is practical and we have always responded to logic and pragmatism. The practical value of changing our names is in identification of names with people. We are an African people and it is logical for us to possess African names. Already we are on the verge of a breakthrough. Young black parents are seeking African names for their children in an attempt to assign meaning to their identity. (1988:27–8)

Euro-Christian names, however, have been seen not only as a method of negating the Africanity of African Americans, but also of inflicting racial blows against them. As Livingston pointed out: 'Names have been used not only to identify a human being but also to vilify, depersonalize and dehumanize. Sam and Sambo, which Dr Puckett identified as common names for enslaved of the seventeenth century, became racist slurs in the twentieth century when black men were commonly summoned by these names' (1975:v). This racial politics of naming in fact came to inspire Puckett (1975) to undertake an extensive study of the origins and usage of different names in the African American experience, tracing some to the American enslavement context and many others to African languages from various parts of the continent.

Unlike their compatriots on the African continent, however, many African Americans who opt for African names do not select them in accordance with any specific African ethnic tradition. Often names have been selected for their symbolic and semantic content even if they are at variance with the ethnic naming systems from which they are derived. First and last African names among African Americans have sometimes come from different ethnic groups and even different countries: Kwame Toure, for example (a Ghanaian first name and Guinean last name). What we are witnessing among African Americans, then, is the pan-Africanization of Africa's naming system as a result of the particular political circumstances of their space and time, circumstances that have forged an African consciousness that transcends the narrower continental ethnic lines of Yorubaness, Zuluness, Amharaness, and the like. The African naming system among African Americans is yet another example of how political economy can be the mother of culture.

But what is in a name, one might ask. European slavery and racialism in the United States of America have generally reduced African Americans to a rootless state with skin pigmentation as the essence of their being. Their identity became 'black' and their personal names became a reminder of ruthless severance from their roots. The struggle for civil rights, therefore, had to include an affirmation of their Africanity, of the historicity of their being; and this new sense of African identity had to be raised to the realm of public knowledge.

Like material objects, however, identities do not become 'public knowledge' until they are named. Without a label to capture our conception of them, they have little social relevance because there is no awareness of their existence in the first place. The emergence of a new label, therefore, carries with it the elevation of a new sense of identity to the domain of 'public knowledge'. It is this important function of bringing historical Africanity and political pan-Africanity to the public sphere that names from African languages came to serve in the African American experience.

The second generalization on the impact of African languages in the African American experience has to do with the area of ceremony. People generally have a very strong attachment to ceremonial activities, especially of a religious nature. Such activities are important symbolic expressions of valued ideas, events, institutions, struggles and sometimes the entire ideological orientation of a people. As a result, ceremonial activities can be important in enhancing a sense of collective identity, and their demise may not augur well for the collective consciousness of a people. There is also a sense in which the infusion of 'foreign' ceremonial symbols undermines some of the binding elements of an independent identity of a particular society and signals its cultural capitulation to the 'other'. And it is against this backdrop that we must understand the emergence of the *Kwanzaa* ceremony among African Americans.

The legacies of European slavery and colonialism have been important factors in the spread of Christianity and in rendering Christmas and the New Year supreme ceremonial symbols of Euro-Christian pre-eminence among Africans. The growing African consciousness among African Americans led to the birth of *Kwanzaa* as a direct antithesis to Christmas/New Year. Inspired by African harvest ceremonies as markers of new temporal cycles, an entire idiom, drawn mainly from Swahili, came into existence to designate *Kwanzaa* principles, practices and artifacts. The *Kwanzaa* ceremony is, of course, itself rooted in a wider ideology of nationhood propounded by Maulana Karenga (1978). This ideology, *Kawaida*, with its various concepts and principles, is again based on an idiom that is entirely Swahili and seeks to unfold a creative motif for African American identity.[5]

If Maulana Karenga has used Swahili as his main linguistic source of African American ideological and ceremonial idiom, however, some other scholars have drawn more from Africa's multilingual heritage. Kariamu Welsh-Asante, for example, uses terms from both Swahili and Shona in her attempt to define the conceptual parameters of African aesthetics (1993). Though relying primarily on Swahili, Dona Marimba Richards also draws from Yoruba and Dagon to critique Eurocentric ideology and articulate an Afrocentric theoretical paradigm (1994). Once again, therefore, African languages have come to serve as an important source of counter-idiom to European intellectual hegemony, and as a source of symbols of African American counter-consciousness that positively (re)affirms Africanity.

We have seen, then, how the racial circumstances that led to the cultural dis-Africanization of African Americans may also have been responsible for the emergence of a new African consciousness. This naturally led to a quest for counter-philosophies, counter-ideologies, and counter-symbols, often inspired by Africa, to give substance to this new consciousness. In this search African languages, too, came to play an important role. Linguistic Africanisms in certain African American dialects of English and the use of aspects of African languages for naming and ceremonial purposes all came to serve as contributing factors to a neo-Africanity in the African diaspora. But precisely because Eurocentricity always attempts to universalize its paradigms, it regards any counter-insurgency as necessarily provincial, subjecting it to attack and derision. 'Afrocentricity', 'Negritude', 'Africanity' and so forth can be regarded as manifestations of nationalism whose essence is rooted in metaphysics and utopianism. On the other hand, nationalism must also be seen as an indispensable dialectical social stage toward liberation. There has been a tendency among (both European and African) Marxists, in particular, to diminish the importance of this kind of African nationalism in favour of the class struggle, but as Terry Eagleton notes:

> Nationalism ... is in a sense like class. To have it, and to feel it, is the only way to end it. If you fail to claim it or give it up too soon, you will merely be cheated, by other classes and by other nations. Nationalism, like class, would thus seem to involve an impossible irony. It is sometimes forgotten that social class, for Karl Marx at least, is itself a form of alienation, cancelling the particularity of any individual life into collective anonymity. Where Marx differs from the commonplace liberal view of such matters is in his belief that to undo this alienation you had to go, not around class, but somehow all the way through it and out the other side. To wish class or nation away, to seek to live sheer irreducible difference now in the manner of some contemporary post-structuralist theory, is to play straight into the hands of the oppressor. (1990:23)

Africans, therefore, must continue to strive to set their own terms of definition and discourse on the global arena, and the attempts to deride their efforts in this regard must be seen as an ideological offensive that needs to be resisted.

Africa's linguistic revolution:
the African American contribution

But African Americans must not be seen merely as *recipients* in their cultural and linguistic relationship with Africa. They have also been philosophical and political contributors to the formation of movements like Negritude, pan-Africanism, and the African personality. Their African heritage led to the emergence of a distinctive type of music, which has in turn been feeding back to Africa. Even hair styles like 'Afro', though arguably originating in the United States of America, became popularized in Africa partly through the African American link. In other words, the global children of Africa have long had a give-and-take relationship with their mother continent.

What, then, are some of the language-related contributions that African Americans can make to Africa? One important contribution may be in the area of national languages. Many African countries are still grappling with the problem of choosing an indigenous national language. There is usually a felt need that the European languages inherited from the colonial tradition should be replaced with local languages at the national and official levels of operation. But the internal power politics of ethnic pluralism has not always made it easy for African policy makers to elevate one language to national and official status. In many instances, there has been concern that the choice of one ethnic language over others may generate fears of ethnic dominance and propel the countries toward political instability.

The African American quest for a linguistic link with Africa may help internationalize certain African languages from individual African countries. If the trend to study African languages like Hausa, Lingala, Wolof, Zulu and so forth continues to become more firmly established, the languages may acquire an international image that may help reduce their ethnic 'essence'. In this way they may eventually become more acceptable as national languages by speakers of other African languages in their respective countries. Likewise, the popularization of a language like Swahili among African Americans may increase its chances of becoming a pan-African language.

The other language-based contribution to Africa is connected with the *Kwanzaa* ceremony. As indicated earlier, this is a ceremony that has been articulated and brought into the sphere of public knowledge through an African language – Swahili. In Africa there is today a quest for a cultural pan-Africanism, and it has sometimes been suggested that different cultural practices could be adopted from different parts of Africa: Swahili from eastern Africa, a particular mode of dress from West Africa, a cuisine from north Africa, music from Zaire (now the Democratic Republic of the Congo) and the diaspora, and so forth. Is it possible that *Kwanzaa*, with its African idiom, will one day be marked throughout global Africa as one of the cultural components of pan-Africanism and African nationalism?

In the area of public holidays and festivals, African nations have come to mark political events in honour of some national achievements (like Independence Day) or of individual leaders (like Kenyatta Day in Kenya). Through external religious influences, they also celebrate 'foreign' cultural festivals like Christmas, and in some countries, *Idd*. But they have yet to establish a holiday to commemorate more indigenous festivals. Again, the question of ethnic diversity is sometimes posed as a problem: which of the many ethnically based festivities should an African country choose as a national symbol without provoking fears of ethnic privilege and dominance? *Kwanzaa* may be the answer.

Finally, African American thinkers may also serve as catalysts of a linguistic revolution in African philosophy. The formal study of philosophy at African universities has been disproportionately in European languages, and virtually all modern African thinkers of note – from Edward W. Blyden to P. J. Hountondji – have conducted their primary discourse in these languages inherited from the colonial era. This linguistic dependence on the imperial languages has been an obstacle to the democratization of knowledge in Africa. In the words of Ali Mazrui, this is a linguistic bondage

> which has made so much of ideological philosophy in Africa hopelessly élitist even when it is doctrinally opposed to élitism. Much of the philosophy of people like Eduardo Mondlane was committed to liberation and morally concerned about ordinary African people. But most of such ideological philosophy had inadvertently erected for itself a linguistic barrier to keep the ordinary people out (1993:16).

In their quest for a peculiarly African linguistic idiom to represent the conceptual core of their ideological philosophies, therefore, some African American thinkers may be prompting an important linguistic shift from European-centred to African-centred paradigms in the formal study of African thought. And this linguistic shift in turn may spur a new beginning in the (re)construction of knowledge in global Africa at large.

Notes

1. I am indebted to Professor Jaffer Kassimali of Hunter College, New York, for providing stimulation and exchanging views and ideas about certain issues discussed in this chapter.
2. It has been estimated by Juma Mutoro of the State University of New York, Albany, that in 1988, for example, there were over a hundred African language programmes in American universities and that almost invariably Swahili was one of those languages.
3. This policy was developed by the Conference on College Composition and Communication (CCCC) – an affiliate of the National Council of Teachers of English – and adopted during its Executive Committee meeting of March 16, 1988. The other two main objectives of the policy are:
   a) To provide resources to enable native and non-native speakers to achieve oral and literate competence in English, the language of wider communication
   b) To support programmes that assert the legitimacy of native languages and dialects and ensure that proficiency in the mother tongue will not be lost.
4. The anthroplogist, Lucy Mair, for example, made the following observations with regard to slavery among the Baganda of East Africa: 'Certain duties, it is true, were specifically allocated to slaves, but, for the greatest part, they shared in the ordinary life of the household, were described by the head as "his children" and a stranger would not be aware that they were his slaves unless this was expressly explained to him.' (1934:31)
5. The idiom includes principles like *umoja* (unity), *kujichagulia* (self-determination), *ujima* (collective responsibility), *nia* (intention), *kuumba* (creativity), *ujamaa* (socialism/ communalism), and *imani* (faith). Molefi Asante's *Afrocentricity* (1988) also relies heavily on an African linguistic idiom. Swahili concepts like *Kawaida* (tradition), *Njia* (the path), *msingi* (foundation), and others constitute an important pillar of his philosophy.

3
Linguistic Eurocentrism &
African Counter-Penetration

Ali Mazrui
& the Global Frontiers of Language

On 30 March 1995, participants at the Annual African Heritage Studies Association Conference held in Philadelphia had the privilege of hearing an Ali Mazrui address that could be described as truly unprecedented. For the first time in his career as an academic Ali Mazrui made an intellectual presentation that was entirely in an African language, Kiswahili, or more specifically in his native variety of the language, Kimvita. And in spite of Mazrui's own apprehensions about his linguistic adequacy to engage in such serious intellectual discourse in a language other than English, once he became less self-conscious and more spontaneous his performance in Kiswahili was as impressive as many in English that I have had occasion to witness.

Mazrui's Kiswahili presentation was in the form of a twenty-minute video-taped dialogue, with me as the interviewer, on a fairly wide range of issues related to the presence of African languages in the corridors of American academia. His interest in language as a socio-political phenomenon has been, of course, one of the most persistent features of Mazrui's intellectual history over the years. And as he became more globalized intellectually, he became increasingly more concerned about linguistic diversity, in general, and the future of African languages, in particular – all as part of his wider focus on the importance of cultural diversity in world affairs.

In the course of the interview we explored his now familiar concept of *counter-penetration* in terms of its relevance to the world of languages. Mazrui has suggested that, rather than pursue a path of disengagement, the Third World may need to use the strategy of *counter-penetration*, on the political, economic and cultural planes, to counteract the growing Eurocentricization of the world and turn Africa from a mere pawn to a significant player in global affairs. Can the promotion of African languages in American academia, then, appropriately be regarded as a form of *linguistic counter-penetration*? In Mazrui's opinion, yes, this exercise does amount to counter-penetration against some dimensions of what may be described as *linguistic Eurocentrism.*

At one level, linguistic counter-penetration could be seen as an aspect of, and a device for, cultural and conceptual counter-penetration. In this case, a distinction may need to be made between counter-penetrating the West through a non-Western language and counter-penetrating the West through a Western language. Kiswahili language and culture, taught to American children, is a case of counter-penetrating the West through a non-Western language. On the other hand, using the English language to influence or even manipulate Western thought can be a case of counter-penetrating the West through a Western language.

Ali Mazrui's uneasiness at making a public presentation in Kiswahili betrays, of course, the extent to which he has been assimilated into the linguistic world of the English language. In intellectual forums he is more at home in English than he is in his native tongue, Kiswahili. But rather than allow English to make him a captive of a Eurocentric world view, Mazrui has turned the language of his assimilation into a tool of counter-penetration. Like many other African scholars based in Western universities, therefore, Mazrui is using a Western language to help reshape the minds of young Americans in their conception of Africa and world affairs.

What is quite unusual about Ali Mazrui as an African political scientist, however, is that partly as a result of his British education he has also assimilated a significant amount of English literature. Mazrui has thus been able to use English literature as a rhetorical device to help him counter-penetrate the West through the instrumentality of the English language. Sometimes Mazrui has used the substance of English literature in a bid to help the West understand Africa better – going back to his essay in the 1960s on 'Obote's Milton and Nyerere's Shakespeare'. He has also exploited William Wordsworth, Alexander Pope, Charles Dickens, George Crabbe, George Orwell and others. And more recently, of course, there has been his paper on 'O. J. Simpson and Shakespeare's Othello: Race and Rage in the Love-Divided' which was also presented at the 1995 meeting of the African Heritage Studies Association. All this could add up to using English literature as a counter-penetrative rhetoric.

Within the realm of his literary activities there is also the strange phenomenon of *The Trial of Christopher Okigbo*. Under a strong emotional crisis, why did Ali Mazrui choose to fictionalize his torment by writing the novel? Were the reasons similar to the ones which stimulated a poetic exchange between Mazrui and his Mombasa family when Mazrui's sons suddenly went blind? In Swahili culture, poetry was a method of giving anguish a literary release. In writing an English novel as a method of seeking literary release, therefore, Ali Mazrui was, perhaps inadvertently, counter-penetrating a European literary mode (the novel) with a typically Swahili literary tradition (versifying anguish).

These are some of the issues that the multiple Mazrui raises about counter-penetration through a Western language, and the relationship between literary assimilation and linguistic counter-penetration. The primary concern in this essay, however, is how Mazrui's ideas help us understand linguistic counter-penetration through African languages, and more specifically, how the very presence of African languages in the West constitutes a form of (macro-)linguistic counter-penetration in response to a specific form of linguistic Eurocentrism.

Linguistic Eurocentrism defined

But what is linguistic Eurocentrism? We can probably distinguish at least five strands. The first strand is *classificational Eurocentrism*. For a long time, Europeans believed that there was a one-to-one correlation between languages and race: European linguists thus proceeded to divide the languages of the world along racial lines. Anthropologists were eager to give contemporary racial distributions a historical substance, and 'many of their attempts were dependent on the implicit assumption that linguistic distributions and interrelations exactly paralleled those of race and could thus be used as a substitute proof' (Henson, 1974:4).

From the above racialist orientation in the study of language naturally emerged the unscientific assumption that the languages of the 'lower' races were somehow more primitive than the languages of the so-called 'higher' races, and this linguistic difference was itself a manifestation of intellectual differences between these racial 'orders'. Some French linguists like Lefevre, for example, promoted the thesis that the stage of evolution of a language correlated with that of its speakers, and that the inflexional languages supposedly characteristic of Indo-European languages demonstrated the more advanced intellectual stage of people of European origin.

But it was not only the languages of the world that were categorized racially; languages existing within the African continent, too, were subjected to this racial imperative of Eurocentrism. African languages were either Semitic (whose speakers were supposedly off-white in pigmentation and second only to speakers of Indo-European languages in their level of civilization); Hamitic, characterizing brown-coloured people with a low civilizational level; and Negritic, encompassing languages of even darker-skinned people with no civilization at all (Faraclas, 1995). It was only fairly recently that the racial presuppositions in the classification of African languages capitulated to more scientific methodology.

Along the same racialist lines, however, there has long been the underlying suggestion that Africa could not have given birth to the family of Semitic languages, the languages which became carriers of universal religious traditions – one of which, Christianity, came to be embraced by Europeans and appropriated by Eurocentric ideology. As a result, it has been assumed all along that the Semitic languages in Africa came originally from the Middle East, in spite of the fact that the contrary is equally if not more plausible from a linguistic point of view. Even though historical linguists no longer seek racial identities for language groupings, the language-race bias has not been completely uninfluential in the quest for linguistic origins.

In this regard, it is to Mazrui's credit that he has been critical of the position that has regarded the Middle East unequivocally as the cradle of Semitic languages. For geographic and demographic reasons Mazrui had already begun to classify Arabic as an African language. Now, for more historical reasons, he ventured to describe Africa as the most ancient Semitic home. Without the benefit of any historical-linguistic methodology, Mazrui was perceptive enough to see the racially motivated bias in the claim that Semitic languages in Africa could only have been the result of a migratory effect from the Middle East.

Even as the racial paradigm of language classification was abandoned, however, the terminology describing different language families and groups in the world continued to be determined by Europeans. This is the realm of *terminological Eurocentrism*. Ali Mazrui once remarked that the West has invented an entire vocabulary which 'has landed us with unprecedented ways of thinking about our planet, a planet we share. This little continent called Europe went around naming this, that and the other, and it stuck. And we cannot think of the world in terms other than those of words they bequeathed to us' (1993:16).

This naming process, however, has affected the world of human languages as much as the language of human experience of the world. All language families, for example, from Indo-European to Afro-Asiatic, from Germanic to Cushitic, have been named by Europeans on the basis of criteria determined by Europeans. Of course, most of the names describing African language groups have been derived

44

from African languages themselves. But the fact remains that it was Europeans, rather than Africans, who selected these general labels to describe the relationship between the different languages. The terminology of language classification, therefore, has continued to be overwhelmingly Eurocentric, even though this belongs, perhaps, to that corpus of 'Eurocentric things' which, in Mazrui's opinion cannot be easily changed.

The third sense of linguistic Eurocentrism is *semantic*. This refers, in particular, to the tendency of European languages to use terms like 'animism', 'tribe', 'primitive' and so forth in describing the African world, and to associate negative images with the terms. With regard to the English language, specifically, Mazrui has argued that 'because of its origins as a language of white-skinned people, it has accumulated a heritage of imagery that had invested black men with negative connotations' (1974:98). But Mazrui's humanism prevents him from recommending a strategy of counter-penetration which would merely invert the black-white metaphor in terms of its connotative meanings. This, to Mazrui, would amount to Eurocentric racism with an African face. Rather, as an African strategy against semantic Eurocentrism, Mazrui proposes the deracialization of the English language. This is the process by which the language would be tamed and domesticated in the direction of greater compatibility with the dignity and experience of people of African descent (1974:99).

Linguistic Eurocentrism can also be *orthographic*. European missionaries and scholars undertook a monumental task when they set out to reduce many hitherto unscripted African languages to writing. Invariably, however, it was the Latin script that came to serve as the foundation of this important exercise. In many instances, the Latinization of African languages was the best one could expect of the missionaries, since their orthographic competence may not have extended beyond the Latin script. There were missionary scholars, however, who were quite well versed in other scripts, especially the Arabic script, which was often acquired as part of a broader agenda to undermine the spread of Islam. Nonetheless, the possibility of using the Arabic script, for example, in writing African languages that have some affinity with Arabic was never entertained. On the contrary, languages like Hausa and Kiswahili, which had adopted the Arabic script centuries before European colonialism were now subjected to orthographic conversion almost overnight. The Arabic script came to be marginalized by the deliberate push of colonial powers in favour of the Latin script. And, in time, literacy too came to be judged in these new terms of orthographic Eurocentrism.

In East Africa, the person who was most prominently associated with the campaign against the orthographic Latinization of Kiswahili was, in fact, Sheikh Al-Amin bin Ali Mazrui, Ali Mazrui's father and the leading Islamic scholar of his time in that entire region. Sheikh Al-Amin considered the Arabic script to be particularly suited to written Kiswahili due to what he believed to be the strong lingo-cultural affinities between the two languages, Arabic and Kiswahili. In a hostile political environment charged with racial and sectarian sentiments, therefore, the colonial agenda to Latinize Kiswahili was regarded as part of a wider attempt to distance the language from its Arabo-Islamic connections.

If his father was in the forefront of the struggle against orthographic penetration of Swahililand by the West, however, Ali Mazrui, himself a son of Swahililand, has more recently been engaged in discussions on *orthographic counter-penetration* of the West. If Europeans have been transporting their Latin script to the Third World, could Third World peoples with established non-Latin scripts now subject

European languages to *their* alphabets? Should Arab-speaking and Amharic-speaking children, for example, learn English in Arabic and Amharic scripts, respectively? While such an experiment may not prevent the expansion of linguistic Eurocentrism, it may empower the non-Latin scripts of Africa sufficiently to ensure their survival for a long time to come.

Finally, there is the *demographic* sense of linguistic Eurocentrism – a strand of linguistic Eurocentrism that has concerned Ali Mazrui probably more than any of the other four. This refers to European linguistic expansionism and linguistic domination of peoples of other nations and nationalities, increasingly resulting in the capitulation of the world to European languages as first or additional media. Within the global constellation of languages European languages have become dominant to the point of marginalizing other languages and rendering some of them virtually extinct. In addition, Eurocentric ideology has presented this global dominance of European languages as both right and desirable. In fact, even in the quest for a supposedly neutral interlanguage, such as Esperanto, there were Eurocentric organizations like the American Philosophical Society which felt that such an artificial medium should be based on 'Aryan' languages (Forster, 1982:55).

The European tongue that has had spectacular global success is, of course, the English language. And in its steady expansion the language has no doubt become a major source of new words that have enriched the vocabularies of several African languages. But, as Ali Mazrui points out, in the process it also:

> distorted educational priorities, diverted resources from indigenous cultures giving English pre-eminence, and diluted the esteem in which indigenous African languages were held. The psychological damage to the colonized African was immense. Most Africans not only seemed to accept that their own languages were fundamentally inferior to the English language; they became convinced that it was not worth doing anything about it (1995:5).

This is the psychological condition that Mazrui describes as *linguistic fatalism.* By marginalizing indigenous languages in national life, English has also contributed to their stultification. And by its psychological impact on the indigenous population, Africans themselves seem to have lost the will to sustain their languages.

In opposing the Esperantist movement Antonio Gramsci once argued that a truly international language can only emerge organically and spontaneously from the ranks of the people, and that such a development was possible only under conditions created by socialist internationalism. In Gramsci's words:

> The Socialists are struggling for the creation of the economic and political conditions necessary to install collectivism and the International. When the International is formed, it is possible that the increased contacts between peoples, the methodical and regular integration of large masses of workers, will slowly bring about a reciprocal adjustment between the Aryo-European languages and will probably extend them throughout the world, because of the influence the new civilization will exert. (1985:30)

But alas, Gramsci's linguistic Eurocentrism notwithstanding, it was the forces of *international capitalism*, rather than those of an anticipated *international socialism* which provided the unprecedented impetus for the globalization of European languages, and especially of the English language.

The question that concerns many people is whether the English language has not, in fact, begun to threaten linguistic diversity in the very cradle of human

46

language, Africa.[1] Will some African languages simply 'die out' as they lose more and more of their speakers to English, leading eventually to the total anglicization of the continent? It has been estimated that, at one time, there were hundreds if not thousands of Native American languages in the USA. The majority of these appear to have fallen into disuse, having 'died out' as a result of the linguistic assimilation of successive generations of their speakers into the world of English. Are African languages likely to suffer the same fate as Native American languages? Is Africa's triple linguistic heritage[2] – encompassing the indigenous tradition, the Islamic legacy and the Western impact – likely to be neutralized by the expansionism of the English language? At the moment this does appear to be a real though by no means an imminent threat. At the same time, however, we should not forget that there are many 'vulnerable' African languages which are sometimes threatened more by 'conquering' African languages like Hausa and Kiswahili than by Euro-languages. It is also interesting that 'minor' African languages are endangered more by post-colonial dynamics of language interaction than by colonial ones.

In spite of the seemingly unimpeded expansion of the English language in Africa, however, there are some politico-economic trends within the continent which may recurrently prompt local languages to fight back and ensure their survival in the short run. These may range from nationalist sentiments against foreign domination to advocacy of ethno-linguistic pluralism as an integral part of the wider campaign against local domination by ethno-autocratic forces.

The diaspora
and Africa's linguistic counter-penetration

Yet another factor that may aid the continued survival of some indigenous African languages is a more global one: *linguistic counter-penetration* engendered by the African diaspora. Just as Western languages have penetrated deep into the African continent, the growth of the African disapora in Canada, Europe and the USA has enabled African languages to begin counter-penetrating the West. Ali Mazrui has drawn a distinction between the older, African diaspora of enslavement and the more recent African diaspora of colonization. Each of these diasporas has contributed to Africa's linguistic counter-penetration in a different way.

The diaspora of enslavement refers to people of African descent who have been dispersed to various parts of the world as a result of the transcontinental slave trade. This diaspora includes the offspring of the millions who were shipped across the Atlantic to the Americas, as well as the offspring of the millions who were transported across the Sahara and the Indian Ocean to the Arab world and, to a lesser extent, to India.

With regard to the language question, in particular, there are similarities and differences between the Western section of the diaspora of enslavement and its Eastern section (that based in the Arab world and Asia). The main similarity is that both sections lost their African linguistic heritage and became assimilated into the linguistic milieu of their enslavers. Thus English became to African Americans what Arabic, for example, became to African Arabians. There is, of course, the phenomenon that has been described by a host of names (including Black English, African American English, Ebonics and so forth) which is part of the African American 'sub-culture' and which is said to manifest a number of linguistic

Africanisms. In the final analysis, however, African American English is more a variety of the English language than of any African language or combination of African languages.

On the other hand – and here we come to the main difference – the Arabic language has also been assimilative in identitarian terms in a way that English has not been. Arabic is among those languages that Mazrui defined as *communalist*, a paradigm which, in the case of Arabic, allows any person who speaks it as a mother tongue to be 'racially' classified as Arab. This absorptive capacity of the Arabic language, among other factors, naturally led to the acquisition of Arab identity among people of African descent in the Arab world, leading ultimately to a recession of their African consciousness. This same analysis can be extended, perhaps, to the African disapora of enslavement in other parts of the Eastern region.

The English language, on the other hand, is among those described by Mazrui as *ecumenical*, languages which, in the particular case of European languages, do not admit into their 'racial' fold people who are not genetically European. In the USA, in the Caribbean, in Britain, and even in parts of Africa, there are literally millions of people of African descent who speak English as their mother tongue. But this sociolinguistic fact alone has not qualified them for European identity. No matter how extensively assimilated African Americans became in linguistic and cultural terms, therefore, the Eurocentric paradigm of identity ensured that they would remain American with qualification.

As indicated in the last chapter, this racial exclusiveness of the indentitarian boundaries of the English language, as well as its semantic Eurocentrism, prompted African Americans to include in their demands for civil rights the right of access to their African linguistic heritage in the corridors of American academia. And this quest to relink with the African linguistic heritage has, in turn, consolidated the global position of some African languages.

In addition to the struggles for civil rights, there were also the anti-war sentiments which helped the fortunes of African languages in American academia. In a personal correspondence with me Ali Mazrui identified three historic movements in the 1960s in the United States: first, the civil rights movement; second, the students' movement; and third the movement against the war in Vietnam. These movements impacted on the destiny of African languages in different ways.

As indicated earlier, the civil rights movement helped the cause of African languages by reactivating Black consciousness and reviving some degree of pan-Africanism. On the other hand, Mazrui regards the concurrent students' movement for academic reforms as having harmed the cause of all language requirements in the syllabuses for degrees. Students' demands for fewer academic regulations included the relaxation of age-old linguistic requirements. All foreign languages were the losers in this aspect of the students' revolution.

If the civil rights movement helped African languages, and the students' movement harmed them, what effect on African languages did the Vietnam War have? US involvement in Vietnam was part of the Cold War, and this Mazrui regards as 'good news' for African languages. The Cold War created a definition of 'national security' in Washington, DC which generated funds for 'area studies', including African studies. Moreover, special status was granted to centres of African studies which taught African languages. The much coveted Title VI status with federal authorities is still not normally granted to any unit without linguistic qualifications.

In Mazrui's opinion, therefore, the concerns for national security precipitated by the Cold War and the clarion call of 'Black is Beautiful' found an unlikely meeting point. Unlike the students' movement, African American nationalism and the Cold War helped to create a greater demand for African languages in the United States.

Even though African Americans were in the forefront of the campaign to get African languages introduced into American academia, however, the languages are now studied by students across racial lines. And, in the opinion of Mazrui, this is as it should be. If the study of African languages is restricted to African Americans, then the whole counter-penetration agenda will have been undermined. If linguistic counter-penetration is to be a response, in part, to linguistic Eurocentrism, then African languages need to become part of the linguistic repertoires of people of European descent. Foreign language proficiency can indeed be used for imperialist ends; but it could also be used for constructive ends. Europeans who learn African languages will have acquired a linguistic window for the comprehension of the African cultural landscape; and armed with this understanding they would probably have been better equipped to participate in the construction of a new and more peaceful world order.

In his television series *The Africans: A Triple Heritage* Mazrui lamented how African Americans have been denied the privilege of nostalgia in their relationship with the continent of their forefathers. They were uprooted in a most brutal way, leaving no record of the exact lingo-cultural communities of their origin in Africa. As a result, Africa increasingly became more of a unified concept than a localized experiential reality to the members of the African diaspora of enslavement. Their efforts, therefore, have predictably led to the establishment of relatively few African languages, especially the more trans-national ones. And precisely because Kiswahili is the most pan-African of the indigenous languages spoken in Africa south of the Sahara, it has tended to be the most popular African language in American academia.

The diaspora that seems to foster a linguistic counter-penetration of the West with a greater multiplicity of African languages is, of course, the diaspora of colonization. This diaspora includes people of African origin who have been dispersed to other parts of the world, especially the West, as a result of conditions precipitated by European colonialism and its aftermath. Colonialism itself may have come to an end in Africa. But the conditions it set in motion, and their multifarious effects, have continued to bedevil the continent to this day. That is why even people who are being 'diasporized' in this post-colonial phase can be regarded as part of the diaspora of colonization. For reasons ranging from the political to the economic the West has been experiencing a growing presence of Africans directly from the continent since the colonial days, Africans who are settling in the West and, perhaps uneasily, regarding it as their new home.

Ironically, it is precisely the European linguistic domination ushered in by colonialism that has created ripe conditions for Africa's own linguistic counter-penetration of the West through the diaspora of colonization. For a long time, African labour could only migrate from one part of a country to another, or at best from one African country to a conterminous one within the same geographical region. But the acquisition of European languages, as additional media, has now accorded African labour the capacity to be mobile on a transcontinental level. With the faculty of the English language, for example, Africans from the Anglophone region of Africa can now migrate more readily than ever before to English-speaking parts of Europe, Canada and the USA, in the process taking with them a whole range of African tongues to their new homes. The diaspora of colonization thus comes to provide the West with a much wider and more readily available African linguistic resource base from which to draw for the benefit of its interested learners.

Documentary counter-penetration: between Ngugi and Mazrui

A special case of African linguistic penetration concerns scholarly publications in African languages in the West. John Innis Mtembezi, an African American Swahilist, has long been producing his Kiswahili publication, *Mfumbuzi*, that covers a wide range of issues of current interest to both continental African and African Americans. Ousseynou Traore, founding editor of *The Literary Griot* has been encouraging critical and theoretical essays in African languages for inclusion in the journal. In an unprecedented move, the Fall 1991 issue of the Yale *Journal of Criticism* carried an article in Gikuyu by the leading Kenyan novelist, Ngugi wa Thiong'o. And more recently Ngugi himself launched *Mutiiri*, an ambitious journalistic project, that uses his native language, Gikuyu.

In connection with *Mutiiri*, in particular, Ali Mazrui made reference, in the introductory part of his Kiswahili video presentation, to an interesting exchange between himself and Ngugi wa Thiong'o. Mazrui's subscription to *Mutiiri* on behalf of The Institute of Global Cultural Studies was apparently accompanied by a personal letter to Ngugi raising the possibility of making *Mutiiri* a Gikuyu-Kiswahili bilingual journal. Noting that no one at his institute could read an exclusively Gikuyu *Mutiiri*, Mazrui felt that the bilingualization of the journal would automatically quadruple its constituency and readership and, subsequently, multiply its own chances of survival in an otherwise unfavourable linguistic environment. Mazrui was of the opinion that in its rapid expansion in Africa Kiswahili has sometimes threatened other African languages. Now, as the second language of bilingual African publications in the West, Kiswahili could perhaps contribute to their consolidation. Such cooperation between African languages, in other words, could strengthen Africa's capacity for the linguistic counter-penetration of the West.

Ngugi, on the other hand, expressed the concern that a bilingual *Mutiiri* would foster a kind of dependency relationship between Gikuyu and Kiswahili that might not be in the developmental interest of Gikuyu. For, to presume that what was intended essentially to be a Gikuyu publication could not survive without the aid of Kiswahili would be to encourage, though indirectly perhaps, the same psychology of linguistic fatalism of which Mazrui himself has been a critic. To Ngugi then – himself an ardent advocate of Kiswahili as a *world* language – Africa's linguistic counter-penetration would be enhanced if African languages *separately* could demonstrate self-sufficiency and self-reliance as media of intellectual, scholarly and technological discourse. Rather than having two or more African languages 'teaming up' to promote one journal, Ngugi recommends the establishment of as many periodicals as possible in individual African languages in accordance with the linguistic proficiency of their founder-editors. In his own case, Ngugi claims to be most proficient in his native tongue, Gikuyu; his *Mutiiri*, therefore, could only appear in Gikuyu. Those most proficient in Kiswahili, for example, should be encouraged to produce a Kiswahili journal.

Between Ali Mazrui and Ngugi wa Thiong'o, then, we have two paradigms of documentary linguistic counter-penetration; one based on linguistic strength founded on linguistic unity, and the other on linguistic credibility founded on the demonstration of individual linguistic capacity. And only time can tell which of these two paradigms will ultimately prove to be in the best interest of Africa's agenda of linguistic counter-penetration of the West.

Conclusion:
linguistic diversity in a polycentric world

Both the diaspora of enslavement and the diaspora of colonization have made important contributions to the survival and promotion of African languages. Typically, the diaspora of enslavement fed into the demand side of African languages, while the diaspora of colonization fed into the supply side of African languages in the West. As African Americans helped to generate the demand for African languages, Africans in America provided some of the teachers of the languages. In the process some African languages have become transcontinental, too, with Arabic, Hausa, Swahili and Yoruba showing the greatest success so far, partly because they have gained from the input of both diasporas.

But are these languages that are being sustained by the African diaspora likely to survive in the West? Will they not ultimately die out as their African pioneers and their descendants get assimilated by the English language? There are two factors that may indeed aid their survival for some time to come. The first factor is, ironically, the state of racism. The persistence of racism in the West is likely to continue breeding strong nationalist sentiments which may encourage diaspora Africans to cling to, or to relink with, their African linguistic heritage. Growing racism in France, for example, has fed the nationalist sentiments of North African immigrants, leading to a kind of lingo-cultural assertion in favour of the continued use of the Arabic language.

The other factor that may help sustain African languages in the West is anti-racism as expressed, in particular, by the growing quest for multiculturalism. Multiculturalism is after all a response to the racialist ideology of Eurocentrism. The multicultural momentum in places like the USA and Britain, therefore, may provide some space for African languages to exist and thrive, and to be constantly rejuvenated by the influx of new immigrants from Africa.

In short, then, aided by the multicultural trend in the West the African diasporas, both of enslavement and of colonization, may continue to play a significant counter-penetrating role in the destiny of African languages. And the internationalization of these languages through the diaspora effect may, in turn, provide part of the impetus for their resistance to annihilation by European linguistic penetration.

Both in Africa and in the West, therefore, there are signs that African languages are not about to fall. Local politico-economic spaces and the tendency in the diaspora towards counter-penetration are likely to empower some of them, in some way or other, and thus augment their resilience. Linguistic diversity across the seas is likely to survive in spite of the seemingly irresistible hegemony of the English language.

Linguistic counter-penetration is, of course, partly based on the belief that *linguistic diversity* is itself a desirable, if not altogether necessary, pursuit of the human community. It is important, however, to recognize the limitations of the ideology of linguistic diversity under the present politico-economic world order. This ideology presupposes that all languages are morally equal, and that, therefore, each has the right to have an unrepressed presence at the global linguistic banquet. In the real world, however, languages are not equal. While some are privileged as the languages of politico-economic power and control, others are marginalized, and others still are pushed to the verge of oblivion.

If global linguistic diversity is to take root, then, it must be built on politico-economic empowerment based on a new world order. For a long time the world was polarized between two politico-economic super-powers, the USA and the Soviet Union. Then the world was essentially bicentric. Now the world is contending with only one super-power, the USA. The world has become virtually unicentric. A linguistically diverse world, however, may require a more polycentric equation, a globe which, in Samir Amin's conception, has multiple centres of politico-economic power and one which is respectful of different economic and social paths of development (1989: 151). Advocates of linguistic and cultural diversity, therefore, may also have to be engaged in a much wider struggle for the politico-economic reorganization of the world system.

A world order that is more balanced politically and economically may not, of course, guarantee a state of linguistic and cultural diversity for all time to come. There may still arise universalistic developments which may privilege some and marginalize other languages and cultures. But in a more balanced world order such universalistic developments are unlikely to be entirely Eurocentric as they have so far been. It will probably be a universalism that is more sensitive to the contributions of the different sections of the global community. Diversity within a polycentric world, therefore, may be a first step towards a healthier universalism built on a multicultural heritage, a universalism that is more in accord with Ali Mazrui's preferred sense of 'a world culture'.

Notes

1. Since, on present evidence, Africa is where the human species originated, it is where human communication is likely to have begun. Of course there has been the suggestion that there was a *homo erectus* population that spread throughout the 'old world' – Africa, Asia and Europe – and that each of these three regions served as an independent stimulus for the evolution of the *homo sapiens*. The implication here, then, is that human language may have developed not from one source, Africa, but from three independent sources.

   This hypothesis, however, clearly overlooks an important historical-linguistic principle: that the area where languages show the greatest divergence and differentiation is where their proto-language is likely to have originated. Africa, therefore, is the most likely home of the human proto-language. For *per capita* today Africa still remains the richest continent in terms of sheer number of languages as well as the variety of language groups. If ever there was a Tower of Babel on this earth, it is likely to have been in Africa.

2. See Chapter 5 of this volume.

4
Language
& the Quest for Liberation

The Legacy of Frantz Fanon

One important dimension in the quest for mental liberation in Africa has often been seen in terms of a deterministic relationship between language, culture and cognition. Language is sometimes regarded as a reservoir of culture which controls human thought and behaviour and sets the boundaries of the world view of its users. In the words of Peter Mwaura:

> Language influences the way in which we perceive reality, evaluate it and conduct ourselves with respect to it. Speakers of different languages and cultures see the universe differently, evaluate it differently, and behave towards its reality differently. Language controls thought and action and speakers of different languages do not have the same world view or perceive the same reality unless they have a similar culture or background. (1980: 27)

The natural deduction drawn from this linguistic determinism, then, is that to overcome a particular perception of reality one first has to escape from the prison house of its corresponding language.

This position on the hegemonic power of language, which is mostly prevalent among some Africans of a neonationalist[1] persuasion, has its origins in what has come to be known as the Sapir-Whorf hypothesis in linguistics. According to Edward Sapir, for example:

> Human beings are very much at the mercy of the particular language which has become the medium of expression for their society.... The fact of the matter is that the 'real world' is to a large extent built up on the language habits of the group. No two languages are ever sufficiently similar to be considered as representing the same reality. (1929:208)

Benjamin Lee Whorf was an even more enthusiastic proponent of linguistic determinism. He claimed that a person's basic ontology is structured by language and that grammar embodies the nascent form of a cultural metaphysics. According to him each language is encoded with a particular mode of thought, a metaphysics that affects the speaker's experience at the level of perception. For this reason he concludes that speakers of different languages will map the world in different ways; the linguist's task is to work out the fragments of a notional grammar (categories of time, space, gender, etc.) and to determine the semantic associations by means of which it is translated into a cultural world view.[2]

These determinists and their followers were especially concerned with the influence of language on its *native* speakers. Native language acquisition itself was partly seen as a gradual process of giving shape to a world view. Different world views emerge out of different communities acquiring and speaking their different native tongues within their respective cultural environments.

Linguistic determinism in the African context

In Africa, however, linguistic determinism has often been extended to second language situations. There has been a basic assumption that the world view 'inherent' in any particular language can be transposed onto the speakers of another, unrelated, language. European languages inherited from the colonial tradition which, in Africa, are usually acquired as second or third languages, often in formal classroom situations, are seen to exercise great control on African thinking and perceptions. Describing the colonial situation, for example, Ngugi wa Thiong'o states:

> The language of an African child's formal education was foreign. The language of the books he read was foreign. Thought in him took the visible form of a foreign language.... [The] colonial child was made to see the world and where he stands in it as seen and defined by or reflected in the culture of the language of imposition. (1986: 17)

This leads Ngugi to conclude that the 'domination of a people's language by languages of the colonising nations was crucial to the domination of the mental universe of the colonised'. (1986: 16) This thesis draws its support from the observation that those who are most proficient in European languages are also the most Westernised culturally.[3]

Against this backdrop, then, mental liberation in Africa has sometimes been seen, at least in part, in terms of reducing the European linguistic hold on the continent and elevating indigenous African languages to a more central position in society. Ngugi's own efforts to write in his native tongue, Gikuyu, are not only an exercise in reaffirming the dignity of African languages, but also a modest attempt to counteract the influence of European languages on African minds.

But how valid is the thesis that English as an additional language, for example, has tended to define the mental universe of its speakers in Africa? Are the European cultural manifestations among Africans who have acquired European languages merely superfluous or are they indicative of a deeper cognitive control by these languages?

Psycholinguists have drawn a distinction between a coordinate bilingual and a compound bilingual. A coordinate bilingual is said to operate in two (or more) languages somewhat independently of each other. In essence a coordinate bilingual 'controls' two cultures and two 'world views' corresponding to the two languages in his/her repertoire. Switching from one language to another means crossing cultural and cognitive boundaries to a different mental universe.

A compound bilingual, on the other hand, it said to operate in the additional language only through the grid of the 'more basic language'. The speaker maintains only one world view 'defined' normally by the first language and through which the additional language is processed. People who acquire additional languages are supposedly inclined more towards compound than coordinate bilingualism.

The African neonationalists who espouse the extreme form of linguistic determinism also seem to regard the bilingualism in African and European languages as essentially compound. But in their case, it is the *additional* European languages which are believed to provide the basic cultural and cognitive grid for the operation of the *native*, African languages, and not the reverse. This is a position that is unlikely to be regarded as tenable in psycholinguistics.

Elsewhere, I have also indicated that linguistic determinism has itself fallen into disrepute over the years,[4] and that the position of the linguistic neonationalists – who see a cause and effect relationship between African languages and mental decolonization – can find little support in the colonial and post-colonial history of language use and language policies in Africa (Mazrui,1992). What the neonationalists have done in fact is make a fetish of language, endowing it with the power of colonization or liberation in a manner that is ahistorical, static and undialectical.

Language and the colonial experience

The bulk of the evidence presented by the neonationalists in support of their thesis is based on the colonial experience. Colonial authorities tend to be regarded as having pursued a monolithic language policy aimed at destroying African languages and establishing the supremacy of European languages for the explicit purpose of controlling the world view of the colonized (Ngugi, 1986: 16). However, this monolithic view of the colonial experience obscures policy differences that ranged from the French goal of linguistic-cultural assimilation to the exclusivist German approach that denied the colonial subject any access to the language of the colonial master. In fact the latter policy contributed significantly to the consolidation of the Swahili language in what was then German East Africa.

Colonial language policies varied according to the identity of the colonizing power: different areas within a single colonial empire, moreover, were sometimes subject to divergent political interests that expressed themselves in language policy. In Chapter 1 of this book Ali Mazrui cites the cases of Franco-Flemish rivalry in the Congo and Anglo-Afrikaner rivalry in South Africa as examples of tensions and conflicts within the ranks of European oppressors in colonial Africa.

In Kenya, the British colonial response to the language issue had to mediate between three colonial forces. A substantial number of Christian missionaries, the so-called Livingstonians, were convinced that spiritual communication with Africans could best be achieved within the 'tribal' context. These missionaries insisted on using indigenous African languages in all their proselytizing and evangelical activities. Ironically, they regarded the preservation of African languages as an essential component of their attempt to capture the African soul.

In contrast to the Livingstonians, colonial administrators had an interest in African education in so far as it could provide them with a substantial pool of potential low-level government employees. For them, imparting the English language, the Christian religion, and a few British social attitudes to the African was a necessary step to ensure the efficient operation of the colonial administrative machinery. Such an education, they felt, should be specifically suited to the African condition, and should disrupt African cultures as little as possible.

In addition to Christian missionaries and colonial administrators, British colonialism in Kenya also responded to the more assertive, aggressive interests of the British settlers, who saw the African primarily as a source of cheap labour for their plantations. These settlers opposed the Europeanization of Africans, lest they became too 'civilized' to accept passively the role of wage labourers. At the same time they opposed the preservation of African cultures in their localized forms because they desired to encourage the cultural proletarianization of the peasants. As a result the British settlers generally preferred the promotion of Kiswahili, a trans-ethnic African language, in the education of Africans because they regarded cultural fusion and 'detribalization' as crucial to the creation of a wage-labour force.

But even when there were no factional differences within a single colony, administrators often chose to maximize the linguistic benefits at their disposal by promoting the use of both European and African languages. In Mozambique, for example, a quasi-assimilationist policy was instituted. One of its major objectives was the promotion of the Portuguese language. A document from the Service For Social Action states that the goal of Portuguese instruction was to instill the desire to learn Portuguese so they will speak of it as 'our language' (quoted by Eduardo de Sousa Ferreira, 1974: 159). Thus, before the beginning of the armed struggle for liberation, broadcasts in Portuguese colonies were exclusively in Portuguese. Once war broke out, however, the Portuguese colonial administration found it necessary to broadcast programmes in languages that Africans could understand. The political psychology behind this linguistic strategy was explained in the following terms:

> The simple fact that our advice and suggestions are being transmitted by an authoritative voice that contacts the peoples in their own language is for the more retarded a guarantee of authenticity, omniscience and infallibility. As he who has been taught to read piously believes in the printed letter, the native believes in the voice that speaks to him in his language over the air. (quoted by Ferreira,1974: 159)

Against this historical backdrop, then, it is evident that neither European languages such as Portuguese, nor African languages such as Chigiryama, are necessarily instruments of cultural bondage or cultural liberation. Throughout the colonial era, European languages served the ends of colonialism, but they did not necessarily do so as a consequence of their imposition on Africans. Sometimes European languages were deemed to serve colonial interests best by being made inaccessible to the African.

Fanon and linguistic alienation

It is true, of course, that wherever European languages and cultures have been imposed on people of colour there have been certain psychological ramifications. This psycholinguistic impact, however, has had less to do with the supposed deterministic power of language on human cognition than on the psychological alienation that results from 'racial' and class domination. It is this latter position that forms the basis of Frantz Fanon's views on language, imperialism and liberation, and it is through this line of reasoning that he was able to escape the linguistic fetishism that characterizes the views of many African neonationalists.

Fanon uses the word alienation to cover a wide range of psychological conditions, from the psycho-existential complex to neurosis, from the inferiority complex of the colonized to the superiority complex of the colonizer. Most of these conditions, however, can be subsumed under a more general definition of alienation as the separation of individuals from their existential conditions, from their individuality and culture. This idea of separation is most clearly described by Fanon in the following words:

> In the man of colour there is a constant effort to run away from his own individuality, to annihilate his own presence. Whenever a man of colour protests, there is alienation. Whenever a man of colour rebukes, there is alienation (1967a: 60).

The phenomenon of alienation, therefore, can be manifested in action as well as in reaction, in submissive behaviour as much as in violent aggression.

The use of language is regarded by Fanon as one of the most powerful possible expressions of alienation. This is because the boundaries of language can serve as important identitarian markers of the self and the other; denial of the self can easily be made public by a shift from one language to another. Underlining this importance of language, Fanon argues:

> I ascribe a basic importance to the phenomenon of language. This is why I find it necessary to begin with this subject, which should provide us with one of the elements in the coloured man's comprehension of the dimensions of the other for it is implicit that to speak is to exist absolutely for the other. (1967a: 17)

Language use, therefore, is not simply an act of communication and the acceptance of the sociocultural presuppositions that make communication possible, but also a means of signifying a certain relationship with the other, with one's interlocutors. To speak a particular language is not only to accept its formal linguistic requirements but also to acknowledge the culture implied by it. In Fanon's words:

> To speak means to be in a position to use a certain syntax, to grasp the morphology of this or that language, but it means above all to assume a culture, to support the weight of a civilization. (1967a: 17–18)

With the acquisition of any language, therefore, comes an entire set of cultural underpinnings.

When the additional language is also the language of the oppressor the world view that it implicitly expresses is often accepted as more valid than one's own. As the oppressed person becomes increasingly proficient in the language of the oppressor, therefore, he/she becomes proportionately estranged from his/her native language and culture. Commenting on the influence of the French language in the Antilles, for example, Fanon says:

> The Negro of the Antilles will be proportionately whiter – that is, he will come closer to being a real human being – in direct ratio to his mastery of the French language. I am not unaware that this is one of man's attitudes face to face with Being. A man who has a language consequently possesses the world expressed and implied by that language. (1967a: 18)

In the above passage Fanon assumes a position that is virtually Whorfian in substance: language is seen as a reservoir of culture that influences the world view of those who control it and directs their behaviour to some extent. Fanon almost seems guilty of the linguistic determinism that has characterized many an African neonationlist.

In fact, however, to Fanon language has this quasi-deterministic psycho-social impact only among those who seek to be the other, to assume the image of the oppressor. This is why elsewhere Fanon reaffirms his position in the following words:

> To speak a language is to take on a world, a culture. The Antilles Negro *who wants to be white* will be the whiter as he gains greater mastery of the cultural tool that language is. (1967a: 38)

In essence, then, a language of the oppressor may influence the cognitive and social orientation of the oppressed only if that person is alienated in the first place. The more isolated a person is from the 'native' self the more (s)he takes on the image of the other.

This state of alienation is a culmination of a peculiar process that a dominated person may go through. Under colonialism, for example, Fanon begins to describe the process with the view that the colonial world is essentially a compartmentalized one, a world divided into two mutually exclusive *zones*. There is a zone for the colonizer, and a zone for the colonized. This zoning – in both its geographical and social manifestations – is maintained by a system of coercion and brute force. The continuation of European domination from a zone that is completely inaccessible to the colonized ultimately leads to a mystification of the European colonizer in the mind of the colonized (1967b: 29-31).

These two zones are in turn mediated by a Manichaean ideology, the ideology of absolute opposites. In this equation the colonizer emerges as the epitome of the good while the colonized embodies everything that is evil. In the words of Fanon:

> The colonial world is a Manichaean world. It is not enough for the settler to delimit physically, that is to say with the help of the army and the police force, the place of the native. As if to show the totalitarian character of colonial exploitation the settler paints the native as a sort of quintessence of evil. Native society is not simply described as a society lacking in values.... The native is declared insensible to ethics; he represents not only the absence of values, but also the negation of values. He is, let us dare to admit, the enemy of values, and in this sense he is the absolute evil. He is the corrosive element, destroying all that comes near him; he is the deforming element, disfiguring all that has to do with beauty or morality; he is the depository of maleficent power, the unconscious and irretrievable instrument of blind forces. (1967b: 32–3)

In short, the colonizer continuously seeks to dehumanize the colonized in his quest for political legitimacy and hegemonic status.

Colonial education and the Christian missionary enterprise become the main agents of perpetrating these racist images of the 'native'. Both these exercises were intended to elevate the culture of the colonizer and debase the culture of the colonized. The process of education led African children to identify with the European explorer, the missionary, 'the bringer of civilization, the white man who carries truth to the savages – an all-white truth' (Fanon, 1967a: 147). Fanon places 'the Christian religion which wages war on embryonic heresies and instincts, and on the evil as yet unborn' on the same level as the DDT insecticide 'which destroys parasites, the bearers of disease'(1967b: 32).

The overall effect of this educational and religious war on the mind is alienation.

As the colonizer becomes increasingly mystified he appears in the eyes of the colonized as the object of moral purity and all that is positive in humanity, in direct contrast to his own stereotyped diabolic, inferior character. 'Guilt and inferiority' according to Fanon 'are the usual consequences of this dialectic. The oppressed then tries to escape these, on the one hand by proclaiming his total and unconditional adoption of the new cultural modes, and on the other hand, by pronouncing an irreversible condemnation of his own cultural style' (1969: 38-39).

This is the stage at which the colonized is said to have *interiorized* the racial stereotypes of the colonizer. The colonized begins to see the language and values of the colonizer as a means of enlightenment and social progress. It is against this backdrop of the political psychology of colonialism that Fanon said:

> Every colonized people … in whose soul an inferiority complex has been created by the death and burial of its local originality – finds itself face to face with the language of the civilizing nation; that is with the culture of the mother country. The colonized is elevated above his jungle status in proportion to his adoption of the mother country's cultural standards. (1967: 18)

The (African) 'self' thus becomes increasingly consumed by the (European) 'other'.

But the colonized gradually find themselves in a state of predicament. They get increasingly alienated from their Africanity as they seek to be European. They even work desperately to perfect their European language speech lest it betrays their African origin. The 'Negro' arriving in France, for example:

> will react against the myth of the R-eating man from Martinique. He will become aware of it, and he will really go to war against it. He will practise not only rolling his R but embroidering it. Furtively observing the slightest reactions of others, listening to his own speech, suspicious of his own tongue, a wretchedly lazy organ – he will lock himself into his room and read aloud for hours – desperately determined to learn *diction*. (Fanon, 1967a: 21)

Upon returning to his native country this 'Negro' has 'forgotten' his native tongue. He can only speak and think in the European language. Narrating the story of a Caribbean African who returns to his father's farm after visiting France, Fanon writes:

> After several months of living in France, a country boy returns to his family. Noticing a farm implement, he asks his father, an old don't-pull-that-kind-of-thing-on-me peasant, 'Tell me, what does one call that apparatus?' His father responded by dropping the tool on the boy's feet, and the amnesia vanishes. Remarkable therapy. (1967a:23–4)

In spite of all the desperate attempts to become European, these Africans never quite attain a European identity. European society never accepts them as full participants; they always remain outsiders. The more European the Africans become in cultural terms, the more they are regarded by European societiy as exotic or even quixotic. Estranged from their Africanity and closed out from European identity, then, they become entrapped in what is essentially a *colonial culture*, a culture which stultifies their thinking and destroys all potential for organic intellectual growth. The colonial context that promotes an inferiority complex on the part of the African has the effect of closing a culture which was once open to organic growth.

Fanon cautions against concluding that colonial relations necessarily lead to the demise of 'native culture'. Rather,

> This culture, once living and open to the future, becomes closed, fixed in the colonial status, caught in the yoke of oppression. Both present and mummified, it testifies against its members. It defines them, in fact, without appeal. The cultural mummification leads to a mummification of individual thinking. The apathy so universally noted among colonial peoples is but the logical consequence of this operation. (1969: 34)

This ossification of individual thinking, then, itself a product of alienation, continues to perpetuate the cycle of alienation, constantly imprisoning the actions and reactions of the dominated person in conceptual terms that have been defined by the dominator.

It is this state of alienation, rather than the supposed deterministic power of language, that entraps the African in a colonial culture and a colonial world view. Fanon does not postulate a one-to-one correlation between specific linguistic items or structures and specific cultural traits or perceptions, as does Benjamin Lee Whorf, for example. Rather he takes language as a totality, as a macro system, and looks at its psychological impact on the colonized in light of the particular social connotations of inferiority and superiority, for example, that it has come to acquire as a direct result of colonial and racial relations of domination. This cycle did not come to an end upon the attainment of political independence in Africa. The neocolonial era that followed it has essentially continued to promote relations of dependence and domination in favour of alienation, albeit through the mediating role of a local bourgeoisie.

That the colonizing effect of language is due to alienation rather than to linguistic determinism is reaffirmed by Fanon when he contrasts the European–African scenario with an intra-European setting. Britons who learn French, for example, may acquire some degree of French culture and an appreciation of a peculiarly French way of looking at some aspects of the world. But in the process the Britons do not get alienated from their existential being, nor colonized mentally by their encounter with the new language. The reason is that between the French and the British there are no colonial or neocolonial relations of domination that could 'inferiorize' the British. In Fanon's view, 'the British do not consider themselves inferior to the French people. The British have not been civilized by the white man' (1967a:11). The colonized and neocolonized African, in contrast, comes to regard Europeanness as something quite superior and as the ultimate key of his/her escape from 'nativism', from 'ignorance' and 'inertia'. Once the colonized are trapped in this psychological predisposition, European languages and cultures become potential tools of perpetuating a state of mental colonization.

Language and the intellectual class

It is not only in the quest to assimilate European languages and cultures, however, that alienation manifests itself. Individuals also can be considered alienated if they turn hostile to that European heritage and seek to return to their 'roots'. This tendency is particularly prominent among intellectuals who Fanon regards as the most alienated social category because 'it has become wonderfully detached from its own thought and has based its consciousness upon foundations which are

60

typically foreign' (1967b: 163). Elsewhere Fanon makes the following comments concerning the African intellectual:

> The educated Negro, slave of the spontaneous and cosmic Negro myth, feels at a given stage that his race no longer understands him. Or that he no longer understands it. Then he congratulates himself on this, and enlarging the difference, the incomprehension, the disharmony, he finds in them the meaning of his real humanity. (1967a: 13)

The intellectuals, therefore, are the most alienated party because they yearn to be the most assimilated.

Gradually, however, some of the intellectuals come to a rude awakening that no matter how unreservedly they seek to adopt European ways of thinking and behaviour, European society has barred them from becoming full and equal members. They come to realize that there are, in fact, definite racial boundaries to linguistic and cultural assimilation. At that point their critical impulse is jolted into action and they embark on an attempt to break out of the prison house of European language and culture.

But this struggle for liberation from European mental enslavement simply propels them to yet another level of alienation that Fanon calls intellectual alienation (1967a: 224) In their aggressive rejection of European linguistic and cultural assimilation they engage in enthusiastic search for a return to the people, to 'native' languages and cultures which they constantly romanticize, all in an attempt to validate their authenticity. And,

> ... when at the height of his intercourse with his people, whatever they were or whatever they are, the intellectual decides to come down into the common paths of real life, he only brings back from his adventuring formulas which are sterile in the extreme. He sets a high value on the customs, traditions and the appearances of his people; but his inevitable, painful experience only seems to be a banal search for exoticism. The sari becomes sacred, the shoes that come from Paris or Italy are left off in favor of pompooties, *while suddenly the language of the ruling power is felt to burn the lips.* [my emphasis] (Fanon, 1967b: 177–8)

This quest, too, is a form of alienation precisely because it is encapsulated in Eurocentric terms of reference. They seek to counterpoise European languages with African languages on the Eurocentric premise that language is a key to high culture and civilization – rather than, say, an instrument of communication and rational thought. It is precisely these considerations that lead Fanon to assert:

> At the very moment when the native intellectual is anxiously trying to create a cultural work he fails to realize that he is utilizing techniques and language which are borrowed from the stranger in his country. . . . Sometimes he has no hesitation in using a dialect in order to show his will to be as near as possible to the people; but the ideas that he expresses and the preoccupations he is taken up with have no common yardstick to measure the *real* situation which the men and women of this country know. (1967b: 180)

In sum, then, the quest for African origins can itself be yet another manifestation of intellectual dependence on the West and estrangement from one's people.

Fanon seems to regard members of the working class as less likely to 'suffer' from the intellectual alienation partly because he thinks they have a more pragmatic orientation towards the issue of language and culture. European languages and cultures are not seen in assimilationist terms that negate their existential being, but in instrumental terms of basic survival. In essence, then, they do not undergo any profound assimilation and, consequently, their Africanity does not become an object of rediscovery. Fanon notes:

> The few working class people I had the chance to know in Paris never took it on themselves to pose the problem of the discovery of the Negro past. They knew they were black, but, they told me, that made no difference in anything. (1967a: 224)

It would not come as a surprise to Fanon, then, that until today the greatest proponents of the move to return to African indigenous languages, cultures and institutions are, in fact, members of the African intelligentsia who, at the same time, happen to be the most alienated.

What all this suggests, then, is that language as an instrument of liberation must be based, not on a reversal of values accorded to European versus African languages on the basis of a preconceived paradigm of linguistic determinism, but on disalienation that seeks to pose new terms of reference altogether. For as long as the struggle for mental liberation is defined in terms that conform to the European ideal of humanity and civilization it will only turn out to be an upward spiral to further alienation and conceptual imprisonment.

Conclusion:
beyond determinism

In terms of the language issue, this disalienation must begin with the rejection of the idea that language, as a reservoir of culture, is a determiner of thought and world views. Language can, of course, serve as a means of gaining access to a culture and society. But more primarily Fanon seems to place language in the realm of capital such that those who control it may wield a certain degree of power. 'Mastery of language', contends Fanon, 'affords remarkable power' to the individual (1967a: 18). This potential power of language, however, can be realized only if one takes a language for what it is: an instrument of communication and rational thought and not a key to enlightenment and civilization as the alienated are wont to do.

Seen form this vantage point, then, language can be a malleable tool in the hands of those who control it to achieve their specific aims and objectives, especially in interpersonal negotiations and struggles for power. In the hands of the oppressed a language of the oppressor can be transmuted to carry new meanings and serve as a weapon of struggle for liberation. It is this view of language that led Fanon to comment on the French language situation in colonial Algeria in the following terms.

> The French language, language of occupation, a vehicle of the oppressing power, seemed doomed for eternity to judge the Algerian in a pejorative way. Every French expression referring to the Algerian had a humiliating content. Every French speech heard was an order, a threat, an insult. The contract between the Algerian and the European is defined by these three spheres. (1967b: 89)

But the Algerians decided to take up arms and change the nature of the contract and relationship with their European oppressors. They gradually liberated this enemy language from its historic meanings. Radio messages in French from the liberation forces now came to assume a more universal dimension of truth and justice. As Fanon put it:

> The French language lost its accursed character, revealing itself to be capable of transmitting, for the benefit of the nation, the messages of truth that the latter awaited. Paradoxically as it may appear, it is the Algerian Revolution, it is the struggle of the Algerian people, that is facilitating the spreading of the French language in the nation. Expressing oneself in French, understanding French, was no longer tantamount to treason or to an impoverishing identification with the occupier. Used by the voice of the combatants, conveying in a positive way the message of the Revolution, the French language also becomes an instrument of liberation…. The 'native' can almost be said to assume responsibility for the language of the occupier. (1967c: 89–90)

The French language thus became 'exorcised' and purged of its oppressive meanings by the forces of liberation.

Prior to the militant stage of Algerian nationalism, accepting the French language was seen as a form of 'cultural treason' against the Algerian people which would only deepen their oppression and colonization. The Arabic language alone was regarded as capable of expressing the nation's existential being and of breaking the mental chains wrought by the French language. By 1956, however, 'the reality of combat and the confusion of the occupier stripped the Arabic language of its sacred character, and the French language of its negative connotations. The new language of the nation could then make itself known through multiple meaningful channels' (1967c: 92). French, then, came to acquire new values that hitherto had been associated exclusively with the Arabic language.

Equally noteworthy, perhaps, was the French oppressors' reaction towards this changed sociolinguistic equation in Algeria. At the beginning, still confined to their deterministic conception of a one-to-one relationship between language, culture and thought, the French regarded the shift from Arabic to French by the Algerian combatants as a vindication of the limits of the Arabic language and the ontological superiority of the French language and its people. To the French authorities, this sociolinguistic shift had, in fact, boundlessly extended the horizons of the French policy of assimilation in their quest to create a truly French Algeria. But as the Algerian Revolution continued to unveil itself through the French language, the oppressors' linguistic thesis gradually collapsed. They could now see clearly that their language had been successfully turned against them. This development ultimately threw the French into a state of total disorientation (1967c: 91).

A more recent example of the semantic transformation of the language of the oppressor is provided by Thomas Sankara, the former revolutionary leader of Burkina Faso, who was executed in a coup led by Blaise Compaore in 1987. Though speaking in a European language, Sankara linguistically appropriated and dialectically inverted the deepest values and ideals of the French and the Americans:

> Rationality, subjectivity, and universality … these are the ideas which had previously been the preserve of the 'white men of means' that wrote the founding document of the bourgeois order … from the notarized title Columbus conferred upon the King and Queen of Spain giving them possession of Hispaniola to the Declaration of Independence to the Rights of Man to the latest

directives sent to the missile batteries in Montana, Sankara's speech took those ideas and claimed them for 'the great, disinherited people of the world'. (Caffentzis, 1990: 3)

By virtue of this inversion of values of the European linguistic discourse, Sankara attracted the hostility of global forces of imperialism.

In Fanon's views, then, Sankara would probably personify the most essential initial step in the struggle for liberation in the Third World. This involves the liberation of people of colour from *themselves*. The oppressed must seek to overcome their state of alienation, to set new terms of reference in asserting their humanity and free will. This process obviously needs a language, both of reflection and of combat.[5]

But this language must not be sought in the ahistorical and artifical contrast that associates European languages with oppression and non-European languages with liberation. For to do so, would be to accept the racist and undialectical terms of reference imposed by European imperialism itself. Rather, the language of liberation can only be a product of a thorough semantic revolution in each and every language that would demystify the process of decolonization, 'reopen' the cultures of the oppressed to organic growth, and counterpoise the message of imperialist domination with a message of resistance and freedom. This kind of language may have been one of Frantz Fanon's greatest achievements and one of his most enduring contributions to the struggle of the 'wretched of the earth' throughout the world. And it is in the quest for this kind of 'linguistic weapon' that Thomas Sankara may have prematurely lost his life.

While global Africans continue to strive to liberate the languages of their oppressors, however, they must also continue with the struggle to 'centre' their own indigenous tongues in their lives. This latter quest is important not because it may assist in the process of mental or cognitive decolonization but more because it may help reduce intellectual dependence on the West.

As we have indicated elsewhere, an important source of intellectual dependence in Africa is the language in which African graduates and scholars are taught. For the time being, it is impossible for an African to be even moderately familiar with the works of Marx or Ricardo without the help of a European language. *Das Kapital* is not yet available in *lingua francas* like Hausa and Kiswahili, let alone in more ethnic-bound languages like Kidigo or Lutooro. In short, major intellectual paradigms of the West are likely to remain unavailable even in a single African language unless there is a genuine educational revolution involving widespread adoption of African languages as media of instruction.

As the matter now stands, an African who has a good command of a European language has probably assimilated other aspects of Western culture as well. The assimilation is due not to any deterministic impact of language, but to the fact that the process of acquiring a European language in Africa is still overwhelmingly through a formal system of Western-style education. And it is partly because of this that the concept of an African Marxist who is not also Westernized is at the present time a socio-linguistic impossibility.

This need not apply to a Chinese or Japanese Marxist. In both China and Japan it is possible to undergo an ideological conversion at a sophisticated level without the explicit mediation of a foreign language. The Japanese range, in particular, goes well beyond ideological and political literature. But today, in non-Arabic speaking Africa, a modern surgeon who does not speak a European language is virtually a sociolinguistic impossibility. So is a modern physicist, zoologist, economist and so forth.

Nor is it simply a case of the surgeon or physicist acquiring an additional skill called a European language which he is capable of discarding when he discusses surgery or physics with fellow professionals in his own society. Professional Japanese scientists or social scientists can organize a conference and discuss professional matters entirely in Japanese. But a conference of African scientists, devoted to scientific matters and conducted primarily in an African language, is not yet possible. (Ali Mazrui and Alamin Mazrui, 1995: 127–8).

It is because of the above considerations that intellectual and scientific dependence in Africa may be inseparable from linguistic dependence. The linguistic quest for liberation, therefore, must not be limited to freeing the European languages from their oppressive meanings in so far as Black and other subjugated people the world over are concerned, but must also seek to promote African languages, especially in academia, as one of the strategies for promoting greater intellectual and scientific independence from the West.

Notes

1. The term 'neonationalist' refers to a group of Africans with a wide range of ideological leanings but united by the belief that the next phase of the African struggle is liberation from neo-colonialism. In the area of language, specifically, the neonationalist thrust has assumed the form of a quest to subvert the authority of the dominant European languages inherited from colonial tradition, either by 'Africanizing' them (e.g. in the novels of Amos Tutuola) or by replacing them with 'indigenous' African languages altogether (e.g. Ngugi wa Thiong'o).
2. The Sapir-Whorf hypothesis has both an extreme and a moderate position. The extreme position claims that language actually *determines* cognition in a culturally specific way. Many linguistic neonationalists in Africa seem to espouse this view. The more moderate position, on the other hand, claims only some influence of these two positions in their writings.
3. It is instructive to note that even colonial administrators who favoured the use of African 'vernaculars' as media of educational instruction tended to invoke a quasi-linguistic determinist position. Westermann, for example once argued:
   > Mental life has evolved in each people in an individual shape and proper mode of expression; in this sense we speak of the soul of people and the most immediate, the most adequate exponent of a people is its language. By taking away a people's language, we cripple or destroy its soul and kill its mental individuality.... Any educational work which does not take into consideration the inseparable unity between African languages and African thinking is based on false principles and must lead to the alienation of the individual from his own self, his past, his traditions, and his people (Quoted by T. P. Gorman, 1974: 449).
4. Eric Lenneberg (1953), Joseph Greenberg (1979), Joshua Fishman (1960), Robert Miller (1968), Einar Haugen (1977) are among those who have called into question the research data that supposedly support the Sapir-Whorf hypothesis. So, after over 30 years of research on the socio-psychology of language Wallace Lambert could only proclaim: 'I am not persuaded by the evidence available that language or culture have any real impact on thought' (1979: 187).
5. Equally important in Fanon's conception of liberation is the issue of violence, including what we may call *linguistic violence*. In Algeria such colonial usage of the French language had manifest negative psychological effects on its victims (Fanon, 1969c: 89). In the period of struggle against imperialism, however, the linguistic violence of the colonial discourse comes to be confronted with the linguistic violence of the nationalist, revolutionary combatants. The oppressive linguistic violence of imperialism and class domination necessarily breeds a counter-linguistic violence in quest for freedom and liberation.

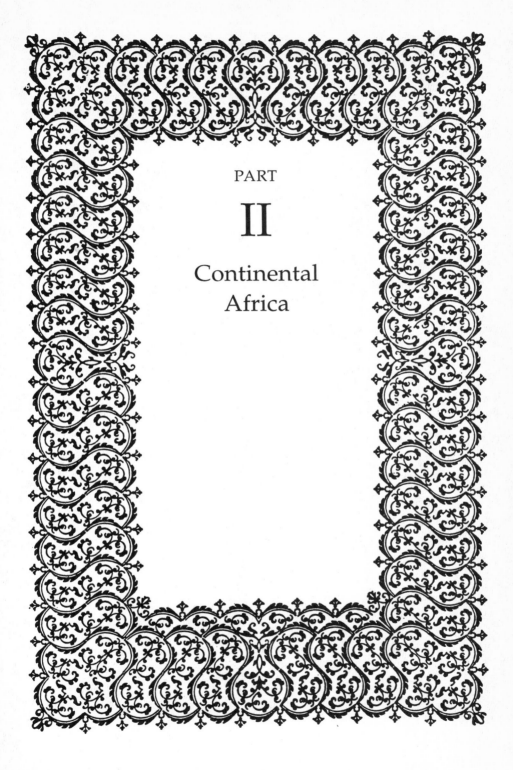

PART

II

Continental
Africa

5
Language in a Multicultural Context

The African Experience

Africa is a grand laboratory of language, a microcosm of the linguistic world. There are African societies which have relied primarily on the oral tradition to this day, and African societies which were literate long before the British Isles evolved into literate communities. Africa today is therefore a living laboratory for the transition from the oral tradition to the written word.

Africa is also a live arena for the interplay between language and religion. In the African context this is particularly marked in the case of the impact of Islam on African languages. Islam has not only helped Arabic, it has sometimes hindered the spread of Kiswahili and Hausa. Religious hostility has spilt over into linguistic hostility. And yet Kiswahili and Hausa are the most widely spread indigenous languages in Africa. How did this happen?

Africa is further a great battleground between Western languages and non-Western languages. English, French and Portuguese have had particularly wide-ranging influence. How have these Western languages interacted with non-Western media in the African arena?

Africa's ethnic heterogeneity is reflected in language. Per capita there is a wider range of languages in Africa than in any other continent in the world. By a strange twist of destiny, there are also more French-speaking, English-speaking and Portuguese-speaking countries in Africa than anywhere else in the world. In terms of ethnic units which use African languages as mother tongues, Africa is a continental Tower of Babel in all its diversity.

Africa is also an acute case of linguistic dependence. Credentials for ruling an African country are disproportionately based on a command of the Euro-imperial language. In Africa south of the Sahara it has become almost impossible to become a Member of Parliament or President without being fluent in at least one of the relevant European languages. How does this relate to the wider world of language and society? Where, for example, do Europe and Asia fit into the metahistory of communication?

Africa can be credited with inventing human language. Asia, on the other hand, sacralized language. And Europe universalized it. Cultural conditions of basic human existence in Africa, as the cradle of humankind, prompted the human language capacity into action prior to the dispersal of the species to other continents. Asia as the cradle of institutionalized religion gave language its sacred imprint. And Europe as the initial centre of international capitalism contributed to the globalization of language. By the turn of the twentieth century these global forces of culture, religion, and political economy had converged on Africa to give rise to what we may call Africa's triple linguistic heritage.

Definitions

Africa's triple linguistic heritage essentially refers to the interaction of indigenous Africa, the Islamic tradition and the Western contribution. This interplay of traditions permits a socio-cultural typology of the languages spoken in Africa into Afro-ethnic, Afro-Islamic, Western and Afro-Western categories. The Afro-ethnic category includes all those languages whose native speakers are predominantly African and which have been shaped only minimally, if at all, by the Arab-Islamic or Euro-Christian impact. It encompasses languages such as Kalabari, Yoruba and Ewe in West Africa, Lingala in Central Africa, Pokot, Luganda and Orominya in East Africa, and Ndebele, Nyanja and Zulu in southern Africa.

Some of the Semitic languages of Ethiopia may be somewhat atypical in this regard, in that Christianity has long been a tradition of their native speakers. In Ethiopia Christianity dates back to the fourth century. But precisely because this Ethiopian brand of Christianity predates the European impact, Ethiopian languages such as Amharic can still be regarded as essentially Afro-ethnic. Afro-ethnic languages, including Berber in North Africa, are found throughout the continent and form the largest category, with estimates ranging from eight hundred to two thousand languages.

Like Afro-ethnic languages, though far less numerous, Afro-Islamic languages are native to Africa in terms of their speakers. But unlike Afro-ethnic languages, the Afro-Islamic languages have been influenced heavily by Islam due to the Islamic identity of their native speakers over centuries and contact with the Arab-Islamic world. The cultures of these people have been infused with an Islamic ethos and traditions, many of which are reflected in their languages.

The major Afro-Islamic language is Arabic. Islam does not recognize a chosen people, but it does insist on a chosen language for ritual. Demographically, there are more native speakers of the language in Africa than there are in Asia. It has been estimated that over 60 per cent of the speakers of Arabic as a first language are in Africa. Furthermore, the varieties of Arabic spoken in Africa have received a peculiarly African imprint. The Arabic dialects of Egypt, Libya and the Maghreb are all different from the colloquial Arabic dialects of Asia. Arabic, therefore, is Afro-Islamic in terms of both its demographic characteristics and the geographical origins of its linguistic peculiarities.

Other Afro-Islamic languages include Swahili, Somali and Nubi in East Africa, and Hausa, Fulfude, Mandinka (and others) in West Africa. In linguistic terms the Islamic quality of these languages is most obvious in their relatively high degree of absorption of Arabic words. These linguistic connections with Arabic are by no means limited to the lexical fields of the religious and spiritual worlds, but also extend to the spheres of politics, economics, education and beyond. But precisely because Arabic at its macro-level is regarded as a religious language, its micro-level influences on other languages can also be regarded as manifestations of a religious imprint in some sense of the word.

The third major component of Africa's triple linguistic heritage is that of Western languages. These are languages whose native speakers are located predominantly in Europe and the Americas; their presence in Africa is linked directly to the trans-Atlantic slave trade and colonial experiences. In this category, then, we may include English, French, Portuguese, Italian and (less widely spread) Spanish and German. Western languages are spoken primarily as additional languages throughout the continent.

There is, finally, the smaller category of Afro-Western languages. This includes Kriyol of Guinea Bissau and Cape Verde Island, Pidgin (English) and Krio of Sierra Leone, in West Africa, and Fanagalo and Afrikaans in Southern Africa. Native speakers of Kriyol and Krio are predominantly African. There is evidence to suggest that West African Pidgin is increasingly becoming creolized as more and more people from the younger generations of West Africans acquire it as a first language.

The exact origins of Afrikaans are uncertain. Did it emerge from pidgin/creole origins or is it merely a result of dialectal differentiation of Dutch? There is no doubt that Afrikaans is a child of the African soil and its native speakers are pre-dominantly located in Africa. For these reasons it can rightly be regarded as an Afro-Western language. Fanagalo, on the other hand, is definitely a pidgin, though of uncertain origin. What is certain is that English, a Western language, played a significant role in its formation. The Afro-Western languages of West Africa are linked to the history of Western slavery and colonialism, while those of Southern Africa are tied to the history of apartheid. Evidence of the emergence of Afro-Western languages in the regions of Africa dominated by Afro-Islamic languages is scant. Even the Afro-Western languages of West Africa seem to be concentrated in predominantly non-Muslim areas.

It is also possible that some of the languages that we have called 'Western' may acquire Afro-Western tendencies. For example, there is a growing population of 'Afro-Saxons' – Africans who, due to the divergent linguistic backgrounds of their parents, grow up speaking English as a mother tongue. As the ranks of such Africans continue to grow, so will the potential of these languages to become Afro-Western.

Characteristics and tendencies

There are other characteristics and tendencies that give additional substance to the distinction between Afro-ethnic, Afro-Islamic, Western and Afro-Western languages. It is to a discussion of these other attributes that we must now turn.

Writing
Of the languages spoken in Africa, the last to be captured in writing were the Afro-ethnic tongues. Although Amharic has had its own alphabet for several centuries, it was not until after the inception of European colonialism that some of the other Afro-ethnic languages, which hitherto had been exclusively oral, were reduced to writing, using the Roman script. In a sense, then, while European colonialism and its language policies often posed a serious threat to Afro-ethnic languages, it accorded some of them a greater capacity for self-preservation through the intro-duction of the written word. There is no doubt that many Afro-ethnic communities developed their own hidden mechanisms to ensure the survival of their languages. But for languages that did get captured in writing, these acquired a new, important tool of linguistic preservation.

In the nineteenth century there were a few attempts, in West Africa especially, to invent indigenous scripts. The better known among these are the *Bamoun* script of Cameroon and the *Vai* script of Sierra Leone. According to Pierre Alexandre, the Bamoun script 'has the special attribute of having run through virtually the entire evolutionary cycle of graphic systems during the entire life of its inventor, the *fon*, or Sultan, of Fournban, Njoya the Great (c. 1880–1933)' (1972: 109). The script is supposed to have started as:

> an initial system of 350 hieroglyphics, each of which represented the notion to which it corresponded in a quite realistic fashion. After several years the designs were simplified: they passed to the stage of ideograms – non-realistic symbols, each corresponding to a notion. In 1911 came an important new advance; the ideograms took on a phonetic value; their number was reduced to 80, with each representing a syllable. Ultimately, in 1918, a final improvement allowed the Bamoun script to pass to the alphabetical stage, wherein each sign corresponds to a phoneme. (Alexandre, 1972: 109)

The Vai script, on the other hand, is said to have been invented in 1830 by one Momolu Duwalu Bukele who transformed 'a preexisting system of ideograms or pictograms into a syllabic system' (Alexandre, 1972: 110).

In terms of our theme of a triple linguistic heritage it is significant that some of these attempts to invent indigenous scripts were not exclusively a response to the need to reduce Africa's dependence on the oral tradition. There also seems to have been an additional motive to set up a writing system that was authentically African and which could distinguish itself from both the Arabic and Roman scripts. In this regard Njoya the Great is supposed to have proclaimed: 'The Muslims and Christians have their writing. The Bamoun must have theirs' (quoted by Alexandre, 1972: 109).

Afro-Islamic languages can take pride in a much longer history of writing than Afro-ethnic languages (except Amharic). Arabic has an even longer literary tradition which pre-dates the birth of Islam itself. With the emergence of Islam, however, both the language and its script acquired a religious essence, even mystique. Prophet Muhammad was reminded by Allah that not only did He reveal the Qur'an to him in the Arabic language (Sura 12, Verse 2 and several others), but that He also tutored humans through the power of the pen and the magic of the written word (Sura 96, Verse 4). The Qur'an, therefore, helped sacralize the Arabic language in its oral as well as its written forms.

The earliest traditions of writing in most other Afro-Islamic languages developed after the Islamization of their native speakers and were, of course, based on the Arabic script. In these instances the script was acquired in the very process of Qur'anic instruction among the believers. Partly for this reason, average members of most Afro-Islamic communities do not make a distinction between the printed and the handwritten versions of the Arabic script. When they do write they often try to approximate the printed script of the Qur'an. Furthermore, the script was used in writing local languages without modification. It was only later that local, Afro-Islamic diagraphs of Arabic developed, but even these were used unsystematically.

Nonetheless, the Arabic script did allow Afro-Islamic languages to have written traditions that antedated those of many other African languages by a couple of centuries or more. A major exception in this regard is Somali which was first (and only recently) written in the Roman script. The widespread use of the Arabic language itself in Somalia, in both its oral and written forms, seems to have served as a disincentive in adopting the Arabic script to write Somali. The few modest attempts to develop a written Somali literature in the Arabic script all failed to take root.

When the Roman script was introduced at the inception of European colonial rule it faced little resistance from the Arabic script except in Arabophone Africa where a longer and more widespread tradition of writing, buttressed by the state, ensured the continuation of literacy in the Arabic script. In most other Afro-Islamic languages, including Fulfulde, Hausa, Kanuri, Mandinka, Nupe, Songhai and Kiswahili, the Arabic script has been giving way to the Roman script.

This is not to suggest that, except in Arabic-speaking Africa, there was absolutely no resistance to orthographic Latinization among speakers of other Afro-Islamic languages. There is evidence, in at least some cases, that Latinization was considered a source of distortion, particularly of the Arabic-derived phonological components of Afro-Islamic languages. In the case of Kiswahili, for example, the renowned East African Muslim theologian, Sheik Al-Amin bin Ali Mazrui (1890–1947), made an impassioned appeal against the orthographic Latinization of the language on account of its inadequacy to represent elements of 'sophisticated' Kiswahili speech, especially Arabic loan words (1931). But such appeals did little to prevent the gradual replacement of the Arabic script by the Latin script. The more aggressive colonial policy to spread the Latin script through the schools, combined with the greater functional diversity that came with it, made the Arabic script in many Afro-Islamic communities a weaker rival to the Latin script.

The increasing number of non-Muslims who were rapidly acquiring some of these Afro-Islamic languages as additional languages were generally precluded from the culture of literacy in the Arabic language. For these non-native speakers of Afro-Islamic languages, the Latin script was the only one accessible. The changing demographic equation of Afro-Islamic languages therefore also helped to popularize the Latin script at the expense of the Arabic.

The introduction of the Latin script in Africa coincided, of course, with the introduction of Western languages themselves. So, while Western languages were the last to join Africa's triple linguistic heritage, they arrived on the continent complete with their own script and with centuries of literary tradition behind them. The Afro-Western offshoots of Western and, of course, African languages did not inherit this literary tradition, however. The only exception to this rule is Afrikaans, which, primarily as an offspring of Dutch, continues to be written in Latin script.

Other Afro-Western languages seem to have inherited the oral tradition from their African 'parentage'. So, in spite of their demonstrated functionality, no serious attempt has been made to develop standardized orthographies for these languages. In Nigeria and Sierra Leone there have been a few plays and prose pieces in Afro-Western languages, using the Latin script. Whether these initiatives will give Afro-Western languages, other than Afrikaans, an acceptable written value in their respective societies remains to be seen.

Poetry

The African language that has the longest documented record of creative writing is probably Amharic, an Afro-ethnic idiom. This claim becomes even more valid if we accept the theory that Amharic is a descendent of Ge'ez, the language of Ethiopia that existed even prior to the Christian era. By the fourth century Ge'ez had developed into a productive literary language. The most impressive and classical literary period of Ge'ez stretched from the thirteenth to the seventeenth centuries, long after it had ceased to be a spoken language of Ethiopia.

Amharic, then, is supposed to have continued with and developed the literary legacy of Ge'ez. There are records of Amharic written verse in honour of Ethiopian kings that can be traced as far back as the fourteenth century. But it was not until the nineteenth century, under the rule of Theodore II, that Amharic fully succeeded in replacing Ge'ez as a literary language of Ethiopia (Ullendorf, 1960: 121–4). Despite this long history of written literature, however, the oral form of literature that characterizes other Afro-ethnic languages continued to flourish in Amharic. Amharic, then, is one of those Afro-ethnic languages with a rich tradition of both oral and written literature, particularly in the poetic genre.

Most other Afro-ethnic languages have, of course, been almost exclusively oral in their literary traditions. More recently there has been some degree of creative writing in Afro-ethnic languages that has been captured in print in the Latin script. The relatively little written so far, however, has tended to be in the areas of prose and drama rather than poetry. And in the oral tradition the tendency has been towards received rather than creative verse. Some Afro-ethnic languages whose native speakers have had long traditions of the institution of monarchy do have relatively rich bodies of oral, creative verse. But mostly such cases are restricted to West African languages like Yoruba and perhaps a few other Afro-ethnic languages.

Afro-Islamic languages, on the other hand, have an impressive record of both oral and written poetry. Much of the oldest poetry that was initially preserved in writing in revised Arabic alphabets is strongly Islamic in content, mood, imagery, nuance and overall orientation. This religiosity of Afro-Islamic poetry is, of course, partly a reflection of the extent to which Islam, as a religion and a civilization, is infused into the cultures of these African communities. Equally important, however, was the pioneering role that the *ulamaa*, the Muslim 'clergy', played in composing written poetry, often with a didactic motive. In the aftermath of Osman Dan Fodio's *jihad* wars, for example, much of the written poetry was directed at eradicating the remnants of 'pagan' culture and inculcating the Islamic ethos. Some of the best poetry of the classical tradition was in fact composed by these *ulamaa* poets. And their compositions were perhaps inspired by the explicit Qur'anic bias in favour of poetry bound by Islam.

Finally, the much talked about poetic elegance of the Qur'an itself, combined with the sub-genre of religious songs, the *qasida*, may have served as a major inspiration to Afro-Islamic poets. There are anecdotes of Arab poets who converted to Islam, during the early period of its emergence, convinced that the superior poetic quality of the Qur'an was proof enough of its divinity. The Qur'an itself alludes to its literary inimitability, sometimes challenging the Arab poets, at the time of its revelation, to produce even a single verse that can match its poetic quality. So, while Muslims accept that the poetic standards of the Qur'an are too high to be attained by mere mortals, its poetic nature may have led to the relative prominence of poetry in the literary imagination of the Muslim world.

As in the case of Amharic, however, the prevalence of written literature in the Arabic script in Afro-Islamic societies did not diminish the value of oral composition. And here, too, especially in the area of oral poetry, Islam has had a visible impact. Even poetry that was thematically non-religious was sometimes pregnant with imagery, words, nuances, and phrases rooted in the Islamic tradition. To a large extent, then, oral as well as written poetry managed to flourish side by side in many Afro-Islamic societies.

A notable exception in this regard has been the Somali language. Though an

Afro-Islamic language, it maintained a strong oral poetic tradition almost to the complete exclusion of written composition. Even the acclaimed nationalist Somali poetry of Sayyid Muhammad Abdille Hassan, basically inspired by Islam, is said to have been composed in an essentially oral mode. We noted above that the Semitic language of Amharic has been the most prominent literary anomaly among Afro-ethnic languages. Among Afro-Islamic languages, on the other hand, it is the Cushitic language of Somali that has proved to be the literary deviation.

If the Afro-ethnic literary tendency has been towards a relatively unproductive oral poetic tradition, and the Afro-Islamic tendency towards a productive oral and written poetic tradition, the Western norm has been a productive, though exclusively written, poetic tradition. Most of the renowned poets – like Christopher Okigbo, Wole Soyinka and Taban Lo Liyong – have adopted Western styles of poetic composition, even though there are some, like the late Okot p'Bitek, who have drawn inspiration from Africa's oral tradition.

Most Afro-Western languages, on the other hand, are yet to develop a poetic tradition. Neither the oral tradition of Afro-ethnic languages nor the written tradition of Western languages seems to have inspired much artistic creativity in Afro-Western languages. Outside the realm of poetry Afro-Western languages seem to show the greatest promise in drama/plays. Nigerian Pidgin and Sierra Leonean Krio are said to have a growing tradition of written plays and theatre. But like Afro-ethnic and Afro-Islamic languages, Afro-Western languages too have their exception, and this is Afrikaans. Being a direct or indirect descendant of Dutch it has continued with the Western literary tradition in poetry as well as in other genres. So, despite its African origins, Afrikaans seems to have ignored the Afro-ethnic base and drawn exclusively from the Western tradition in the creation of its literary legacy.

Geographical distribution

The languages that have the widest geographical spread in Africa are, of course, Western languages. Geographical spread is not the same as numerical spread. Arabic has more speakers than has any other language in Africa. But English has been the most successful in terms of geographical spread. Not only is it spoken in several African countries across the continent, but it also appears to be expanding rapidly, both geographically and in number of speakers. In this respect, Africa is responding to the global status of English as the primary language of science, aviation, sports, and increasingly even literature and the theatre.

The other Western language that has a wide geographical base in Africa is French. Over twenty African countries have adopted French as the main language of national business. Both English and French, therefore, have a firm *international* status within the African continent. Less international among Western languages are Portuguese, Italian, Spanish and German. But whatever the case, it is primarily through these Western languages that Africa is linked linguistically to the rest of the world.

Afro-Western languages, on the other hand, have tended to be *transnational* and *national* in geographic status. Pidgin English is spoken in sections of Nigeria, Ghana, and Cameroon. Krio is the *de facto* national language of Sierra Leone. Fanagalo is found in South Africa, and to some extent in Zambia and Zimbabwe. Afrikaans is widely spread in South Africa in spite of local resistance against it in favour of English.

Unlike Western and Afro-Western languages, most Afro-ethnic languages can be said to be *subnational*, geographically limited to specific regions within nation-state boundaries. There are, of course, a number of Afro-ethnic *lingua francas*, but many of these are again regional. The proportion of Afro-ethnic languages which are national or transnational is rather small. This would include Amharic (Ethiopia and Eritrea), Bemba (Zambia and Zimbabwe), Kituba (the Democratic Republic of the Congo and Congo), Lingala (the DRC, Congo, Angola, Central African Republic, Sudan and Uganda), Lwena (Angola, the DRC and Zambia), Nyanja or Chewa (Malawi and Zambia), and Sango (Central African Republic, Cameroon, Chad, Congo and the DRC).

Like Afro-Western languages, virtually all Afro-Islamic languages are either *national* or *transnational* in their geographic status. Arabic is spoken across the northern part of the continent, from Egypt to Mauritania, and there are pockets of Arabic speakers in both West and East Africa. In the non-Arab but Muslim country of Somalia, Arabic serves as an important national language. And in the Sudan, Arabic is spreading to the southern half of the country at a faster rate than is the Islamic religion. The Southern Sudanese are less likely to go to the mosque than to pronounce with sophistication the Arabic words *Insha'Allah* (If Allah, God, Wills).

Somali is another transnational Afro-Islamic language. It is spoken in Somalia, Djibouti, Kenya and the contested Ogaden region of Ethiopia. Though spoken across national boundaries, however, Somali is not a lingua franca in that it is limited to people who are ethnically Somali. In the Ogaden region there are non-Somali 'settlers' who speak Somali as an additional language, but these constitute a small minority. Somali, therefore, remains an Afro-Islamic language which, though transnational, essentially has ethnic limits.

At the other extreme is Kiswahili. It is a transnational lingua franca that is spoken widely throughout East and Central Africa, and is the declared national language of Tanzania and Kenya. The majority of Kiswahili speakers, however, use it as an additional language. Though an increasing number of East Africans (especially Tanzanians) are growing up speaking Kiswahili as a first language, those who do speak it as such constitute a rather small percentage of the total number of its speakers. The destiny of Kiswahili has long ceased to be in the hands of its native speakers.

Most other Afro-Islamic languages fall somewhere in between Somali and Kiswahili. They are either *national* (Wolof in Senegambia) or *transnational* (Hausa, Fulfulde, Songai, Mandinka). Unlike Somali they are all lingua francas; they are used by substantial numbers of ethnically heterogeneous speakers to facilitate inter-ethnic communication. But unlike Kiswahili, each of these Afro-Islamic languages has a majority of native speakers. Both native and non-native speakers, therefore, are contributing to shaping the destiny of these Afro-Islamic languages.

As intimated above, the Western languages, English and French, are the continent's most successful lingua francas. Between Afro-ethnic and Afro-Islamic languages, however, the latter seem to have been more successful lingua francas in terms of numbers of speakers. For example, the five top lingua francas in terms of speakers are all Afro-Islamic languages. These are Arabic, Kiswahili, Hausa, Fulfulde and Mandinka (Thea Bruhn, 1984: 10–11). In addition, Arabic, Kiswahili and Hausa are all on the increase in respect of the numbers of their speakers, contributing to the decline of sister Afro-Islamic languages such as Fulfulde and Mandinka.

Demographic distribution

Even though Western languages, especially English and French, have been the most international of Africa's lingua francas, they have tended to be limited demographically to the continent's urban, 'educated' population. The chances of an 'uneducated' peasant, from some rural area, speaking a Western language are almost nil. The tendency for Western languages to flourish in urban areas increases their chances of acquisition by urban residents generally. Entrenched as these languages are in the African milieu, their authenticity derives from their linkage with the metropolitan areas. London and Paris, rather than Monrovia or Dakar, are considered the cultural centres of (African) English and (African) French respectively.[3]

Afro-ethnic languages, on the other hand tend to be overwhelmingly *rural* in two senses of the term. First, the most 'ethnic' forms of Afro-ethnic languages are usually considered to be based in rural areas.[1] This, however, is not quite true of languages like Amharic. The majority of Afro-ethnic languages are definitely rural in this specific sense of *linguistic value*. Second, Afro-ethnic languages tend to be rural in a demographic sense. Speakers of Afro-ethnic languages are usually located in rural areas; but even those who reside in urban areas tend to regard the rural homeland as their real home.[2] For the majority of Afro-ethnic languages the rural hold is still predominant.

Afro-ethnic and Western languages, therefore, almost represent opposite poles of the demographic spectrum, spread between the 'lower' rural classes, and the 'upper' urban classes. It is between these two poles of the demographic spectrum that we can locate Afro-Islamic and Afro-Western languages. Afro-Islamic languages are primarily urban in two senses of the word. First it is the urban areas that are considered the cultural centres of Afro-Islamic languages. The rural versions of Afro-Islamic languages are sometimes perceived as less 'cultured' and less 'pure' than certain urban varieties. This particular linguistic urban–rural equation, however, applies mostly in native-speaking areas of Afro-Islamic languages. Second, Afro-Islamic languages are oriented towards the urban in the composition of their speakers. In areas where they predominate, Afro-Islamic languages often tend to facilitate rural–urban migration. And, unlike Western languages, Afro-Islamic languages are more firmly based on the urban 'masses' than on the urban élite. Outside the ranks of their native speakers, then, the destiny of most Afro-Islamic languages depends on the dynamics of the urban masses.

Like Afro-Islamic languages, Afro-Western languages are essentially urban phenomena. Fanagalo and West African Pidgin (English) are also languages of the masses. Middle-class and even upper-class Nigerians in the south may be very proficient in Pidgin but it is the urban lower classes who are more dependent on it for urban survival. Sierra Leonian Krio had élitist connotations, but it seems to be changing rapidly with increasing recognition as the country's *de facto* national language. The only Afro-Western language that is élitist, and exclusively so, is Afrikaans. Its strongest demographic base is the Afrikaners themselves and a large section of the so-called 'coloured' population.

English as an African language: the post-colonial balance sheet

As the twentieth century comes to a close the English language is arguably the most widespread language on the African continent. It is the official language of fewer countries than French, but English is spoken by a larger number of individual

Africans. More and more now learn it simply because it is the most important language *globally*.

The credentials of English as an African language are perhaps to be traced to Liberia, home of the continent's first *Afro-Saxonism* as a fusion of African biological ancestry with Anglo-cultural inheritance. At the very minimum an Afro-Saxon individual is a person of African descent whose mother tongue is the English language. From the 1820s onwards Liberia became the home of African American returnees whose first language was English or a version of it. A new African 'tribe' was born in the nineteenth century: the Americo-Liberians, whose language was a dialect of the English language.

But at about the same time as the birth of Liberia the British were beginning to carry out their imperial designs upon other parts of Africa. Huge portions of Africa subsequently fell under the British flag. The English language seemed destined to play a decisive role in this newly colonized Africa. We now know that Britain colonized nearly twenty countries which came to adopt English as the main language of national business. This included the largest African country in population, Nigeria, which accommodates one out of every four Black Africans living today. English is also the language of national business in South Africa, the continent's most industrialized state. Even ancient Ethiopia, for centuries totally dependent on indigenous languages, has witnessed a rapid expansion of the English language in the second half of the twentieth century.

We might therefore distinguish between four categories of countries in relation to the English language. *Category A* applies to countries where English is the language of both society and the state. This category includes such 'Afro-Saxon' Caribbean countries as Jamaica, Barbados, Afro-Trinidad and Afro-Guyana. Americo-Liberians fit that pattern of Afro-West Indians.

Category B countries are those where English is the language of the state but not of society. This applies to the majority of African members of the [British] Commonwealth, countries previously ruled by Britain and retaining English as the main language of governmental political business. This includes Nigeria, South Africa, Tanzania and some fifteen other African countries.

Outside Africa *Category B* also includes countries previously ruled by the United States (such as the Philippines), or by Australia (such as Papua New Guinea). Within Africa Category B countries include one (Namibia) previously ruled by South Africa.

English is the language of neither society nor state in our third category of societies. *Category C* is made up of countries which seem to need English in specialized vital areas of activity. Outside Africa, Japan needs English in major areas of commercial, industrial, and trade activity. Mexico needs English because of activities arising out of its proximity to the United States.

It is possible to argue that Sudan (Khartoum) once belonged to Category B, with extensive use of English in governmental, legislative, and north–south activities. Sudan in the 1990s may have moved more decisively into Category C – as the role of Arabic has expanded even in universities at the expense of the English language.

Somalia is a Category C country which needs English for other reasons, including the legacy of British Somaliland in the north. Mozambique and Angola are Category C countries since English continues to rise in importance, partly because of the proximity of South Africa as a big neighbour, and partly because Southern Africa as a whole is disproportionately Anglophone. In a sense Egypt has belonged to Category C for most of the twentieth century.

Category D societies are those which rely mainly on a world language other than English for their specialized activities. Most of the Francophone African countries belong to Category D, in which English is merely incidental. The Republic of Cameroon, where a part of the country is Anglophone, is one Francophone exception. The Democratic Republic of the Congo may be a Category C country rather than a Category D. English is more important in the DRC than it is in most other Francophone countries.

Mauritius is basically Euro-bilingual, where both the English language and a version of the French language (sometimes a Creole) are spoken. A few African countries may be difficult to categorize because they are on the borderline in one respect or another. But our four categories nevertheless cover almost all the post-colonial societies of Africa.

The English language serves other paradoxical roles in Africa. It has both enriched and stultified many indigenous languages. English has enriched them by being a major source of loan words – ranging from more universal words like radio, bicycle, socialism, democracy, and lorry to words for family relationships like cousin, nephew, and niece.

In some cases English has played a part in turning oral languages into written languages – transferring its borrowed Roman/Latin alphabet to languages like Luganda, Igbo, Kikuyu as well as to previously Arabized literary languages like Hausa and Kiswahili. As indicated earlier, the written tradition is usually more stabilizing for languages than the oral tradition. Indirectly English has helped stabilize some indigenous languages by helping them become written traditions.

But English has also stultified and weakened indigenous languages by marginal-izing most of them in national life and in the educational system. The huge imperial prestige enjoyed by the English language distorted educational opportunities, diverted resources from indigenous cultures towards giving English pre-eminence, and diluted the esteem in which indigenous African languages were held. The psychological damage to the colonized African was immense. Most Africans not only seemed to accept that their own languages were fundamentally inferior to the English language, they became convinced that it was not worth doing anything about it. Linguistic fatalism is still part of the post-colonial condition in Africa. Nonetheless, it is still premature to suggest that the more indigenous languages of Africa have lost the struggle for survival.

Functional distribution: complementarity and competition

Most sociolinguistic studies on Africa recognize a three-way distinction between 'vernacular' languages that serve as media of intra-ethnic communication and solidarity, vehicular languages of inter-ethnic communication and integration, and official languages of administration and national communication. This division roughly coincides with Africa's triple linguistic heritage. Afro-ethnic languages facilitate intra-ethnic communicative and socio-psychological needs in non-formal, and many formal, domains of discourse. Afro-Islamic and Afro-Western languages facilitate *inter-ethnic* communication with limited socio-psychological value. Western languages can also be considered as inter-ethnic media of communication, but mainly among the élite. In addition, Western languages are predominant in official domains nationally, and in meeting Africa's international communication needs.

But this picture of linguistic complementarity between Afro-ethnic, Afro-Islamic, Afro-Western and Western languages tells only part of the story. The other part is a story of linguistic competition. With regard to Western languages, for example, there is a growing number of young educated Africans who, finding it difficult to secure white collar jobs, are being forced to accept more menial jobs which, until recently, were taken only by the uneducated. This new class of African youth is gradually extending the realm of Western languages from the office to the market-place.[4] Whatever the case, there is evidence that Western languages have begun to encroach on domains that had hitherto been considered the exclusive monopoly of their competitors.

On the other hand, domains that previously have been tied to Western languages are being penetrated, especially by Afro-Islamic languages. The case of Kiswahili in Tanzania is self-evident. By the time of its independence in 1961, Tanzania was like most other African countries in its dependence on the Western official language, English. By 1967, however, Kiswahili had replaced English in internal administration, the courts and primary education. It is also gradually replacing English in secondary education, even though its progress there is delayed by the lack of adequate instructional materials. English continues to be used as the medium of instruction in most subjects at the university level, but even here it is acknowledged that English is on the decline in terms of both the number and the competence of its speakers.

Kiswahili has made less headway in neighbouring Kenya. In competition with Afro-ethnic languages it is commonly used in the lower levels of governmental administration, and in competition with English in Parliament. Hitherto English was the only compulsory language in Kenyan schools. More recently, however, the Kenya government has made Kiswahili a compulsory and examinable subject in both primary and secondary schools. This move may have long-term implications for the potential of Kiswahili to compete with English as we witness an increasing number of graduates, constituting a potential educational élite, who are proficient in Kiswahili.

Somali is another Afro-Islamic language which has made notable gains in competition with Western languages. It seems unlikely, however, that Somali will be able to follow Tanzania's example of replacing Western languages with Afro-Islamic ones in the educational sphere in the near future. In the Maghreb, French has been facing some competition from Arabic. The Arabization programmes adopted by Algeria, Morocco and Tunisia all have, as their principal objective, the gradual phasing out of French and its replacement by Arabic. In general, the Maghreb has moved much more indecisively in implementing the Arabization programme than Tanzania has with Kiswahili or Somalia with Somali. In Egypt, Libya, and to a lesser extent, Sudan, Arabic is basically triumphant. Across the board, Western languages have faced their stiffest competition from Afro-Islamic languages.

Afro-ethnic languages were probably the most marginalized by colonial language policies. Despite the fact that some of them came to be written, they were less well placed to compete with Western languages.[5] Language policies in some African countries, however, continue to favour the use of Afro-ethnic languages in lower primary education. A number of Afro-ethnic languages are also offered for study at some African universities and they often serve as the unsanctioned official *oral* media. Written official communication may invariably be in Western languages, but oral official communication may often be conducted in Afro-ethnic languages – depending, of course, on the linguistic background of the interlocutors.[6] In some cases, Afro-ethnic languages are in competition with Afro-Islamic languages. In the Democratic Republic of the Congo, Lingala is in competition with Kiswahili, with Lingala seemingly gaining the upper hand for the time being. In Nigeria, Hausa is facing competition from both Igbo and Yoruba. In short, in spite of the many difficulties that Afro-ethnic languages may face, they have continued to demonstrate tremendous resilience and a competitive spirit.

Against this demographic background, the forces of complementarity and competition in linguistic function have had certain effects on the languages themselves and on their speakers. By virtue of their role as vehicular languages, many Afro-Islamic languages (and Afro-ethnic lingua francas) were already highly differentiated along the horizontal demographic plane. The varieties of Kiswahili, for example, have formed a continuum from the primary dialects of native speakers to the pidginized varieties of the DRC. European languages, as languages of the élite acquired through formal instruction, have so far maintained relatively homogeneous normative standards. But as their demographic base stretches downward, and the streets and market-places become probable avenues for their acquisition, are they likely to undergo a downwards differentiation along the vertical demographic plane?

Africans are already well known for their strong tendency towards polylingualism. Richard Fardon and Graham Furhiss even claim that 'Africans have been talented linguists throughout history. Monolingualism has never been the norm it is in much of Europe' (1991: 23). The forces of functional complementarity definitely encourage polylingualism. Complete overlap in function may stimulate a gradual trend towards unilingualism. But an uncertain situation of partial complementarity and partial competition may prompt an even higher incidence of polylingualism. In short, the interplay between complementarity and competition in the roles and functions of languages in Africa may trigger sociolingusitic dynamics in the overall interest of the emergent world language system.

Foreign relations: between language and religion

In the previous sections we have demonstrated that religious, economic and political forces have combined to affect the destiny of the religious, economic and political processes and institutions on the continent. Religion, economics, politics and language, therefore, have all complemented each other in shaping the future of individual African countries.

But what about the international level of African affairs? Have any of the above forces been more important than others in determining the foreign policies of African nations? By all indications, economic and political considerations constitute the backbone of much of Africa's foreign policy with the West. Issues of bilateral or multilateral assistance, superpower ideologies and differences, North–South tensions on the servicing, and actual payment, of debts and so forth seem to dominate the foreign policy agendas of most African countries.

But behind the apparent predominance of political and economic factors in Africa's foreign relations, there are the cultural forces of language and religion. Is one of these two forces more important than the other in shaping foreign policy in Africa? Our contention here is that language has been a greater determinant of foreign policy than religion, for the following reasons:

1. The formulation of foreign policy is usually in the hands of the élite. The masses may form part of foreign policy considerations but are unlikely to participate in policy formulation. Western languages, therefore, come to assume a disproportionate importance precisely because African élite assimilation of Western languages is more permanent than élite conversion to foreign religions. Members of the élite may, and sometimes do, give up one religion or religious sect for another. In addition, there will probably always be more Africans who receive international acclaim for their contributions in Western languages than for their achievements in Western religions. There is a sense, then, in which élite formulation of foreign policy will be bound somewhat by their linguistic assimilation.

2. The second point is directly related to the first one. Western languages as media of reading and communication are more relevant in learning about foreign affairs than are religions. An élite that is competent in Portuguese alone is likely to learn more about the Portuguese-speaking world than about the French- or English-speaking worlds. Through these linguistically-based constraints on the flow of information, then, Western languages continue to exercise their influence on the foreign policies of individual African states. In general, Western languages are keys to major sources of information relevant for foreign policy.

3. Language is important not only in orienting the élite, in foreign policy formulation, toward particular Western countries, but also in the formation of the future élite. Throughout Africa Western languages rather than Western religions influence the choice of the country in which the next élite is educated. Students from Kenya and Nigeria, irrespective of their religious backgrounds, are more likely to seek admission into American and English universities than into French and Portuguese universities.

4. Finally, within Africa itself birds of the same linguistic feather are more likely to stick together than birds of the same religious feather. African nations are never referred to by religious categories like Islamic, Catholic or Protestant except when one is explicitly talking about the religious composition of their populations. But it is quite common, and seemingly quite acceptable, to categorize African nations by reference to Western languages. We often talk of Anglophone, Francophone, and Lusophone Africa, for example, but seldom of Christian or Islamic Africa. Likewise, cooperation between African states has often followed these divisions based on Western languages.

The above considerations do indicate, then, that Africa's relations with the West are affected more by language than by religion. This is in sharp contrast to Africa's relations with the Middle East. Senegal, a Francophone country, stands the chance of establishing more enduring foreign relations with Oman, a semi-Anglophone nation, than would Sierra Leone, for example, another Anglophone country. The predominantly Muslim nation of Oman would respond more favourably to Senegal because of its predominance of Muslims – in an influential position over Christians – than to Sierra Leone with its uninfluential Muslim minority. Uganda under Idi Amin (a Muslim head of state) had firmer relations with Saudi Arabia than under Milton Obote (a Christian head of state).

Conclusion

We started this essay with a triple observation. Africa invented language; Asia sacralized language; and Europe universalized it. Since, on present evidence, Africa is where the human species originated, it is where human communication began. Our concern in this chapter has been with the religions of Christianity and Islam and their effect on language. The Qur'an is the most widely read book in its *original language* in human history. The Christian Bible is the most widely read book in *translation* in history. Both books have had consequences for the history of literacy, idiom and vocabulary in African languages.

If Africa invented language and Asia sacralized it, the historical role of Europe has been in universalizing language. Europeans and people of European descent have gone further than any other people in history towards turning some of their languages into *global* successes.

Within this global triple heritage of Africa, Asia and Europe in relation to language, we have put forward a narrower triple heritage within the African continent itself, one concerning the cultural interplay within Africa between *indigenous, Islamic* and *Western* legacies. Indigenous culture is part of the genesis of language. Islamic culture is part of Asia's role in sacralizing language. As for the Western impact on Africa, that is one aspect of Europe's role in universalizing language.

Apart from Amharic in Ethiopia, indigenous Afro-ethnic languages are usually sub-national in distribution (the Igbo language in Nigeria, for example). Afro-Islamic languages are national or transnational (Somali and Kiswahili languages). Western languages are widely used as official languages (e.g. French in the Democratic Republic of the Congo, for example). The intermediate category of Afro-Western languages (creolized or pidginized European tongues) tend to be sub-national in distributive scale.

In the light of this comparative distribution the languages most extensively used in *national* politics in Africa are Afro-Islamic and European. Political speeches given in European and Afro-Islamic languages probably account for the bulk of speech making at the national level, although numerically the great majority of languages in Africa are Afro-ethnic. With only a tenth of the population of the world, Africa has about a quarter of its languages – most of them Afro-ethnic in our sense. But although numerous, and perhaps because of being numerous, Afro-ethnic languages have a lesser role in national politics than either European languages or Afro-Islamic languages. Afro-ethnic languages are also used less often as languages of command in the armed forces, precisely because the security forces are usually multi-ethnic in composition and need a Western or Afro-Islamic lingua franca.

The contradictions of Africa's triple heritage continue to condition the interplay between language and power in the stark realities of post-colonial history. In East Africa Western technology is creating competition for Western languages. Greater use of Kiswahili on Radio Tanzania, for example, has squeezed out English almost completely from the Tanzanian airwaves. Nonetheless, the role of Western technology in spreading languages is part of the West's globalizing role. In the future Africa may or may not invent new languages. Asia may or may not sacralize any additional languages. What is certain is the West's continuing role in the universalization of language – with Africa as one persistent linguistic constituency.

Notes

1. To study the 'most authentic' Kikuyu, one would not go to Nairobi, for example, but to rural Kikuyuland.
2. The case of Afro-ethnic lingua francas like Lingala and Bemba is less clear since their inter-ethnic

role is most pronounced in the urban milieu.

3. One is more likely to go to cities like Cairo, Kano and Mombasa to study the 'cultured' varieties of Arabic, Hausa and Kiswahili, respectively, than to rural areas.

4. In a country like Kenya, for example, it is not at all uncommon to find domestic workers, hawkers, shoe-shine boys, and so forth, who are sufficiently proficient in English to conduct their business exclusively in the language. Foreigners in Kenya who learn Kiswahili and seek to practise it with the 'common man' in the streets of Nairobi meet with a lot of frustration. Apparently their African interlocutors usually take these as opportunities to practise and improve their own English.

5. Amharic, in Ethiopia, is one of the few exceptions in this regard. Having succeeded in resisting the colonial fold, Amharic continued to hold its own, and has given in to Western languages only in the area of higher education. The competition offered by most other Afro-ethnic languages, however, is more modest.

6. In addition, there is a growing body of creative and non-creative literature in Afro-ethnic languages. The attempts to write in Afro-ethnic languages by prominent writers such as Ngugi wa Thiong'o and Mazisi Kunene are helping to elevate their social status and to render them potentially more competitive.

6
Language Planning
& Gender Planning

Some African Perspectives

Language planning is usually part of wider social engineering and is used in order to achieve other goals such as political participation or national integration. But are there occasions when there is an inversion of cause and effect – when language planning emerges as a consequence of some other social planning, in some other area of endeavour?

Among such areas is *gender planning*. One idea is to plan for guaranteed female participation in Parliament in the new wave of democratization in Africa. Africa is accustomed to racial reservation of seats in those countries which had a significant number of white settlers. Zimbabwe's first decade of independence included seats in Parliament reserved exclusively for the white minority. Should Africa now experiment with gender reservation – seats set aside for women?

Phase I of such a gender plan could be an arrangement in which both the Parliamentary candidates for those seats and those who vote for those seats have to be women. Phase II would be the stage when the candidates still have to be women, but the voters for these gender seats are now both men and women. The female candidates would need to cultivate the male voters in their constituencies as well as the women. The third phase would be the abolition of the reserved seats for women altogether, but only when the political system has reached a stage at which female participation needs no special protection. Even during the stages when there are reserved gender seats, other women would be free to compete with men for the remaining seats on the common electoral roll.

What is clear is that this entire gender Parliamentary planning has language consequences. In most African countries the language of debate in Parliament is the ex-colonial Parliamentary language. Also, in most of those countries far more men speak a European language than women. A strategy of increasing female participation in politics may require either a review of the language policy of Parliament (with the possibility of changing it) or a longer-term campaign to make it easier for women to learn the ex-colonial European languages. Changing the language policy of the legislature may be easier to implement without waiting a long time. The legislature would have to permit debate in one or two indigenous languages, as well as in the relevant European tongue. A system of simultaneous translation would have to be installed.

85

The other solution would involve making it easier to learn a European language simply as a language and not as part of the pursuit of a comprehensive educational qualification. Most Africans learn the language of their former imperial masters not as an independent skill but in pursuit of a more comprehensive school certificate, or a bachelor's degree or its equivalent. The new policy would establish language-learning centres in their own right, and pay special attention to the hours which are convenient to mothers and to the working patterns of women more generally.

A systematic convergence between gender planning and language planning will be easier in a country like Tanzania where an indigenous language, Kiswahili, is the main language of politics and public life. Tanzania is also among the first countries in sub-Saharan Africa to consider the reservation of seats for women in Parliament.

In South Africa the African National Congress has considered reserving seats for women on its own National Executive, but that idea has been shelved for the time being. In Parliament the struggle had been to try and get black representation at all, male or female. The issue remained primarily *race* rather than gender. The first multiracial elections in history took place in April 1994.

Is there such a concept as *de-planning* language? In South Africa the Soweto rebellion of young people in 1976 against the Afrikaans language was, in part, an effort to break down the Euro-bilingual plan of teaching African children both English and Afrikaans. The students regarded Afrikaans as the language of oppression, and wanted it knocked out of the educational grand design.

But since the students were not in a position to provide an alternative national educational plan, and the South African situation was politically fluid anyhow, a process of *de facto* de-planning in language was under way. Again, the central issue in the politics of the country remained race rather than gender, even after the 1994 multiracial elections.

As for the role of language in African diplomacy, there has been a surprising level of female participation despite the fact that there are far fewer African women who are fluent in European languages than men. While African ministries of foreign affairs do not have gender reservation of ambassadorships, there has been more affirmative action in favour of women in diplomatic posts than in most other areas of African public life. For one thing, having women in highly visible international roles is one way of impressing the Western world with regard to progress in the status of women in African societies.

And so three forms of planning converge: gender planning (affirmative action in favour of women), diplomatic planning (ways of cultivating Western sensibilities) and language planning (learning the European languages which African diplomats need for their work on the world stage).

Female diplomats and European languages

African women have made their mark on African foreign services more firmly than on African Parliaments. Here a paradox emerges. While European languages in Africa are essentially instruments of élite formation, in diplomacy they serve the reverse role of gender equalization. In the wider society European languages help to deepen disparities between groups. But in diplomacy those languages help to narrow the gulf of privilege between men and women.

European languages have been a crucial factor in the development of African foreign services. Competence in two European languages (Euro-bilingualism) is often a major credential for rapid promotion in the diplomatic service. While almost all educated Africans are at least bilingual (combining an African language with a European one) very few are Euro-bilingual (competent in two European languages). The diplomatic service puts a premium on that dual Euro-skill.

But the African woman who makes it diplomatically does not necessarily have to be Euro-bilingual. Indeed, it was not entirely accidental that the first African woman to be a major diplomatic success had the English language as her *mother* tongue. This was the Liberian woman, Angie Elizabeth Brooks, who in 1969 became President of the United Nations General Assembly. She was then one of only two women to have served in that capacity – the first had been Madame Pandit of the Nehru family in India (Indira Gandhi's aunt). From an African perspective, Angie Brooks's achievement would have been inconceivable without her command of the English language.

Ambassador Brooks had blazed other diplomatic trails before – including her appointment as the first woman and the first African to preside over the United Nations Trusteeship Council. When she took on the presidency of the General Assembly itself in 1969 Ms Brooks affirmed: 'I am proud of my continent, my country and my sex.' Before long international diplomacy was confirmed as one of the first prestigious professions to open its doors to African women. The language issue was crucial.

Uganda's Elizabeth Bagaya (Princess of Toro) served as Idi Amin's Roving Ambassador and Delegate to the United Nations and later as Foreign Minister in the 1970s. But Princess Elizabeth was too independent to last in such a capacity under such a volatile military regime. Under a different president she later served as Ambassador to the United States. Had she spoken only the Rutooro language of her traditional kingdom, Toro, Princess Elizabeth would never have made it in the Uganda foreign service.

Uganda has had other women in prominent diplomatic roles, ranging from Bonn (Ambassador Bernadette Olowo) to Ottawa (High Commissioner Anna Amailuk). In the late 1980s these diplomats included Freda Blick as Ambassador to France. At least one European language was again indispensable.

Kenyan women who have served in quasi-diplomatic roles over the years have included Margaret Kenyatta (the late President's daughter), Grace Ogot, the novelist, and others. The Kenyan Foreign Service has also included high-ranking women officials and diplomats – often serving both Africa and their own country. Not even Kiswahili (let alone their ethnic languages) would have been enough to give them an international role.

At the time of Zambia's independence in 1964 the country's most highly publicized woman was not a diplomat at all. She was Alice Lenshina, the prophetess who led the Lumpa Church. Alice's defiance of Zambia's government and ruling party precipitated serious civil conflict. Her movement refused to declare allegiance to either the government or the ruling party. In Alice's case a European language was an aversion.

Other women in Zambia since then have assumed quasi-diplomatic roles from time to time – including Mrs Mutumba Bull, both as a minister and as a scholar. Such women have served both their country and the continent in the Euro-colonial language.

Certain spouses of African leaders in this period developed a high diplomatic and political visibility of their own. In the 1980s the late Mrs Sally Mugabe became active in a number of humanitarian and international causes. She had to be articulate in a European language (English).

Another African presidential spouse who was diplomatically active for a while was Mrs Jehan Anwar Sadat of Egypt. Among conservative Muslim men in the Middle East, Mrs Sadat's public posture and visibility were often a liability rather than an asset. But to many women in the Arab world Mrs Sadat became, at least for a while, a role model. Linguistically, she combined Arabic with Western credentials.

In Southern Africa as a whole in this period, pan-Africanism has been at its most tumultuous, both politically and in gender relations. In the Republic of South Africa the most spectacular spouse of any race in the 1980s was Winnie Mandela. Although she had neither a direct diplomatic role nor an official political office in the struggle against apartheid, Winnie Mandela became the most famous African woman of the 1980s. She found herself in the middle of a variety of historical and pan-African processes in her part of the continent. In the 1990s she partially fell from political grace. The English language was intricately interwoven in her national and international fate.

Pan-Africanism has traditionally been viewed as relations of unity between Africans across *territorial* boundaries. But pan-Africanism should be redefined to include relations of unity between Africans across the divide of *gender*. It is not enough to transcend the divisions of nationality and the territorial legacy of the scramble for Africa. There is a need to transcend an even older divide between Africans – the political gap between men and women in the realm of public affairs. In both cases Euro-languages are crucially relevant.

The big question was whether a woman Secretary-General of the Organization of African Unity (OAU) would come *before* or *after* the first woman president of an African country. Both jobs necessitate competence in at least one European language for the foreseeable future. In July 1993 Africa took a step towards those goals. Two Francophone African countries chose women for prime ministers – the first female heads of government in post-colonial African history. Mrs Sylvie Kinigi in Burundi and Ms Agathe Uwilingiyimana in Rwanda, each country polarized ethnically for so long between Hutu and Tutsi, took a momentous step toward narrowing the gap between genders. Unfortunately these new developments in gender relations were overwhelmed in 1994 by the much older ethnic tensions between Hutu and Tutsi. At least half a million people died in the Rwanda genocide of 1994. The genocide was ended by an army of Rwandan exiles penetrating Rwanda from Uganda. These were English-speaking Rwandan Tutsi. The rest of the country was French-speaking. This language issue influenced the policy of France towards Rwanda and its new Anglophone rulers. France was for a while hostile to the new government in Kigali.

Meanwhile, the other lingo-gender paradox has persisted all over Africa. The same European languages which have been responsible for creating disparities of privilege in the wider African society may be contributing towards narrowing disparities between genders in the diplomatic arena. And language planning remains inextricably intertwined with other areas of social engineering.

Pre-planning gender roles

Only the state in Africa – when all is said and done – is strong enough to make the necessary *cultural readjustment* on the gender question. Only the state can enable the market to benefit from fuller female participation in the economy. In Muslim Africa, Tunisia is one of the places where progress has gone the furthest in improving female participation, even in the professions. But this has often meant promoting bilingualism in French and Arabic. In Algeria until 1989 – where state socialism had also been attempted with the strong hand of government power – women's rights did fall short of the expectations of the revolution, but are still substantial in terms of public participation. Algeria even had women airplane pilots – a rather unusual situation in the Muslim world. But a change in language policy in Algeria from emphasis on French to emphasis on Arabic seemed to slow down female empowerment. This was because linguistic Arabization was often accompanied by Islamic traditionalism. Since the aborted election of 1992 the country has been plunged into civil conflict.

In much of Black Africa women traditionally have been almost natural entrepreneurs. In addition to their triple trusteeship of catering, water supply and subsistence cultivation, women have also entered the arena of trade and marketing. But more recently African women are becoming less and less entrepreneurial in response to four wider processes of social change. These processes are, first, the enlargement of the scale of African economies; second, the internationalization of those economies; third, the mechanization of production; and fourth, the Westernization of supportive values and roles. European colonial languages played a disproportionate role in facilitating national economic activities and international economic relations.

Ethno-economies and sub-regional marketing still allow considerable room for women. But as African patterns of production and exchange have become more integrated into national economies, the role of women therein has narrowed. An even more marginalizing factor for the economic role of women has been the internationalization of African trade and investment patterns. In spite of the new involvement of East African women in trading with Arabian Gulf countries, citizens who deal with transnational corporations are more likely to be men than women. Competence in European languages has again favoured men. Ugandans who sit on boards of directors or who manage international subsidiaries are more likely to be men than women. The same applies to east Africans who control the Central Bank or who become advisers to the World Bank or the International Monetary Fund (IMF). Production of food crops for local markets still leaves women in control in many parts of East Africa. Production of cash crops for export tends to increase male dominance.

Advancing technology and complex organization in African economies are also likely to favour men. There is a cultural presumption against women as technicians or engineers. Women may be involved extensively in a tea plantation in picking the tea leaves, but not in planning the original planting of the trees or in handling the tractor.

As for the Westernization of supportive values, these range from rules of credit to the language of economic discourse. The problem is not simply whether an African man is more likely to get credit from a bank than an African woman. At least as basic is the fact that a Westernized English-speaking African woman is much more likely to get credit than a non-Westernized female competent only in an African language. Let us look more closely at the cultural and historical background to this trend of declining female entrepreneurship.

Africa since the colonial period has witnessed significant changes in the roles and functions of men and women. In many traditional cultures there has been a belief that God made woman the custodian of fire, water, and earth. God himself took charge of the fourth element of the universe – the omnipresent air. Custody of fire entailed responsibility for making energy available. And the greatest source of energy in rural Africa remains firewood. The African woman became disproportionately responsible for finding and carrying huge bundles of firewood, though quite often it was men who initially chopped down the big trees. Custody of water involved a liquid which was a symbol of both survival and cleanliness. The African woman became responsible for ensuring that this critical substance was available for the family. She has trekked long distances to fetch water. But where a well needed to be dug, it was often the man who did the digging. The custody of earth has been part of a doctrine of *dual fertility*. Woman ensures the survival of this generation by maintaining a central role in cultivation – and preserving the fertility of the soil. Woman ensures the arrival of the next generation in her role as mother – the fertility of the womb. Dual fertility becomes an aspect of the triple custodial role of African womanhood, though always in partnership with the African man.[1]

What has happened to this doctrine of triple custody in the period since 1935? Different elements of the colonial experience affected the roles of men and women in Africa in different ways. Many social trends had linguistic consequences. Among the factors which increased the women's role on the land was wage labour for the men. Faced with an African population reluctant to work for somebody else for low wages, colonial rulers had already experimented with both forced labour and taxation as a way of inducing Africans (especially men) to join the colonial workforce.

According to Margaret Jean Hay, it was some time before wage labour for men began to affect women's role on the land. Hay's own work was among Luo women in Kenya:

> By 1930 a large number of men had left Kowe at least once for outside employment.... More than half of this group stayed away for periods of fifteen years or more.... This growing export of labour from the province might be thought to have increased the burden of agricultural work for women.... As early as 1910, administrators lamented the fact that Nyanza was becoming the labour pool of the entire colony.... Yet the short-term migrants of the 1920s were usually unmarried youths, who played a relatively minor role in the local economy beyond occasional herding and the conquest of cattle in war. Furthermore, the short-term labour migrants could and often did arrange to be away during the slack periods in the agriculture cycle.... Thus labour migration in the period before 1930 actually removed little labour from the local economy and did not significantly alter the sexual division of labour. (Hay, 1976: 98-9)

But Margaret Hay goes on to demonstrate how the Great Depression and the Second World War changed the situation as migrant labour and conscription of males took an increasingly larger proportion of men away from the land. Migration created the need for new languages. This was compounded by the growth of mining industries like the gold mining at Kowe from 1934 onwards:

> The long-term absence of men had an impact on the sexual division of labour, with women and children assuming a greater share of agricultural work than ever before.... The thirties represent a transition with regard to the sexual division of labour, and it was clearly the women who bore the burden of the transition in rural areas. (Hay, 1976: 105)

Women in this period, from the 1930s onwards, became more deeply involved as 'custodians of earth'. In southern Africa the migrations of men to the mines became even more dramatic. By the 1950s a remarkable bifurcation was taking place in some South African societies – a division between a male multilingual proletariat (industrial working class) and a female, often unilingual peasantry. The old South Africa's regulations against families joining their husbands in the mines exacerbated this tendency towards *gender-apartheid*, the segregation of the sexes. Many women in the front-line states (FLS) of Southern Africa had to fulfil their triple role as custodians of fire, water, and earth in greater isolation than ever. But language implications were always present. Migrant male workers learnt more languages than their sedentary women back home.

The wars of liberation in Southern Africa from the 1960s took their own toll. Some of the fighters did have their wives with them. Indeed, liberation armies like ZANLA and ZIPRA in Zimbabwe and FRELIMO in Mozambique included a few female fighters. But on the whole the impact of the wars was disruptive of family life and the traditional sexual division of labour.

After independence there were counter-revolutionary wars among some of the front-line states. The most artificial of the post-colonial wars was that of Mozambique, initiated by the so-called Mozambique National Resistance (MNR or RENAMO). The movement was originally created by reactionary white Rhodesians to punish Samora Machel for his support of Robert Mugabe's forces in Zimbabwe. After Zimbabwe's independence the Mozambique National Resistance became a surrogate army for reactionary whites in the Republic of South Africa – committing a variety of acts of sabotage against the fragile post-colonial economy of Mozambique. The linguistic implications were as mucky as the dreadful warfare.

Again, there were also implications for relations between the genders. In addition to the usual disruptive consequences of war for the family, the MNR, by the mid-1980s, had inflicted enough damage on the infrastructure in Mozambique to prevent many migrant workers getting home to their families in the intervals in between their contracts with the South African industries and mines. The miners often remained on the border between South Africa and Mozambique, waiting for their next opportunity to return to the mines, without ever having found the transportation to get to their families in the distant villages of Mozambique. This problem continued well into the 1990s.

It is not absolutely clear how this situation has affected the doctrine of 'dual fertility' in relation to the role of the African woman. One possibility is that the extra long absences of the husbands reduced fertility rates in some communities like Mozambique. The other scenario is that the pattern of migrant labour in Southern Africa generally initiated a tendency towards *de facto* polyandry. The woman who was left behind aquired over time a *de facto* extra husband. The two husbands took their turn over time with the woman. The migrant labourer from the mines had conjugal priority between mining contracts if he did manage to get to the village. He also had prior claim to the new babies unless agreed otherwise.[2]

If the more widespread pattern is that of declining fertility as a result of extra-long absences of husbands, the principle of 'dual fertility' has reduced the social function of the fertility of the womb and increased the woman's involvement in matters pertaining to the fertility of the soil. On the other hand, if the more significant tendency in mining communities in Southern Africa is towards *de facto* polyandry, a whole new nexus of social relationships may be in the making in Southern Africa even after apartheid.[3]

The gender of technology

Other changes in Africa during this period which affected relationships between men and women have included the impact of new technologies on gender roles. Cultivation with the hoe still left the African woman centrally involved in agriculture. But cultivation with the tractor was often a prescription for male dominance.

> When you see a farmer
> On bended knee
> Tilling land
> For the family
> The chances are
> It is a *she*

> When you see a tractor
> Passing by
> And the driver
> Waves you 'Hi'
> The chances are that
> It is a *he*!

Mechanization of agriculture in Africa has tended to marginalize women. Their role as 'custodians of earth' is threatened by male prerogatives in new and more advanced technologies. It is true that greater male involvement in agriculture could help reduce the heavy burdens of work undertaken by women on the land. On the other hand, there is no reason why this relief in workload for women should not come through better technology. Tractors were not invented to be driven solely by men.

Another threat to the central role of the African woman in the economy in this period has come from the nature of Western education. We are back to the Euro-colonial languages. It is true that the Westernized African woman is usually more mobile and with more freedom for her own interests than is her traditional sister. But a transition from custodian of fire, water, and earth to keeper of the typewriter is definitely a form of marginalization for African womanhood. Typing, even in the elegant French language, is less fundamental for survival than cultivation. The Westernized African woman in the second half of the twentieth century has tended to be more free, better equipped with at least one European language, but less important for African economies than the traditional woman in rural areas.

The third threat to the role of the African woman in this period came, once again, with the internationalization of African economies. As we have indicated, the colonial and post-colonial tendencies towards enlargement of economic scale have pushed women increasingly to the side in international decision making. It is true that Nigerian women, especially, have refused to be marginalized completely even in international trade. But, on the whole, the Euro-glottal males have taken over the governing boards.

Gender planning and cultural adjustment

What are the policy implications of all these trends? One central imperative is indeed to arrest the marginalization of women and to cultivate further their entrepreneurial potential. *Cultural adjustment* is the imperative.

Traditionally women as custodians of earth have emphasized food cultivation. But from now on greater involvement of women in the production of cash crops for export is one way of linking tradition to modernity – and preventing Africa's economic internationalization from resulting in the marginalization of African women.

But support for traditional market women in food production and local food trade need not suffer as a result of the new androgynization of cash-crop production. Credit facilities should be made available in such a manner that there is equity not only between men and women but also between Euro-glottal Westernized and Afro-glottal, non-Westernized females. As matters now stand, traditionalist Afro-glottal non-Westernized women are often at a disadvantage when assessed for credit-worthiness. The system should stop disadvantaging women who cannot speak a European language.

On the other hand, a higher proportion of non-Westernized Afro-glottal women are involved in agricultural production than their Westernized sisters. Indeed, cultural Westernization of women – though improving their credit-worthiness – tends to decrease women's direct economic productivity. A balance has to be struck between the two categories of women (Westernized and non-Westernized) in relation to both credit and production.

Preventing technology from marginalizing women is yet another imperative. Special programmes for women in technical training – from driving tractors to repairing a lorry engine – should be inaugurated. It will not happen on its own. Such shifts in the cultural aspects of technology need to be addressed purposefully. Effective participation of women in the world of economic entrepreneurship requires their upliftment in the world of technical and mechanical skills as well. Higher forms of technical training in Africa require competence in Euro-colonial languages.

Women as custodians of fire make them the greatest users of firewood on the continent. But should not women also be centrally involved in forest management and reforestation? Wood should increasingly be approached as an integrated industry, sensitized to the needs of environmental protection and ecological balance. Women as the greatest users of firewood should also be among the leading planters of trees for reforestation. This would not be incompatible with their involvement in the commercial aspects of wood more generally. Carpentry and furniture-making are crafts which cry out for greater female involvement than has been achieved so far. Culturally, women are often the selectors of furniture and trustees of the domestic infrastructure of the family. And yet it is an anomaly that African women have played a limited role in designing furniture or making it. This is an area of entrepreneurship which beckons the female participant to become more involved. Do African women have to be Euro-glottal to perform these tasks?

As traditional custodians of water, do women have any special role in this era of faucets and dams? Africa's women, as we indicated, still trek long distances in some rural areas for their water. But water-related industries, surprisingly, are still male-dominated. This includes the whole infrasturcture of water supply in urban areas. Even commercialized laundry and dry cleaning operations for the élite and for foreigners in African towns are still usually owned and managed by men, even when women do most of the washing and ironing. The soap manufacturing industry is also male-owned and male-managed, even when the consumers are overwhelmingly women. One question which arises is whether these water-related industries are appropriate areas of linking tradition to modernity in Africa's gender roles. Do they need language planning?

Conclusion

What is at stake is the tapping of female talent where it was previously under-utilized. What is at stake is also the androgynization of entrepreneurship. Once again the imperative is cultural adjustment. And part of that involves language planning.

Can the traditional custodian of fire be the innovative consumer of hydroelectric power? Can the traditional trustee of water be the new creative user of the high dam? Can the traditional trustee of earth take control of a new (and more creative) green revolution? The future of the continent depends upon a new sexual equation in the whole economic process. The future of the continent depends more fundamentally on cultural than on a structural adjustment. Language policy and language planning are likely to be basic elements in that cultural adjustment.

The underlying moral of Africa's experience is that language planning is always an aspect of a wider design of social engineering. As we have indicated, language policy has often been an instrument of national integration or promoting political participation. In this paper we have linked language to gender politics and history. The search for answers is eternal. The need for planning is one response.

Notes

1. I am indebted to the late Okot p'Bitek, the Ugandan anthropologist and poet, for stimulation and information about myths and womanhood in northern Uganda. Okot and I also discussed similarities and differences between African concepts of matter and the ideas of Empedocles, the Greek philosopher of the fifth century BC.
2. There is no doubt such arrangements occur in Mozambique. What is not clear is how widespread *de facto* polyandry is becoming in Southern Africa. For how long will it continue after the end of official apartheid?
3. I am indebted to the field research and interviews in Southern Africa which accompanied the BBC/WETA television project, 'The Africans: A Triple Heritage: (1985-86)'. I am also grateful to the work associated with Vol. VIII of the UNESCO General History of Africa, *Africa Since 1935* (Edited by Ali A. Mazrui, assisted by C. Wondji) (London: Heinemann and Berkeley, CA: University of California Press, 1993).

7
Language Policy
& the Foundations of Democracy

An African Perspective

Most African nations can be described as linguistically heterogeneous and, in the name of pragmatism, have pursued linguistic practices in favour of their respective European or Western languages inherited from the colonial tradition. Until the 1990s most of these countries were under either military rule or single-party regimes. Indeed, about two thirds of African countries had military governments of one type or another, some having been subject to several military coups and counter-coups. Others were either *de facto* one-party states, after 'voluntary' dissolution of opposition parties, or *de jure* one-party states through acts of Parliament which made opposition parties illegal. In spite of their recurrent claim to the contrary, in political practice the majority of these nations tended more towards autocracy than towards democracy. Terms like 'popular democracy' and 'one-party democracy' that were in vogue in these nations were often intended to mask authoritarian practices.

Yet it is precisely in some of these quasi-autocratic societies that the most successful experiments in language planning in Africa have taken place. Inspired by its policy of socialism (*Ujamaa*) and self-reliance (*kujitegemea*), for example, the one-party civilian government of Tanzania made a decisive move to adopt Kiswahili as its national and official language, and proceeded to invest tremendous financial and human resources in its development to meet various linguistic needs of the state and the society at large. The personal rule of the country's first president, Julius K. Nyerere, and the unchallenged authority of the ruling and only political party, the CCM (*Chama cha Mapinduzi* or Revolutionary Party), were some of the key factors that ensured the success of Tanzania's Swahilization policy after the Arusha Declaration in 1967 had oriented the country officially towards a socialist path.

Kenya's record in the promotion of Kiswahili has been less impressive than that of Tanzania. But even the modest achievements that it has been able to attain over the years would probably not have taken root without the personal push of its successive presidents and the uncontested power that one-party rule accorded them. Jomo Kenyatta, the first President of Kenya, was very keen to see Kiswahili introduced as the official language of Parliamentary discussion, which hitherto had been conducted exclusively in the English language. The Parliamentary motion intended to effect his presidential wish was frustrated repeatedly as long as democratic procedures of the house were left to decide on the matter. It took Jomo Kenyatta's dictatorial intervention to introduce Kiswahili into the national assembly in 1974 (Republic of Kenya, 1974: Column 20–1).

Among military regimes, Somalia offers a good example of government concern with the language question. Unlike most other African countries Somalia is relatively homogeneous linguistically, with virtually all its citizens being proficient in the Somali language. But because the language had no established orthography by the time the country became independent in 1960, Arabic, English and Italian, all 'foreign' to the country, were adopted as the official languages. In 1972, however, a military decree of president Mohammed Siad Barre replaced these foreign languages with Somali as the official language, imposed the Latin script on the language, and set in motion an ambitious literacy campaign in the Somali language (Laitin, 1977). Somalia's linguistic landscape was thus transformed almost overnight through the intervention of a military dictatorship.

In Uganda, there was recurrent debate over several years on the possible promotion of Kiswahili as the national language of the country. The two multi-party but shaky regimes under Milton Obote (1962–71 and 1980–85) failed to deal with this question in any decisive way, leaving English as the *de facto* official and national language of Uganda. Again, it took a military dictator in the person of Idi Amina Dada to alter this situation in 1972 by declaring Kiswahili the national language and introducing it as a major language of Uganda's radio and television (Mazrui and Mazrui, 1993: 281). Once again, therefore, the authoritarian arm of a dictator came to offer a way out of a problem that the democratic atmosphere was unable to resolve. The picture that emerges from these examples, then, is that in Africa the fortunes of language policy in favour of African languages are linked to the survival of autocratic regimes.

None of these instances of attempted language planning, however, was designed to aid the democratic process or establish a democratic tradition. The need for mass mobilization and the desire to close the linguistic gap between the élite and the masses in pursuit of quasi-egalitarian aims are some of the factors that inspired the specific language efforts of both Somalia and Tanzania. The choice of Kiswahili in both Uganda and Kenya, on the other hand, was influenced more by nationalist and pan-African concerns. The autocratic tendency of these single-party and military regimes could hardly be expected to have prompted a democratic motive in the adoption of their respective language policies.

Since 1990, however, the political situation in Africa has changed somewhat as some military and single-party autocracies began to give way to the politics of pluralism. Many autocrats have capitulated to popular demands for democratic change from the local populations as well as from the international community. Even hardened dictators like Kamuzu Banda of Malawi found it an uphill task to contain the movement for democratic reform. It now seems unlikely that Africa will again witness a proliferation of single-party regimes and military dictatorships on the scale that was experienced up to 1990.

The question that concerns us here, then, is whether language can be planned to help in guiding Africa in its path towards democracy. Do certain language choices have a greater potential than others in promoting a democratic tradition? What kinds of language engineering efforts are necessary to enrich the capacity of African languages to accommodate the dynamics of a democratic political system? These are questions that require a closer look at the forces that constitute the foundations of democracy.

Foundations of democracy

For democracy to survive and flourish it needs to be built upon certain systemic, material, social and cultural foundations. The systemic foundation has to do with the extent to which a political system is structured to allow democratic principles to operate with minimum impediments. While there is little agreement on the exact meaning of democracy, some of its more commonly cited principles include: the existence of a range of alternatives from which people can choose when making decisions, popular participation by the governed, political accountability of the governors, openness and transparency in the process, and fairness and justice as guiding aims.

Does the system, legally and otherwise, allow for the existence of an unrestricted number of groups or political parties through which people can express their preferences? How free are these groups in fielding candidates and contesting elections and political power? Are there any features of the system which preclude a certain class of people from participating in decision making, either directly or indirectly through their representatives? Does the system enable the people to know what the various organs of government are doing and is it open to ideas and criticism from the governed? These are some of the questions that relate specifically to the systemic or institutional level of democratic foundations.

The material foundation of democracy is concerned with the economic well-being of society. There is a wealth of empirical evidence that establishes a correlation between a country's economic development and the existence and stability of democracy. A strong and flourishing economy that meets the basic needs of its population is more likely to sustain a democratic atmosphere than a weak and depressed economy. In the words of Afrifa K. Gitonga:

> The infrastructure of democracy lies in the economy – the system of production, distribution and consumption of material goods and services. To this extent, democracy is served by the existence of a healthy and prosperous economy. The reverse is also true: a weak and badly functioning economy is a mortal danger for democracy. Therefore, as a first requirement, the solidly anchored democratic system should enable the people to get, in quality and quantity, an adequate supply of goods (food, shelter, clothing) and services (education, security, entertainment), to meet and satisfy their material, social and other needs, wants and desires. (1987: 19)

Economic declines and crises, therefore, have often led to the demise of democratic governments and the rise of authoritarian regimes of one sort or another.

An equally important condition of democracy is the extent to which a society is integrated. This is what we call the social foundation of democracy. A democratic system of competing parties presumes, to some extent, that 'the people of a nation would have so profound an agreement on the fundamentals of their society that different political parties could alternate in and out of power without changing the country's basic social and political system' (Harvey Wheeler, 1968: 48). This agreement on fundamentals, however, without which further political development is hampered, can only come about if a society has achieved a reasonable degree of integration at the vertical and horizontal levels.

Vertically, the ideal situation for democratic growth is probably one in which there is a high degree of socio-economic equality among the citizens of a country.

However, though an important quest of some Third World nations, an egalitarian order has not been particularly easy to establish. Class-based societies, therefore, have continued to be the norm. In a society where there are extreme socio-economic disparities – in which a small proportion of the population is extremely rich and the rest live in conditions of deprivation, with nothing in between – democracy is unlikely to survive as an enduring system. Yet this is the prevailing social structure in most African countries. A more conducive class structure for democracy is one in which there is a more gradual gradation between the very top and the very bottom of the hierarchy. While such a structure may not promote socio-economic equality, it does reduce levels of inequality and provides for a more integrated society upon which democracy partly thrives.

At the horizontal level is the quest for integration across ethnic boundaries. Most African nations are ethnically heterogeneous. These ethnic groups operate, to one degree or another, with slightly different though overlapping sets of fundamentals as far as the prevailing political system is concerned. The success of democracy, therefore, will partly depend on the 'softness' of ethnic boundaries and the creation of a more unified political community.

The fourth foundation of democracy falls in the realm of culture. The values, beliefs and attitudes of the people which orient their political behaviour are fundamental in determining the prospects for democratic change in a particular society. Subsumed under the wider notion of political culture is a 'culture of democracy' without which acquisition a society is unlikely to achieve a significant level of democracy. To quote Afrifa K. Gitonga once again:

> other things being equal, the amount or degree of democracy in any given society is directly proportional to the degree of acculturation of the people in democratic values, attitudes and beliefs. For democracy to exist, survive and prosper, it requires that the people be bathed in and drenched with the democratic ethos. (1987: 22)

Through changes in material conditions, through educational and media influences, therefore, people come to acquire elements of a political culture that are necessary for the survival of democracy.

If these systemic, economic, social and cultural factors constitute the foundations of democracy, then, how can they benefit from the language phenomenon? Can language be planned to somehow assist in the promotion and consolidation of these four pillars of democracy? It is to these questions that we must now turn.

Democracy and language policy

Each of the foundational levels of democracy raises certain questions about language policy. How these questions are handled may determine the extent to which language could serve as an aid to democracy in the long run.

The systemic level
Among the areas that are most directly related to language at the systemic level is popular participation, that is, the involvement of people in public affairs and policy making at different levels. The degree of people's participation will, of course, depend on how free, open, transparent and fair the system is.

One dimension of political participation has to do with the electoral process through which the people can vote for candidates to legislative assemblies, parties to political power, and for major and critical issues of governmental policy. But, in order to orient people away from voting on the basis of personal or ethnic allegiances, the system ought to be designed to encourage politicians to seek support outside their ethnic homelands. Under these circumstances then, the choice of the primary language of politics would be based on two principles: providing the politician with access to trans-ethnic mass opinion and creating for him/her a national constituency; and providing the masses with linguistic space for involvement in national agitation for specific issues, policies and reforms. This once again raises the issue of cultivating a national language or national languages from the indigenous pool. To the extent that the majority of the constituents have no proficiency in the ex-colonial languages, these Western languages become poor instruments for seeking national support from the people and for promoting their involvement in national politics.

Politicians may, of course, opt to use European languages outside their ethnic areas and to communicate with the people through interpreters. But if candidates can reach their constituents only through interpreters not only may they remain relatively unknowable, but they will also reduce tremendously their chances of benefiting directly from the reactions of the constituents.

The use of interpreters in active politics is a predicament that Milton Obote, who was then president of Uganda, once commented on in the following terms:

> Obviously I have no alternative [to using English] but I lose a lot especially as far as the Party is concerned. The Uganda People's Congress welcomes everybody and some of the greatest and most dedicated workers are those who do not speak English. And yet the Party leader cannot call his great dedicated worker and say 'Thank you' in a language that the man will understand. It has to be translated. (1967: 5)

A political candidate, therefore, must try to reach his/her multi-ethnic constituents directly and personally, or he/she may never reach them at all. The handicap of reaching one's constituents only through an interpreter carries a serious risk of political alienation. And such alienation between the political élite and the mass of the people certainly cannot be in the interest of democracy.

The other dimension of political participation concerns legislative assemblies at the national level as well as at the more local level. In most African countries parliamentary discussions, in particular, are undertaken in the ex-colonial (European) languages. This state of affairs reduces the pool of élite recruitment and of those who can participate in the legislature to a tiny minority who are conversant with European languages. By limiting political participation, therefore, this linguistic restriction will tend to attenuate the democratic base of a society.

A good example of a country that has achieved a considerable degree of democratization through deliberate language choice and language policy is Tanzania. Replacing English with its national lingua franca, Kiswahili, as the sole language of parliamentary business, both written and oral, has enabled the country to extend political participation in its Legislative Assembly to all classes of people. The 'common man' can now compete with members of the educated élite for parliamentary seats, and use his/her Kiswahili oratorical skills effectively to influence legislative decisions.

Across the border in Kenya, parliament took a bilingual path after shifting in 1974 from a monolingual policy based on the English language. At present, even though the legislation itself continues to come before parliament written in English, both English and Kiswahili serve as the languages of debate in the legislature. In the process, then, both English and Kiswahili have become necessary qualifications in the Kenyan Parliament. Legislators must have some competence in both English and Kiswahili to participate fully in parliamentary proceedings.

This policy, which requires that a candidate be able to speak *both* English *and* Kiswahili, has a technical advantage in that a Member of Parliament who speaks both languages is better equipped to deal with parliamentary bills, and is perhaps politically more sophisticated than a person who is at home only with Kiswahili. But from the point of view of democracy, this policy narrows the boundaries of political recruitment even further, since there are probably fewer Kenyans who are bilingual in both English and Kiswahili than those who have English but not Kiswahili in their linguistic repertoires.

From the democratic point of view, then, there may be a case, in many African nations, for adopting a policy which requires that each candidate for parliament be able to speak *either* the European language of the former colonizer *or* one or more African lingua francas. This recommendation may necessitate the installation of a system of simultaneous translation in the national assembly. There is a precedent for this in mainland Tanzania on the eve of independence when both Kiswahili and English were full-fledged parliamentary languages. The great advantage of this policy is that it would greatly widen the section of the population from which parliamentarians could be drawn. By extending the boundaries of political recruitment it would foster greater political participation. More Africans would be qualified to be active in national politics than is the case at present.

But any policy that involves the adoption of an African language in parliament would require deliberate efforts towards language expansion at the lexical level. New terms will need to be coined and popularized to cater for the articulation of parliamentary procedures as well as of substantive legislative issues.

The economic level

In looking at the relationship between language and economic growth, David Laitin poses the following question:

> Do countries that have a single speech community whose language is the sole official language of the state perform better economically than countries with diverse speech communities that rely on a foreign language for important government business?... Correlation analysis involving all countries of the world suggests that there is a positive statistical relationship between societies with diverse speech communities and low level economic development.... Scholars who provide policy advice accept these results and argue that economic development presupposes the settlement of the language question and therefore depends upon agreement on a single national language. (1992: 53-4)

Laitin then goes on to question this proposition and concludes that 'any advice assuming that changes in language diversity would yield changes in economic development is scientifically suspect'. He further argues that data based on socio-economic indicators from forty African countries demonstrate no obvious statistical relationship between language diversity and economic growth (1992: 54).

But if one avoids the kind of linguistic determinism alluded to above, it is possible to argue that, other things being equal, the presence of a national lingua franca would favour economic development to a greater extent than a situation of

100

linguistic diversity without a common language that is widely understood by the people. In the first place a language of wider communication may aid the consolidation of the national market by making it somewhat easier for the entrepreneurial class to reach the consumer through advertising and other marketing strategies. A common, national language, therefore, can serve as an important link between capital and the market, between production and consumption, in a way that indirectly helps economic growth.

Secondly, a language of wider communication may be better suited to the mass mobilization and organization of labour for economic development than a linguistically heterogeneous situation that is unmediated by a more common language. Even though Tanzania's *Ujamaa* experiment was to some extent a failure, there is little doubt that the country would have found it a lot more difficult to mobilize its population for socialist economic production without the facilitating role of Kiswahili. Mass mobilization for socialist development was a reasonable goal in Tanzania partly because the government had access to a mass medium of linguistic communication.

Thirdly, there is the role of language in the dissemination of information on the technology of production. Peasant agriculture still constitutes the mainstay of economic production in Africa and most of the people involved in this sphere are not proficient in European languages. Information on fertilizer, high-yielding seeds, new farming methods and implements that may be crucial to economic productivity and efficiency is best relayed in one or more local African languages than in European languages which few understand. Knowledge of production methods that is essential to the development of a healthy economy can only be acquired through the language or languages understood by the producers.

Fourth, the ability of the people to contribute to economic development depends, to some extent, on their physical well-being. This relates to the reproduction of human labour and requires not only the availability of an efficient medical system, but also, and more importantly, that people be constantly informed about issues of public health and preventive measures against all sorts of common health problems. The construction of a healthy society economically, therefore, will be aided by the existence of a healthy society physically. In this respect, local languages that have been significantly 'developed' to deal effectively with concepts and issues of public health will be a significant contribution to the reproduction of labour necessary for a successful economy.

The fifth consideration has to do with the African quest to reduce dependence on the West. Dependence has increasingly been seen as one of the factors behind Africa's economic misfortunes (Offiong, 1982). If this is true, then Africa's heavy reliance on European languages, informed partly by the belief that such languages are crucial to the continent's technological advancement and modernization, is likely to deepen this dependence. African leaders may be more easily inclined to run to foreign experts for assistance partly because of the dependence on foreign languages. The use of African languages as national and official languages, therefore, is likely to make it more difficult to seek Western expertise and to reduce Western penetration of Africa. By learning to modernize without (linguistic and cultural) Westernization, Africa may improve its own chances of more organic economic and political development.

With regard to 'linguistic dissociation' from the West as a way of reducing dependence, David Laitin draws the example of Japan. In Japan, where linguistic barriers have been particularly high, argues Laitin, there was incentive to separate the 'technical' from the 'western', making more probable the development of distinct organizations and market strategies, and with it the potential to break the hegemony of the economic order dominated by the advanced industrial states of the west. By this agreement, while policies of linguistic association [that favour the maintenance of European languages] might induce 'catch-up' [with the more economically advanced countries], policies of linguistic dissociation [i.e. support for vernaculars] might induce challenge [to their economic domination]. (1983: 38)

Such a challenge might lead to a level of innovativeness based on local resources and ideas that would put Africa on a healthier and more organic path of economic development.

Finally, policies that favour the use of indigenous languages as official media may also help in retaining the human resources Africa needs for its economic development. One of the factors that threaten African economies is the out-flux of African expertise to the West – the so-called brain-drain. Local experts trained in local languages and with limited facility in European languages are likely to find it more difficult to get employment opportunities in Europe and America (Godfrey, 1976; Laitin, 1992: 56). The negative effects of the brain-drain on African economies might thus be reduced by the kinds of linguistic policies that African governments choose to pursue.

The economic foundation of democracy, therefore, seems to favour the choice, development and promotion of one or more indigenous African languages understood widely by the people.

The social level

The rise of competitive multi-party politics is likely to have a direct bearing on the language situation in specific African countries in two fundamental ways. There is, first, the relationship between ethnicity and political pluralism. Multi-party politics in many African countries has tended to assume an ethnic character to one degree or another. Different political parties often tend to derive their popular support from different ethnic groups. This ethnicization of politics in a plural society may exert pressure on party leaders and functionaries to invoke certain symbols of ethnic identity partly as a way of seeking and maintaining the allegiance of members of particular ethnic groups. Other things being equal, then, the inclination of politicians to use local, ethnically-bounded languages when addressing audiences from different parts of a country may be stronger in a multi-party polity than in a single-party system. Ethnic languages become symbols of solidarity and support, of cultivating a patron-client relationship, between political parties and different sections of the electorate.

In addition to this inherent ethno-linguistic pull of political pluralism in Africa, there is the class basis of multi-party democracy. While the struggle for democracy has enjoyed the support of people from various classes, the leading advocates of multi-partyism in most African nations have tended to come from the ranks of the professional middle class – lawyers, teachers, journalists, etc. Issues that have to do with the rights and freedoms of the individual are of more direct concern to the élite than to the mass of the people. The lower classes in Africa support the democratic struggle not necessarily for its own sake, but with the understanding that political reform is a path towards the improvement of their economic well-being. In sum, the democratic struggle in Africa is essentially a petit-bourgeois struggle.

Yet it is precisely this class of the professional élite that is most linguistically and culturally alienated from the masses. Its members have had the longest exposure to educational institutions which continue to serve as some of the main agents of Western acculturation, and they are the most proficient in European languages. If the ethnic factor in multi-party politics tends to encourage the use of ethnic languages, therefore, the class factor may end up strengthening the position of Western languages. In both Kenya and Tanzania, for example, the opening up of the political space since 1990 has been marked by a significant increase in the proportion of English newspapers and magazines relative to those printed in Kiswahili.

The socio-linguistic consequences of multi-partyism, then, may include a heightened sense of consciousness and a less integrated society at the horizontal level, and increasing élite isolation and a less integrated society at the vertical level. Both these are tendencies that need to be taken into consideration in language planning efforts for democratic change.

We define horizontal integration simply in terms of social communication and interaction across ethnic and geographical divisions of the society as a whole. We define vertical integration as a process of interaction between different strata of the society, especially between the élite and the masses.

European languages like English and French in Africa may indeed aid the process of integration at the upper horizontal level. This is when there is greater contact, communication and interaction among the élite. European languages are a great asset in facilitating horizontal interaction of the educated élite across ethnic and geographical boundaries.

European languages, however, are a liability when it comes to vertical integration. In effect they exacerbate the problem of 'élite closure' by reinforcing the language barriers between the élite and the masses. Vertical integration, then, is assisted more by a policy that favours the use of African languages, which allow the rulers to communicate with the ruled and vice versa. African languages which facilitate the process by which the élite successfully penetrates the masses, and the masses have adequate access to the élite, are a definite advantage in the quest for vertical integration.

African lingua francas like Hausa in West Africa, Kiswahili in East Africa, and Lingala in Central Africa are also important in fostering lower horizontal integration. This concerns the degree to which the masses are in contact with each other and are able to establish a linguistic basis for sustained interaction.

In performing horizontally integrative functions at the lower level, African lingua francas serve as the main languages of trade unionism and organized labour to facilitate social communication between workers and peasants from different geographical areas and ethnic groups. And to the extent that these functions are expanding the wage sector of the economy, facilitating the circulation of money across the country as a whole, promoting a consciousness of a national economy, and defining the boundaries of the national market-place of goods and labour, African lingua francas can also be said to be involved in the process of socio-economic consolidation.

In essence, then, African countries that adopt policies which favour the promotion and development of local lingua francas will be contributing, to some extent, to the process of social and economic integration. Linguistic media that advance horizontal interaction across ethnic lines and vertical interaction across class lines help in the creation of a more integrated society which constitutes one of the foundations of democracy.

The cultural level

Can language be planned to promote a political culture that could sustain a democratic tradition? One of the most prominent theories on the relationship between language and culture is that of linguistic relativity pioneered by Edward Sapir and Benjamin Lee Whorf (Sapir, 1929; Whorf, 1956). In its extreme form, their thesis is deterministic, arguing that language determines a people's world view and directs human behaviour in a culturally specific manner. Language is thus viewed as a kind of prison house, and users of different languages are said to perceive the world and respond to it in different ways. By implication, therefore, differences in political culture are, to some extent, the result of linguistic differences that mark different communities. A culture of autocracy and a culture of democracy would thus be regarded as orientations produced by two different language systems.

This deterministic thesis has, for all practical purposes, been discredited from a theoretical as well as an empirical point of view. There is little evidence of irrefutable scientific validity that demonstrates causality between language, culture and cognition. And the rise of the universalist school of thought spearheaded by Noam Chomsky (1968), with its emphasis on innate cognitive structures, contributed to undermining the credibility of linguistic determinism even further.

This, however, is not to deny the fact that language and culture are interrelated phenomena and that they do tend to influence each other to one degree or another. Language may not determine the world view of a people, but it could serve as an indicator of certain aspects of their culture. It is true that language often lags behind cultural, social and material developments, but partly out of its own dynamism, and partly out of deliberate human effort, it manages to 'catch up' with these developments. More importantly for our purposes language can be planned so that, in combination with other forces in society, it can contribute to the emergence of a new ethos. The experience of countries like East Germany, Tanzania and what, until recently, constituted the Soviet Union, are quite instructive in this regard. Language engineering became part of a more comprehensive strategy intended to direct people towards socialist thinking and a socialist world view in these societies that were hitherto quasi-capitalistic.

As African countries seek to create the political institutions, economic structures and social dynamics that are necessary for genuine democratic development, therefore, they also need to consolidate the cultural foundation of democracy through the instrumentality of education, the media and language planning. Language planning for a democratic culture needs to be directed to accomplish three main objectives: *to enable national language(s) to express the socio-cultural diversity existing in a particular country.* A language that is representative of the national character is better placed to articulate the competing claims of different interest groups than one that is culturally bound in ethnic, class or sectarian confines. A language that is limited in its capacity to express the interests and concerns of any particular section of a national society is equally limited in its potential to foster a democratic culture. The second objective is *to seek to neutralize linguistically based prejudices and negative stereotypes against particular group(s) in the nation.* A language that perpetuates the image of a particular group of citizens as being somewhat inferior and less deserving undermines the foundations of a democratic culture. Jacqeline Adhiambo-Oduol, for example, shows how discrimination against women is supported by language and language use in Kenya, and concludes that:

there exists in Kenya a world view that discriminates against women through language use. Language is thus an aspect of the life of the Kenyan woman that is blind to the gender dimension. It is therefore an aspect that has to be re-examined if women are to attain development. Men and women in Kenya must recognize language as a tool that can be used to deny or allow women to have their democratic rights. (1993: 46)

In essence, then, language planning needs to be directed towards making the national language(s) gender-sensitive as well as sensitive to other group and subcultural differences. The third and final objective is *to expand the lexical scope of national language(s) to include fundamental precepts of democracy*, like openness, transparency, political pluralism, accountability, popular participation, fairness and so forth. If properly harnessed to other non-linguistic strategies, these linguistically induced tenets may become part of a new value system that contributes to the cultural foundation of democracy.

Conclusion

The democratic path in Africa, then, reveals a certain interplay, sometimes conflicting, sometimes complementary, between Western languages, African lingua francas and the more localized ethnic languages. One of the most important contributions of Western languages is at the cultural level of democratic foundations. The notional dimension of liberal democratic culture, on the one hand, and the technological orientation necessary for efficient capitalist economic production, on the other, have been introduced to the African élite mainly through the instrumentality of Western languages.

But the Western languages have also contributed to the social foundation of democracy. They have served to promote horizontal integration among the élite from various ethnic groups. While ethnic consciousness may indeed have increased among the African élite since the end of European colonialism on the continent, ethnic behaviour seems to have decreased. In social behaviour members of the élite from different ethnic groups are increasingly moving closer to each other and away from their more 'traditional' ethnic compatriots from the rural areas.

What is obvious, however, is that in their contribution to democratic foundations, Western languages have been strongly class-bound. Since these languages are still acquired predominantly in a formal set-up they come to be confined to the schooled from whose ranks the élite is continuously formed. As a result, relatively few people become the beneficiaries of the Western linguistic contribution to the cultural foundation of democracy. So restricted, Western languages ultimately have the effect of exacerbating the communication and cultural gap between the élite and the mass of the people. In the final analysis, then, as Western languages continue to play an integrative role horizontally among the élite, they serve a disjunctive function vertically in the relationship between the élite and the masses.

But the process of democracy is aided not only by forces of social integration sufficient to lead to some agreement on certain political fundamentals, but also by the existence of political pluralism and the availability of choice. Ideally, integration in a democratic order should not proceed to a point of obliterating political divergences, because, in so doing, it deprives the population of the possibility of democratic choice. The development of democracy need not, of course, be dependent on a precondition of political pluralism; nor does political pluralism necessarily give rise to a democratic tradition. But, all things being equal, a democracy built upon political pluralism is perhaps more democratic than one based on complete political convergence.

Impressionistically, it appears that political pluralism in the present democratic momentum in Africa has tended to assume an overtly ethnic character. The democratic opening of the political space may be encouraging the articulation, in ethnic languages, of rights and interests of particular ethnic groups, especially those that had hitherto felt repressed by their respective African regimes. And the ethnicization of party politics, partly a product of the ethnocratic tendency in African leadership, may lead to the growing use of ethnic languages in practical politics. All this may be contributing to a national climate of political pluralism. What is less certain, however, is whether this ethnic orientation of political pluralism will eventually serve to undermine social integration at the horizontal level as well as the democratic process in general in Africa. Are ethnic languages likely to encourage pluralism without contributing to democracy? This is a sociolinguistic situation that is still unfolding.

But ethnic languages are not only the vehicles of members of various ethnic groups. They are also *ipso facto* the languages of the masses. It is through these languages that notional aspects of the culture of democracy can be paraphrased and passed on to the people. It is also through these languages that labour can be mobilized at the local level, and the people can gain knowledge of new and relevant technologies of production and reproduction whose understanding may be important to economic development and integration. In the absence of local lingua francas, therefore, the ethnically-bounded languages may make an important contribution to the consolidation of both the cultural and economic foundations of democracy.

The languages that encompass the widest scope in terms of their potential to contribute to democratic foundations, however, are probably the local lingua francas. At the systemic level we have shown that whereas Western languages continue to be given the most prominent role in most African parliaments, it is the African lingua francas which can widen political participation across the lines of social class. It is also the African lingua francas that have the greatest capacity to consolidate national and regional markets, mobilize labour at the national level, disseminate information to the mass of the people on issues relevant to economic production, and assist in reducing dependence, on the one hand, and the brain-drain, on the other. All this may strengthen the economic foundation of democracy.

At the social level, African lingua francas can serve an integrative function at the lower horizontal level. And if a particular lingua franca is offered as a school subject, as is Kiswahili in both Tanzania and Kenya, making it accessible to the emerging élite, it may also be a factor in vertical integration between the élite and the masses. In this regard, African lingua francas are probably unlike Western languages which may be integrative at the upper horizontal level but potentially disjunctive at the vertical level; they are also unlike ethnic languages which may lack an integrative potential altogether at both the horizontal and vertical planes.

Finally, at the cultural level, African lingua francas may not have introduced the essential notions of democracy to the national élites of various African countries, but they may indeed be effective media of adapting these notions to local conditions and carrying them to the people.

It appears, then, that democracy would develop on firmer foundations on the systemic, economic, social, and cultural planes if African nations pursued language policies that reduced dependence on Western languages, pushed African languages more towards the centre of the political and economic arenas, and consolidated the use and development of their local languages of wider communication.

8
Language Policy & the Rule of Law in 'Anglophone' Africa

The 1990s can be described as Africa's decade of popular struggles for reform from autocratic forms of government to more democratic political orders. An important tradition that needs to accompany this democratic trend is the rule of law. We may define the rule of law as the dimension which seeks to ensure that governmental decisions are impersonal and subject to legal restraints, and the dimension which guarantees to the individual freedom from arbitrary government and entitles that individual to 'due process of law'.

There has been some theoretical debate as to whether the rule of law is not, in fact, inherently conservative because of its tendency to impose certain closures on legislative action. According to this view , then, the rule of law is incompatible with the more dynamic mission of democracy. Our own position, however, is more in conformity with that of Yash Ghai, one of Africa's leading constitutional lawyers, that 'modern notions of the rule of law have become suffused with democratic values and practices and that in the contemporary African situation the rule of law, far from being threatened by democracy, cannot be sustained without it' (1992: 5). There is a sense, then, in which democracy and the rule of law can be regarded as mutually dependent partners in Africa's political development.

There are certain factors, however, which help turn the rule of law into an enduring system. One of these factors is cultural and has to do with the interplay between language and legal traditions. The legal traditions of virtually all 'Anglophone' African countries today have been shaped, in part, by the British colonial experience. From this colonial history the region inherited much of its present legal establishment and it continues to draw most of its lessons and precedents directly from Britain or from the Commonwealth.

The judicial arrangement in many of these countries also provides for African customary law and, in some cases, for Islamic law. Both Kenya and Nigeria, for example, have this tripartite legal structure, that reflects the triple heritage drawn from the indigenous tradition, the Islamic legacy and the Western influence. But the indigenous and Islamic elements are often confined to a few aspects of personal law, like marriage and divorce. In the final analysis, therefore, it is the Western contribution that has remained the dominant legal mode throughout the region.

In addition to the substance of the law, however, Anglophone Africa also inherited the linguistic medium of its law, English, from Britain. Many African countries are linguistically heterogeneous, each containing several indigenous languages within its borders. The majority of these languages can be regarded as ethnic in the sense of being confined demographically to speakers from the respective ethnic groups. A few African nations are also endowed with trans-ethnic languages from the local pool – Kiswahili being one of the most successful among them.

In spite of this rich linguistic heritage, however, and perhaps because of it, English has continued to feature as the primary language of legal discourse almost throughout Anglophone Africa. Though spoken and understood by a minority, English is the major official language, in policy as well as in practice. It is the medium of educational instruction, the instrument of civil administration, the language of parliamentary discussion, the link with the international community of nations and the perceived key to socio-economic advancement. But precisely because the legal culture is itself derived from the British legal experience, the English language finds one of its most natural environments in Africa's legal system.

The relationship between the English language and the law almost throughout Anglophone Africa, therefore, is one of maximum *convergence*. Every right, every civil liberty, every law in the constitution has to be interpreted in terms of its meaning in the ex-colonial language. Anglophone African constitutional law is almost entirely Eurocentric in this linguistic sense. Precisely because of the excessive centrality of the English language, African languages have remained marginalized, and their relationship to non-customary law has been marked by a state of relative *divergence*.

Of course, all societies assume that for the law to enjoy adequate 'majesty', some social distance has to be cultivated deliberately. The British developed a tradition of judges wearing wigs, and lawyers wearing black robes. Both the British and the Americans also cultivated the language of 'Your honour' when addressing the judge (sometimes 'My Lord' in British courts).

Moreover, legal language in the West has often included direct Latin words and phrases and an even larger number of Anglicized Latinisms. Phrases like *post mortem, sub judice, de jure* and *de facto* have become commonplace. What all this means is that some degree of social distance from ordinary language is not only inevitable but has often been deliberately cultivated to give the law greater judicial majesty.

But there comes a time when the majesty of the law goes too far and becomes the alienation of the law from the people. The role of the English language in the judicial systems of Anglophone Africa constitutes such an alienation of the law. The British wigs still adorn Black judges, the British black robes still give solemnity to African lawyers. The Latin phrases and Anglicized Latinisms still abound in Africa as in Britain. And on top of all that, the English language itself continues to be fundamentally alien in all African countries. This is more than social distance for the law. The 'majesty' of the law crosses the line into stark alienation from the people whom it seeks to serve.

This lingo-legal equation has had certain adverse implications for the rule of law in much of Africa. It has affected law making as well as law enforcement, legal ideology and legal rights, judicial staffing as well as the administration of justice. And it is to a discussion of some of these implications that we must now turn.

Linguistic exclusion and the legislative process

The problem of the rule of law often begins with the practice of linguistic exclusion that is prevalent in virtually all African national assemblies entrusted with the making of the law. By linguistic exclusion we mean the policy that, intentionally or inadvertently, seeks to keep out some languages from certain domains of society. Almost throughout Anglophone Africa, the English language is the primary language of legislation, as African languages continue to be excluded as media of national legislatures. The English language is a fundamental requirement for participation in Anglophone African parliaments, and some countries even administer English proficiency tests for parliamentary candidates.

This practice of linguistic exclusion has a dual effect on the lingo-legal configuration. First, it denies African languages the opportunity to develop a legislative register that is compatible with the prevailing parliamentary tradition inherited from the colonial experience. Discussions on parliamentary bills and parliamentary procedures are conducted almost exclusively in the English language. There is thus the persistent anomaly that virtually all constitutions in Anglophone Africa are in English, a language spoken by very few of the citizens governed by those constitutions.

The linguistic gap between the constitution and the citizenry deepens the remoteness of the constitution, and may be a contributory factor to the perceived irrelevance of the constitutional order in most African countries. It is extremely rare that African constitutions are available in African languages. Most African languages have remained, therefore, poor in constitutional vocabulary, lacking even such basic terms as 'fundamental law,' 'the bill of rights,' 'the right to privacy,' 'civil liberties,' or 'secular state'.

Citizens of the United States of America are constantly bombarded with terms like 'separation of church and state' and 'the First Amendment'. How many African languages can even translate such concepts? The exclusion of Africa's indigenous languages from the legislative process itself, therefore, has contributed to the acute state of divergence between the languages and the law.

Africa is paying a higher price for this Euro-constitutionalism than Africa realizes. The fact that the African constitutions are almost exclusively in European languages may have slowed down the development of a new constitutional culture in Africa. African citizens are not learning to think in constitutional terms partly because they live in political systems that stifle the development of indigenous constitutional vocabulary. This lingo-legal divergence may have created a conceptual void in the intellectual universe of the average citizen.

The second effect of the practice of linguistic exclusion in African parliaments is that it has denied the majority that lack proficiency in English their democratic right of participation in the formulation of the laws. Can Africa really talk of democracy as 'rule by the people' when the majority lack the opportunity to participate in making the very laws used to govern them, or cannot even understand what goes on in their own parliaments? The right of participation in Africa's law-making bodies, therefore, has been closed to the majority of citizens precisely because their languages have been denied a role in these institutions.

With respect to language and the legislative process Tanzania and Kenya offer somewhat different examples from the rest of Anglophone Africa because of the special place of Kiswahili within their borders. In both countries Kiswahili is a dynamic trans-ethnic language used as an additional language, to one degree or another, by a plurality of citizens. In addition, its initial history as the language of Islamic law and jurisprudence in East Africa, and the more recent efforts of Tanzania and, to a lesser extent, Kenya to 'modernize' the language, have endowed Kiswahili with an appreciable wealth of legal terms to augment its potential as a language of parliament. And this is a potential that has been recognized by both Tanzania and Kenya.

In Tanzania, the parliament or *Bunge* has indeed been Swahilized all the way since the Arusha Declaration of 1967. This Swahilization of the legislative process in Tanzania has resulted in greater democratization partly because it has made possible a wider participation of its citizenry in the *Bunge*. Kiswahili has made it possible to mobilize more people into the law-making process of the country. This has in turn helped to enrich the language in terms of legal and constitutional vocabulary. A more democratic parliamentary system often enriches the language in which it conducts its business.

Across the border in Kenya English continued to be the exclusive language of its parliament until 1974 when the country's first president, Mzee Jomo Kenyatta, ordered the instant use of Kiswahili as the exclusive language of parliamentary debate. But since President Daniel Arap Moi came to power in 1978 the Kenyan legislature has been a bilingual one, using both English and Kiswahili in its *oral* deliberations.

Although Kiswahili is now one of the languages of debate in the legislature, however, the legislation itself continues to come before parliament written exclusively in the English language. Documents written in English could now be the subject of debate either in English or Kiswahili. For those opting to use Kiswahili, then, this anomaly between the written word and oral practice has created complications of its own, from phrase to phrase, clause to clause.

The official version of the constitution as fundamental law in Kenya, therefore, continues to be in the English language. A constitutional point which comes before the courts has to be resolved by interpreting phrases and words in the English version. What a particular clause of the constitution means can be resolved by a judge who understands no Kiswahili at all. Indeed, the judicial system of Kenya is based on the assumption that many of the most senior judges might be completely illiterate in Kiswahili.

The language requirement for candidates standing for parliamentary elections in Kenya has been adjusted to reflect a more bilingual character of the house. The original requirement at the time of independence was competence in the English language. Since 1978, however, candidates are required to demonstrate their competence in both English and Kiswahili. In the Kenyan situation, then, every Member of Parliament needs a capacity to read English but not necessarily to speak it; and a capacity to understand Kiswahili but not necessarily to read or even speak it. The legislation continues to come before parliamentarians written in the English language, while the debate which follows may be conducted in Kiswahili or English.

Partly because both English and Kiswahili continue to be necessary qualifications in the Kenyan parliament, however, the decision to make Kiswahili one of the media of parliamentary debate has had less effect on broadening participation than it might have had. If linguistic qualifications for membership of the Kenyan parliament had been based more purely on competence in Kiswahili, this would immediately have broadened the number of potential legislators. This follows from the simple statistic that the number of Kenyans who are competent in Kiswahili is several times greater than the number of those whose competency is restricted to the English language. The full Swahilization of the Kenyan parliament would, therefore, have democratized the legislative process considerably.

In any case, Tanzania and, to a lesser extent, Kenya have been able to demonstrate the potential of an African language, Kiswahili, to play a significant role in the legislative system. In the process the language itself has been enriched, and more citizens who seek participation in the legislative assembly have come to rely on its widening horizons.

The English language and judicial dependence

Like the legislature, the judiciary in Anglophone Africa is also faced with certain lingo-legal problems. But at the level of human-power there may also be some advantages in the interplay between the English language and the judiciary. On the pan-African side, for example, it has enabled lawyers from one part of Africa and the African diaspora to serve in another part. It is not at all unusual in some African countries to find some of the highest-ranking judges coming from other parts of the black world. One of the top judges in Tanzania was at one time from the West Indies. In Uganda, a Nigerian judge, Sir Udo Udoma, was indeed Chief Justice in the critical years after independence. Kenya's chief justices, on the other hand, have included Cecil Miller from Guyana, and Justice Fred Kwasi Apaloo of Ghana. The fact that English has been the language of law and constitutionalism in the Commonwealth has sometimes facilitated the interchange of lawyers and judges across huge distances. There have been occasions, then, when pan-Africanism has been among the beneficiaries of this lingo-legal convergence.

Furthermore, the centrality of English in the legal system has sometimes enabled lawyers from one part of Africa or the Commonwealth to help defend dissidents in another part of Africa. It has also enabled African lawyers to construct networks of solidarity with other 'jurists' internationally. In Nigeria and Kenya, lawyers have been in the vanguard of defending human rights and democratic processes, and have been protected from excessive government revenge partly by the international networking of jurists and constitutionalists from the Anglophone world.

It would appear, however, that the losses precipitated by the marriage between the English language and the English-derived legal system far outweigh the gains. And one of the negative effects of this lingo-legal convergence has been the promotion of a dependence syndrome. Former British colonies have sometimes been excessively dependent on the metropole (the former colonial power) even for the recruitment of judges for African courts. Kenya is one Anglophone African country which has been particularly slow in replacing expatriate judges with African ones. Out of the seven chief justices who have served on the Kenyan bench since the nation's independence in 1963, for example, all but three have been expatriates.

The problem of expatriate judges poses intricate problems for this whole issue of 'the rule of law'. Is one truly being 'judged by one's peers' if foreigners still constitute a major proportion of the judicial establishment? Of the three branches of government (executive, legislative and judiciary) the judicial branch has often been the least Africanized. While politicians have to use African languages in some context or other, judges and lawyers in most Anglophone African nations need not know a single word of an indigenous language. And dependence on expatriate judges only contributes to making this lingo-legal anomaly a more enduring phenomenon.

There is the vexing question of whether expatriate judges are more likely to be independent of the executive branch than local judges. This used to be a popular belief at one time. It was assumed that a judge in Uganda who was a British citizen, for example, was more likely to stand up to the dictatorial government of the day than was a local Ugandan judge. The language policy which enabled British citizens to serve in African judiciaries, therefore, was regarded as an asset for the rule of law.

Empirically, on the other hand, the record of expatriate judges has been mixed. It is true that one brave expatriate judge in Uganda under Idi Amin gave a ruling against the regime and then fled the country – rather than compromise. In Kenya, too, there was a case of a British judge who resigned in protest against excessive executive interference in judicial affairs by the government of President Daniel Arap Moi. On the other hand, expatriate judges in some countries, like Malawi and Kenya, have routinely acted as if they were an extension of the executive branch – leading to rumours of massive government manipulation of the judiciary.

Nor should it be forgotten that some local African justices have been known to stand up to their own governments even at great personal risk. One of the more tragic cases was that of Chief Justice Benedicto Kiwanuka of Uganda who, in 1972, gave a ruling contrary to President Idi Amin's preference – and paid the supreme price for it. The Chief Justice was picked up from his own chambers in Kampala by military thugs, and was never seen again. He was a martyr to the rule of law – and he was a native son.

The convergence (between the English language and the legal tradition inherited from Britain) may still be important in safeguarding the rule of law in Africa; but the distinction between expatriate and local judges may be far less relevant than once was assumed. A reformation of language policies in Africa, therefore, has to be sensitive to the imperative of reducing judicial dependence resulting from this lingo-legal convergence without necessarily undermining the gains accruing from it.

Law as command and language as rights

The law inevitably has a dual role – the law as command and the law as protector of rights. The law as command prescribes what individuals and institutions should or should not do – ranging from paying taxes to refraining from rape. The law as protector of rights insists on civil liberties, entitlements, legitimacy and due process.

Similarly, language can have a dual role. It can serve as a language of command or as a language of rights. How has the English language performed in these roles in Africa?

An imperial language in the colonial context inevitably begins much more as a language of command than as a language of rights. English in Britain was of course already a language of both command and rights for British people – but in the colonies it took a while before the colonized subjects looked to the English language for the articulation of their own moral demands and rights.

While in policy making Britain was not entirely insensitive to some basic human rights of her subjects, Britain did not encourage discourse on human rights or civil liberties *within* the colonies until rather late in the colonial period. That is why

English remained for so long a language of command rather than of rights within the Empire.

In the legal system also, in the colonies the domain of rights was initially relatively narrow. But as the imperial system was liberalized, *law as command* began to find a new equilibrium with *law as rights*. In all phases of transition the English language was the primary medium of both command and rights.

The question has arisen as to whether the primacy of the English language has itself caused a curtailment of legal and political rights. The paradox is that while the English language has introduced Africa to new concepts of rights, the English language itself is often an impediment to the realization of the very rights it has helped to initiate.

In South Africa two Euro-Imperial languages came to serve drastically divergent roles. Afrikaans (linked to Dutch) was widely perceived by people of colour as a language of command. The English language, on the other hand, was accepted widely by the same people of colour as a language of rights. Concepts like democracy, self-determination, human rights, and civil liberties reached the South African masses partly through the English language. Yet even in South Africa the question nevertheless persists as to whether the English language becomes an impediment to the rights it espouses itself. Is African self-determination hampered by the primacy of the English language in Anglophone Africa? Is the rule of law compromised when indigenous African languages are marginalized by the English language?

Not using indigenous African languages in the legal process is damaging not only to the rule of law but also, of course, to the indigenous languages themselves. The languages are marginalized in some of the fundamental areas of civil society – law and order, governance and civil liberties. In some circumstances indigenous languages are condemned to being languages of command rather than languages of rights. This happened to Kiswahili in Uganda, first under Idi Amin's military rule (1971–79), and then under Tanzania's military occupation of Uganda (1979–81). Kiswahili was widely used to order the population around. In Buganda especially Kiswahili was viewed much more as a language of command than a language of rights. Northern Uganda was more ambivalent about Kiswahili in these periods.

Linguistic rights and legal rights

Within the more general realm of cultural rights we may distinguish a more specific category that is purely linguistic. Linguistic rights may take the form of the *right of language(s)* or the *right to languages*. The former refers to the right of each and every language in a multilingual society to exist and the equality of opportunity for it to 'develop' legal and other technological limbs and to flourish. Government policies that deliberately seek to suppress some languages – as was the case in Ethiopia under Emperor Haile Selassie, or in Malawi under President Kamuzu Banda – would be in violation of the right of language(s); so would policies which deprive certain languages of material and logistical opportunities for 'development' and 'modernization.'

The internationally acclaimed Kenyan creative writer and cultural critic, Ngugi wa Thiong'o, can be described as an advocate of linguistic rights in this specific sense of the right of languages as defined above. His recently launched Gikuyu journal, *Mutiiri*, is an exercise in linguistic vindication intended to demonstrate that African languages, too, have the capacity for abstract, intellectual and scientific thought. But it is also a forum that provides the Gikuyu language with the opportunity to grow in a particular direction.

Sometimes colonial-cum-missionary policies were more sensitive to the rights of language(s) than most post-colonial Anglophone African governments have endeavoured to be. There were some serious attempts to codify African languages and standardize them, in an attempt to augment their capacity for growth and development. Missionary establishments were sometimes involved in preparing African languages for new functions in society in a way that has been virtually unmatched in Africa's post-colonial experience. In many instances, therefore, post-colonial governments in Africa have been more guilty of violating the rights of indigenous languages than were their colonial predecessors.

We talk of the right of language(s) as a *collective* right. Its violation automatically affects entire linguistic communities. The right to language(s) on the other hand, is more of an *individual* right. Within a particular linguistic constellation, it refers to the right to use the language one is most proficient in, as well as the right of access to the language(s) of empowerment and socio-economic advancement. A policy that prevents one from using Yoruba in the legislature, for example, would be in violation of that person's right to language. If, for political, economic or other reasons, a person is denied access to a language, a language variety, or language skill that is crucial to his/her upliftment above the poverty level, then his/her individual right to language has again been violated.

Colonial governments in Anglophone Africa were often more guilty of violating the right *to* language(s) than of violating the right of languages. African students were often punished for using their mother tongues, for example, within the school compound. There was some control over how large a population of Africans should be allowed to acquire English, and how much English they should be allowed to acquire, at a time when the language was becoming increasingly critical for upward socio-economic mobility. All these were instances of violation of the right to language(s).

There is, of course, an obvious link between the rights of language(s) and the right to language(s). The violation of the collective right of a particular language to exist, for example, necessarily encroaches on the individual right of access to that language.

There is also an interconnection between linguistic rights and some other kinds of rights. Certain political and economic rights, for example, are dependent on the promotion of certain linguistic rights. As indicated earlier, the English-only policy which denies people the right to use their first languages in the legislature, for example, also limits the political right to parliamentary participation of those who lack proficiency in English.

Non-linguistic rights which interact with linguistic rights and which are of particular concern to us here are what we may call *legal rights*. Broadly defined, these are all rights provided under the law of a particular country, be they political, economic, social or cultural. Here, however, we are more interested in a narrower definition of legal rights. This refers specifically to the rights of litigants intended to ensure a degree of fair play in the legal process and in the administration of justice. The right of an arrested person to remain silent, and the right of an accused person to legal representation are examples of rights that are exclusively legal in this narrower sense of the term.

Among these rights there are two which usually make explicit reference to language. These are:

1. The right to personal liberty, which stipulates that an arrested or detained person should be informed, *in a language that he/she understands*, of the facts of, and grounds for, his/her arrest or detention, and
2. The right to a fair hearing, under which provision a person charged with a criminal offence is entitled to detailed information, *in a language that he/she understands*, on the nature of the offence and to have , without payment, the assistance of an interpreter.

The interplay between language and the law that is implicit in the provisions of both these rights – the right to personal liberty and the right to a fair hearing – raises certain fundamental problems in the administration of justice. In the first place, those who are the most vulnerable to arrest - the poor - are also the most ignorant of their legal rights partly because the law itself is not accessible in the ethnic languages in which they are most proficient. To this day, for example, Willy Mutunga's *The Rights of An Arrested Person* (1991) exists only in the English language. The text has not been translated even into a major trans-ethnic African language like Kiswahili. The poor, thus, are barred linguistically from acquiring a knowledge of their most basic legal rights.

The ramifications of this lingo-legal problem may begin even before the accused appears in court. The law in most Anglophone African countries provides that police interrogation and recording of the statement of a suspect be in a language in which he/she is sufficiently proficient. In a number of cases it is even mandatory that the statement of inquiry of the accused be recorded in his/her first language if the crime carries capital punishment. The essence of this provion, however, is immediately undermined by the requirement that the interrogating police officer, who has normally received no skills training in translation, undertake an English rendering of the statement for presentation in court. The same body, the police department, which is charged with the responsiblity of prosecuting the accused in court, is thus given the licence to translate his/her statement from one language to another without the training to carry out such a task.

The court room: between interpretation and recording

The reliance on expatriate judges, the prevalence of advocates who are alienated from their African linguistic roots and, above all, the lingo-legal divergence between African languages and the Eurocentric legal tradition have combined to make interpretation virtually indispensable in the judicial process as well.

In most Anglophone African courts English is the primary official medium of judicial proceedings. In Kenya, for example, Cap. 8 of the Judicature Act, Section 198(4) of the Criminal Procedure Code and Section 86(1) of the Civil Procedure Act all indicate that English shall be be the language of the High Court and Court of Appeal. In all such instances, then, an accused person who does not understand English is automatically at the mercy of the interpreter. But the task of interpretation in African judicial set-ups is replete with problems precipitated by factors that are inherent to the process of interpretation itself, and by factors that have more to do with those who have been entrusted with the responsibility of interpreting – the professional interpreters.

Interpretation, the *oral* transfer of meaning from one language to another, permits communication between two or more persons who do not share the same language. In Anglophone African courts of law interpretation normally makes it possible for defendants and witnesses who do not speak English to hear the proceedings to which they are a party, and for judges, attorneys and assessors or juries to understand the testimony of the non-English speakers.

The process of interpretation, however, involves not only linguistic factors, but also extra-linguistic parameters. To interpret is initially to comprehend perfectly the message so as to be able to detach it from its verbal support and reconstitute it subsequently, with its entire semantic, emotional and aesthetic baggage, with all its nuances, in another language. This involves a constant exchange and interchange of mentalities, of one cultural universe with another.

A competent interpreter, then, would be one who (1) has a native or near-native proficiency in both the source and target languages; (2) has knowledge of the court registers and legal jargons of both languages; (3) is communicatively competent – that is, sensitive to linguistic variations based on factors like class, gender, domains, contexts and social situations, geographical background, relationship to authority, orality and literacy, in both source and target languages; and (4) is knowledgeable about the cultures that are associated with both the source and receptor languages.

What has been described above is, of course, an ideal situation that is not easy to reproduce in actual practice. And this problem is highly aggravated in Africa by the great multiplicity of languages in most countries. But our contention here is that the linguistic policies of most Anglophone African governments do not help us move any closer to this ideal. Court interpreters in Africa receive little training in the skill and their bilingualism in the relevant languages is often presumed sufficient for this onerous task that is central to the adminstration of justice. But, as indicated earlier, bilingualism, or proficiency in two or more languages, is only one qualification of a competent court interpreter.

In his study of the adminstration of justice in the rural areas, a prominent Kenyan advocate of the high court has singled out the use of the English language in the courts as one major aspect of the judicial system that serves to alienate the courts from the rural people. He comments further that:

> Although there are interpreters, it is also true that almost all the interpreters are poorly trained, and usually picked from among the clerical staff of the courts. In the course of interpretation the litigant loses personal touch and expression to the court and therefore does not follow properly the proceedings of the court in his own case.... In the end, what is finally produced is a story quite different from what the litigant had intended to say. Judgement is based on that misunderstood story. (M. M. Kioga, 1992: 79)

In the final analysis, then, the judicial ideal that 'justice must not only be done, but must also be *heard* to be done' is seriously compromised.

The problems of court interpretation are further aggravated by the system of court reporting prevalent in virtually all Anglophone African countries. In most Western countries there are court reporters who are charged by law with the responsibility of making verbatim transcriptions of legal proceedings. The basic assumption here is that verbatim recording of trial proceedings exerts a profound influence on the adminstration of justice, and that without it the ability of an appellate counsel to protect the basic rights of his/her client is seriously impaired. There is thus the presumption that an accurate record of an oral event can be made by writing down exactly what has been said.

It is now widely understood, however, that in any movement from the oral to the written, even in the so-called verbatim transcription, certain discrepancies are bound to occur between spoken language and written language. Some of these are directly related to differences that are inherent in the spoken and written word. Other are due to the cultural climate within which court reporters operate, and, more particularly, to the beliefs and attitudes which reporters hold about language and about their profession.

Despite these discrepancies, however, there is little doubt that, as a way of promoting the ideal of accurate recording of proceedings, verbatim transcription is superior to freer transcription. Yet it is precisely this liberal form of court recording that prevails throughout Anglophone Africa. The system of verbatim transcription in this region has been part of the recording tradition of the legislature, but not of the judiciary. In the judiciary recording is the responsibility of the magistrate or judge who is totally free to decide what and how to record as (s)he continues to concentrate on the flow of arguments in the proceedings. What appears in the written record, therefore, may be at great variance with the oral event. And the consequences of this kind of reporting may be even worse when it seeks to record interpreted speech from one language to another.

Equally important in assessing the impact of justice is the role of the interpreter. It is often assumed that the interpreter is an unobtrusive element, a neutral, or even passive verbal representative of participants in the court room, whose presence does not have an impact of its own on the progression of a judicial event. But as Susan Berk-Seligson has convincingly demonstrated, the prevalent judicial assumption about court interpreters is simply not true, and

> the court interpreter plays a far more active verbal role than the system could ever imagine.... The interpreter's verbal role is very much tied to the linguistic control of 'legitimate' participants in judicial proceedings, a degree of control that is tantamount to linguistic coercion. (1992: 156)

Even the best-trained interpreter, therefore, is ultimately an intrusive party in the judicial process, constantly usurping the powers of judges and attorneys through linguistic manipulation, and influencing the outcome of a case. From the point of view of the accused in many parts of Africa, this problem is aggravated by the fact that he/she has little freedom of choice of interpreters. The interpreter is virtually imposed on the participants.

The linguistic problem of the courtroom, however, affects not only the litigants, advocates, judges and interpreters; it also has a definite impact on the jury. The Anglo-American concept of justice puts a special premium on the jury system as a factor in 'due process'. The British use the jury system in certain categories of cases, with special reference to homicide. The United States uses the jury system in a much wider range of cases. Perhaps some 80 per cent of the jury trials in the world may occur in the United States.

The United States' influence led to some experimentation with the jury system in Liberia. The British were more cautious in passing on the jury system to their African colonies, in spite of British belief in 'verdict by one's peers'. In most African colonies the jury system was replaced by a system of assessors, who advised the judge on the basis of the facts of the case.

In South Africa and Southern Rhodesia (now Zimbabwe) a jury system was introduced, at least for the white population. The experiment has had repercussions for the post-apartheid and post-colonial period in Anglophone Southern Africa.

But in both the jury system and the system of assessors the clash between indigenous and Euro-imperial languages has been a central factor. What languages were the jurors and the assessors listening to from the witness box? What difference did the interpretation of the evidence make to the jurors and assessors? What impact did the linguistic divergence have on whether or not the evidence allowed for a 'reasonable doubt'? After all, if there was indeed a reasonable doubt, the legal process is supposed to acquit the accused. Linguistic confusion can make it hard to ascertain if there is indeed reasonable doubt.

On the other hand, there are countries where the English language may simply be better for the jury system than any indigenous language. Such countries include Uganda where the most widely spoken indigenous language (Luganda) is regarded with suspicion and hostility by most non-Baganda.

Language and equality before law

One fundamental principle of the judiciary is the presumption of equality before the law. The central idea here is that in considering cases of litigants before it, the court will not be influenced by differences of race, ethnicity, gender, class, religion and so forth, in the administration of justice. The presumed equality, however, can be described only as moral in character. In the real world there is little equality before the law. Some people are definitely more underprivileged than others, and this state of inequality ultimately impacts on the administration of justice.

One area of disadvantage is, of course, linguistic, and is directly related to the work of the British sociologist, Basil Bernstein. In 1971 Bernstein came up with his rather controversial dichotomy between 'restricted code' and 'elaborated code'. In very broad terms, socialization processes as determined by social class background are said to impose a certain degree of code differentiation on a language, and the different codes, in turn, come to function as stabilizers of the social structure. The restricted code, for example, is regarded as a product of social patterns within lower class life – overcrowded homes offering a limited variety of social situations, work relations that require physical manipulation rather than symbolic organization and control, assertion that tends to be collective rather than individual, and a community environment having little intellectual stimulation. These and other conditions of the lower class, Bernstein believed, tend to generate 'a particular form of communication [a restricted code] which will shape the children' (1971: 143).

Many aspects of Bernstein's dichotomy have since been criticized and discredited from both a theoretical and empirical point of view; and Gordon (1981) offers a good summary of some of these major critical works. Nonetheless there are still areas of Bernstein's hypothesis which seem to have defied refutation. Of particular significance among these is the distinction Bernstein draws between universalistic meanings and particularistic meanings. Universalistic meanings are those in which principles and operations are made linguistically explicit and the meanings are less tied to context. Particularistic meanings, on the other hand, are those in which principles and meanings are relatively implicit linguistically; these meanings tend to be context bound. Where meanings are particularistic we say they are tied to local relations and local social structures; they are embedded in the context and may be restricted to those who share similar experiences (Bernstein, 1972: 163).

Having made this distinction, Bernstein goes on to argue that social conditions orient a child towards speech codes which control access to relatively context-tied

119

or relatively context-independent meanings. 'Where codes are elaborated the socialized has more access to the grounds of his own socialization, and so can enter into reflexive relation to the social order he has taken over. Where codes are restricted, the socialized has less access to the grounds of his own socialization and thus reflexiveness may be limited in range. One of the effects of the class system is to limit access to the elaborated code' (1972a: 164).

This linguistic phenomenon described by Bernstein, then, may have some direct bearing on the question of language and the law in the urban areas of African nations. As indicated earlier, those charged with criminal offences disproportionately come from the African underclass living under urban slum conditions somewhat similar to those described by Bernstein – overcrowded homes and localities, limited avenues through which the human creative impulse could find expression, job occupations which tend towards the physical rather than the intellectual. These social conditions, which have been developing since the colonial days, may have begun to influence socialization patterns, and subsequently may have led to language differentiation into codes quite akin to Bernstein's elaborated and restricted codes at the level of semantic explicitness/implicitness.

If this extension of Bernstein's proposition to the African urban scene is valid, then, it is easy to see how it might affect the administration of justice in Africa. The legal arena of the court is one which is naturally married to elaborated codes where meanings are universalistic. As Weissbourd and Mertz rightly claim, 'Law ... makes explicit what in ordinary speech is left implicit and presupposed' (1985: 648). Without legal representation, therefore, members of the urban underclass, who are presumably limited to the semantically particularistic communicative mode, would be disadvantaged linguistically in defending themselves against charges proffered against them. On the other hand, to have legal representation normally would imply placing oneself at the mercy of a process of court interpretation, which, as demonstrated above, is so flawed that it cannot guarantee fair play and justice for the accused.

Eurocentricity in legal culture

To the extent that language is an aspect of culture, the predominance of European languages in African courts renders the African judiciary culturally Eurocentric. But language is also a reflection and an expression of culture. In linguistic circles there is today renewed interest in the Sapir-Whorf hypothesis – the relativist conception of language that posits some correlation between language and cognition within conceptual boundaries that are defined by particular cultures. Informed by this sociolinguistic hypothesis, Abiodun Goke-Pariola, for example, has wondered whether a process of Eurocentric cultural distortion does not, in fact, enter into cases revolving around such culturally specific institutions as marriage, the family, 'witchcraft' and the like (1993: 174).

But language is cultural not only referentially in terms of what it expresses, but also ideologically in terms of how it is reflected upon by its native speakers. This is the realm of linguistic ideology – the sets of beliefs about language held by its users as a rationalization or justification of perceived language structure and usage.

This thesis on the relationship between language structure and linguistic ideology also traces its origins to the Sapir-Whorf hypothesis. Benjamin Lee Whorf, in particular, proposed that the language users' native ideology of linguistic reference, of how, for example, language serves as a system of segmenting and classifying the universe of experience, is systematically related to the grammatical structure of language (1978:139–40).

Silverstein (1979) attempts to extend Whorf's view on the semantico-referential plane to the more pragmatic function of language – to the way language gives its users a sense that it may effectively be used to achieve a particular goal, as well as the way established patterns of language actually function to refer to the context of speech. From his study of the structure of language use, then, Silverstein concludes that 'people not only speak about, or refer to the world "out there" – outside of language – they also presuppose (or reflect on) or create (or fashion) a good deal of social reality by the very activity of using language' (1979: 194).

Some of the research in this linguistic tradition has concentrated on the way in which the use of language in legal arenas not only restructures the relationship of interacting parties, but also contributes to the (re)construction of legal ideologies. Weissbourd and Elizabeth Mertz (1985), for example, have attempted to demonstrate that the subconscious reflection on language structure by native speakers and the structure of discourse in the courtoom ultimately affect legal ideologies in a culturally circumscribed manner.

Weissbourd and Mertz begin with the premise that the Anglo-American legal system which has been inherited throughout Anglophone Africa is biased towards minimizing the role of *context* in the decision-making process. It concentrates, rather, on rules deductively applied and upon rules specifying *prerequisite* elements of situations. It is a system that favours 'abstractness' with a tendency to perceive legal rules as part of a fixed system that can be applied to statically conceived facts. Extending this proposition to language, Weissbourd and Mertz argue that whereas 'in its appellate courts, in its law schools, in the way its law-makers talk about law, the Anglo-American system contrasts a system of rule with unanalyzable contextual factors, legal systems of other cultures tend to look to the actual dynamics of contextual (linguistic) interaction for underlying truths' (1985: 649).

This legal ideology of Anglo-America is aided, in part, by a kind of legal training and practice, based primarily on the English language, that puts a heavy premium on the written word. It is true, of course, that the court process is primarily oral in its deliberations; but the decisions of the court tend to rely disproportionately on the body of written rules that are statically codified in the European language.

Yet the majority of the accused who appear before the court have no knowledge of the English language nor of the written word. Their linguistic proficiency is limited to local languages within the oral mode. There is the mistaken assumption that the written word is merely a modal replication of the spoken word. But, in fact, the two are bound by different 'discourse cultures'. The notion of presupposable truth arising from the kind of abstraction and 'objectification' engendered by written communication, for example, is more difficult to attain in oral communication. Truth in the oral tradition is seen to emerge from the ongoing process of creative use of speech and from the ongoing force of rhetoric itself.

But precisely because of the written-English bias of the Western legal system which Anglophone Africa has inherited from the colonial experience, many litigants who are bound to the oral-indigenous linguistic tradition are precluded from making any real contribution to the (re)construction of the legal process. Africa's legal ideology continues to be overwhelmingly Eurocentric partly because, linguistically, it continues to marginalize the less Europeanized members of society, and those who are best placed to contribute towards its Africanization.

Conclusion

From the foregoing it is clear that the linguistic policies pursued by Anglophone African countries have had a direct bearing on the rule of law. They have rendered the law excessively Eurocentric, both linguistically and culturally, thereby alienating the majority whose conduct it seeks to regulate and who are, in any case, better placed to Africanize it. Often they have had negative implications for the administration of justice and the formulation of laws. And they have continued to interfere with people's rights – from the right of participation in parliament to the right of a fair hearing in the courts of law.

One of the most important lingusitic rights provided in virtually all the constitutions of Anglophone African countries is that of the *freedom of speech*. It is through this right that individuals can make their own contributions to the (re)shaping of their community and the laws and legal systems that govern them. Yet, the kinds of exclusionary linguistic policies prevalent in Africa, especially in legal institutions, seriously constrain the exercise of this right. For, when the law insists on a particular European language in parliament and in the courts of law, when the majority can only communicate through the intermediation of a third party, when the standards of linguistic propriety in legal bodies are unfamiliar to the majority, then what we have is not freedom of speech, but the denial of voice. And such linguistic denial is, ultimately, a form of excommunication that deprives individuals of their right to participate in turning the rule of law into the democratic principle that it ought to be.

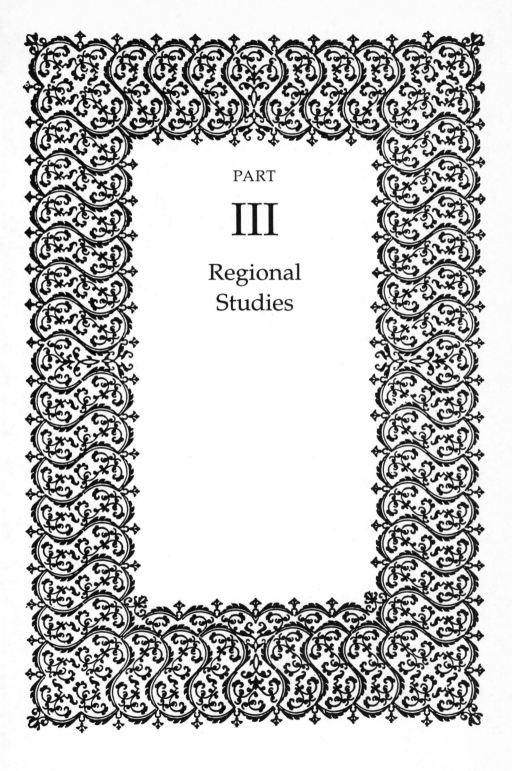

PART

III

Regional
Studies

9
Dominant Languages in a Plural Society

English & Kiswahili in Post-Colonial East Africa

English, an ex-colonial language, and Kiswahili, an African lingua franca, share the characteristic of being the most influential trans-ethnic languages in East Africa.[1] From the religious to the secular, from the state level to the household domain, these languages have become virtually indispensable in the day-to-day lives of many East Africans.

The histories of English and Kiswahili, however, show significant variation from one East African country to another. In this paper, we intend to explore the sociopolitical dynamics of these two languages in the East African countries of Kenya, Tanzania and Uganda, along three interrelated parameters.

First is the confluence of three cultures in the region, the coming together of indigenous, Islamic, and Western traditions. The Arab-Islamic encounter with the 'land of Zanj' and the Western impact on Africa have contributed to the histories of English and Kiswahili in complex ways and have posed many challenges to their continued development. How, then, have these languages responded to these challenges, and what kinds of sociolinguistic configurations have resulted from these responses?

The second parameter has to do with power relations. Trans-ethnic languages in Africa can be either imperial, hegemonic, or preponderant. An imperial language is one which came with a dominant external power and has yet to develop a large enough number of native speakers from the indigenous population. English in many African countries is, of course, still imperial.

A hegemonic language, on the other hand, is a dominant indigenous or indigenized tongue with a large and powerful constituency of native speakers. Amharic in Ethiopia, and perhaps the Arabic language in Sudan, are hegemonic in this respect. Both the speakers of the language and the language itself are powerful forces in the society at large.

On the other hand, a preponderant language is triumphant itself but its native speakers are not necessarily so. A preponderant language in our sense is an indigenous tongue which is very widespread as a second language but whose native speakers are not numerous enough or otherwise powerful enough in society to be politically threatening. Kiswahili in Kenya and Tanzania is a preponderant language in this regard. What then are the chances that English may some day become a preponderant language in East Africa?

The third important parameter in our discussion of the political sociology of English and Kiswahili in East Africa, is that of sociolinguistic value. Languages relate to values of sentiment and instrumentality. The instrumental value can include both a collective scale (as in national integration) and an individual scale (in promoting the goals and aspirations of individual users, for example). In addition, both the instrumental and the sentimental values of a language can be spread generally in society, or can be specific to a particular profession or occupation like the army or civil service. How, then, have English and Kiswahili balanced out by the measurements of sentiment and instrumentality in East Africa?

The making of a preponderant language

Kiswahili has gone through four stages in its development. These are the *Islamic* stage, when the language culturally and idiomatically was associated closely with Islam; the *ecumenical* stage, when the language also came to serve the purposes of Christianity; the *secular* stage, when the main influences on the language have been non-religious and when its role has been overwhelmingly secular; and, finally, the *universalist* stage when the language has become the most widely used African language internationally and is becoming the medium of scientific discourse and technology.

This history has gone hand in hand with Kiswahili's growing sociolinguistic value, accumulating layers and layers of sentiment and instrumentality, which have in turn enhanced its development into a preponderant language. It is this political sociology of Kiswahili that we should now look at more closely from an historical point of view, examining some of its wider societal implications.

Centuries of East African contact with the Arab-Islamic world, and the Islamic identity of the native speakers of Kiswahili, gave the language a peculiarly Islamic imprint. In a sense, this encounter between the indigenous and Islamic traditions led to the emergence of an Afro-Islamic language, Kiswahili. The culture of the Waswahili (Swahili people) has been infused with an Islamic ethos and traditions, many of which are reflected in the language. The high proportion of words of Arabic origin in Kiswahili is often an expression of the once Islamic quality of the language. As a native language Kiswahili had, of course, both instrumental and sentimental values among its native speakers from quite early on.

The encounter with the Arab-Islamic world also led to the use of the Arabic script in writing and the emergence of a rich poetic tradition, much of which was inspired by Islamic themes. The overall impact of these linguistic influences was the development of a Kiswahili metalanguage, at least in the domains of religion and poetry. Though still at the Islamic stage, therefore, the language had begun to demonstrate its universal potential in metalinguistic discourse in a limited number of domains.

But the contact with the Arab-Islamic world was not merely religious and cultural. It was also economic. The Arabs were at the centre of the Indian Ocean trade network which penetrated deep into the African continent as far as what is today the Democratic Republic of the Congo in Central Africa. In the process Kiswahili became an important trade language, spreading by a process of 'contagion' (to use Jean Laponce's term, 1993) well beyond the borders of its native speakers. Gradually Kiswahili came to be acquired as an important lingua franca in inter-ethnic communication. The preponderant status was at hand.

In this early phase, Kiswahili as an additional language was essentially instrumental in its sociolinguistic value; it had little, if any, sentimental value. Its language value, moreover, was more individual than collective. Its use as an additional language was prompted more directly by individual needs and aspirations and only indirectly by collective concerns. But with the inception of European colonial rule Kiswahili quickly came to acquire a collective instrumental value.

With a wide geographic and demographic base, an expanding vocabulary scope, and a relatively rich written tradition, Kiswahili became a prime candidate in the European colonial quest for a solution to the 'problem' linguistic diversity posed to their missionary and administrative needs of communication with the 'natives' in East Africa. Concerted efforts were made, therefore, by some missionaries and British administrative personnel and agencies to standardize Kiswahili, codify it using the Latin script, and promote it through creative writing, the mass media, and the school. If the spread of Kiswahili prior to the inception of colonial rule was based primarily on the process of conduction – through diverse, informal, and face-to-face contacts – this was now complemented by a process of radiation (Laponce, 1993) from above through statal, para-statal, and other centralized agencies. In addition to being a horizontal means of communication between various people in society, therefore, Kiswahili also became an instrument of nation building, colonial state formation, and vertical mediation between the government and the wider society.

The further development of Kiswahili, however, did not depend only on the impetus from missionary and colonial activities. The language also gained its own momentum by expanding and diversifying its functions in the wake of new economic processes, political structures, social dynamics, and cultural institutions that were generated by East Africa's encounter with the West. In this regard one of the earliest changes in Kiswahili's social roles was its acquisition of an ecumenical function in addition to its more traditional functions of facilitating trade transactions and inter-ethnic communications. As suggested earlier, in the popular consciousness of many East Africans, Kiswahili was associated strongly with the religion of Islam. Conversion to Islam and the use of Kiswahili had in fact become almost inseparable.

This tendency to associate Kiswahili with Islam was not only due to the religious background of its native speakers, or to the Islamic character of much of the language's vocabulary, nuancing and poetry. It was also due to the fact that Kiswahili was almost the only African language in the region to be used for Islamic purposes. No doubt Arabic continued to serve as the language of religion for a number of East African Muslims. Non-Muslim Africans who adhered to their own traditional religions normally would use their own ethnic languages for religious purposes. There is a sense, then, in which even as a second language Kiswahili came to have a strong sentimental value as a symbol of East African Islamic identity.

The colonial introduction of Christianity quickly changed this linguistic-religious equation. Christianity was, of course, an African religion long before it was introduced in most parts of Europe. But in the geographical region of our focus in this paper, essentially Christianity was a product of contact with the West. Christian missionary efforts to develop Kiswahili were intended to put the language to the service of Christianity. There were, indeed, some Christian missionaries who deemed Kiswahili to be suspect for evangelical and proselytization work precisely because of its links with Islam. For some other missionaries, however, Kiswahili's Islamic orientation, combined with its status as a lingua franca, made it particularly suited to East African Christianity. The fact that Kiswahili was already a medium of Islamic monotheism, with much of the imagery of the Old Testament, facilitated its use among Africans of the Christian faith.

In addition Kiswahili came to play a wider range of secular functions. Even though Kiswahili, as an additional language, was already playing a secular role prior to the inception of colonialism, it was under European colonialism that it demonstrated its wider secular potential. The secular stage in the history of Kiswahili was now in full bloom. Increasingly Kiswahili came to facilitate the development of trans-ethnic allegiances, class formation, labour unions, and expanding political participation (Mazrui and Zirimu, 1990, Chapter 12).

Kiswahili and political integration

In terms of forging new, trans-ethnic linkages Kiswahili's role is linked partly to the process of urbanization. Urbanization in East Africa has been a major factor behind the erosion of ethnic custom and ritual, though it has not necessarily diluted ethnic loyalty and identity. The groups from different ethnic origins intermingled in places like Dar-es-Salaam in Tanzania, Jinja in Uganda and Mombasa in Kenya. Although many rural customs have declined in these urban and semi-urban conditions, the different ethnic groups which have organized themselves to meet the needs of their ethnic compatriots have interacted with those compatriots in their own ethnic languages. In the scramble for limited opportunities and resources in the cities and towns, the pull of ethnic loyalty has remained strong. Ethnic behaviour may have declined, but ethnic loyalty has remained strong.

Kiswahili, then, has been an important facilitating factor behind urbanization, contributing to decreasing ethnic behaviour, and has served as a lingua franca among the different ethnic communities. Rural to urban migration and urban functionality in certain regions of East Africa came to rely quite heavily on some proficiency in Kiswahili. The language has also been, quite often, the most important medium of the workplace and the marketplace in the towns. This role of Kiswahili has also contributed to the expansion of the network of allegiances and to the erosion of the ancestral traditions of village life.

After the Second World War, towns and cities became major centres for the new politics of African nationalism. A growing 'race' consciousness was spreading among black East Africans. They were sensing not merely their own original ethnic identity as Kikuyu, Acholi, or Sukuma. They were recognizing, in a new way, that they were black people sharing a history of exploitation and domination by people belonging to another 'race'. Kiswahili played an important part in this new phenomenon of African nationalism. Africans in Dar-es-Salaam, Zanzibar, and Nairobi heard speeches from the new breed of African politicians, agitating for African rights in Kiswahili. Politics in Kenya and Tanzania especially became national politics, with Kiswahili as a lingua franca. In addition to its collective instrumental value of political integration, therefore, Kiswahili began to acquire a sentimental value as a language of African nationalism.

In addition to the racial boundaries of the new nationalism in East Africa there were also the emerging territorial boundaries. East Africans were thinking of themselves not merely as black people belonging to the African continent, but also as Tanzanians, Ugandans, and Kenyans. A new complex relationship based on territorial nationality was being born. Through Kiswahili national radio programmes and national newspapers the language played its part in this process.

Yet another role Kiswahili has played in reducing ethnic behaviour in East Africa lies in the emergence of national armies and security forces. Recruitment into the armed forces was, and continues to be, substantially trans-ethnic. Ethnic inter-mingling in the barracks, accompanied by new military routines and drills, contributed to the erosion of ethnic customs within each group. The army, the police, and the paramilitary forces in Kenya have all utilized Kiswahili as the primary language of command. So, of course, have the security forces of Tanzania, including the National Service, which recruits, for limited periods, young people from all parts of the country. In Uganda, too, Kiswahili has continued to feature as the language of the military despite the massive convulsions that have taken place in the country over the years.

In broadening the social horizon of East Africans the role of Kiswahili also included facilitating class formation. In both Kenya and Tanzania, Kiswahili played a significant role in the history of proletarianization, in the emergence of a modern working class. Kiswahili not only facilitated labour migration in East Africa, but very often became the primary language of interaction at the place of work. When the British were agonizing over a language policy in East Africa, the colonial settlers, who were the main employers of African labour, generally preferred the promotion of Kiswahili. They saw in it, as a lingua franca, an instrument of some degree of 'detribalization' that was necessary in the formation of a proletariat.

The interplay between working conditions and diversified ethnicity charac-teristic of some urban areas also sharpened class consciousness and necessitated an effective lingua franca. Kiswahili thus came to be an important tool of organized labour agitation and militant collective bargaining. In its formation and consolida-tion the trade union movement in East Africa came to depend, in no small way, on Kiswahili.

Kiswahili also made possible wider political participation among East Africans. As it evolved into the primary language of politics in Tanzania and Kenya especially, it became part of the process through which the masses in these countries became increasingly involved in national agitation for African rights. A national political constituency emerged partly because a national lingua franca was operating in those societies.

After independence Tanzania went a stage further. Kiswahili was made the only medium of parliamentary discourse. This Swahilization of the political process in Tanzania has resulted in wider participation and broader political recruitment, and has enriched the language in terms of political vocabulary and metaphor.

Today Tanzania is also the most successful case of the use of Kiswahili for national integration. Tanzania is often castigated for the failure of its socialist experiment, but it is seldom given credit for its success in national integration on the mainland. Kiswahili is part and parcel of that integrative triumph.

But it was not only in the political sphere that post-colonial Tanzania made greater use of Kiswahili. Prior to independence, English was the official language of the country. Its acquisition meant greater employment prospects for its citizens. After independence and after Tanzania's move to the left with the 1967 Arusha Declaration in particular, Kiswahili was made the language of official business and the medium of instruction in primary schools. In addition to its sentimental value as the language of Tanzania's sovereignty and national identity, and its multifarious instrumental value in the economic, political and social spheres, therefore, Kiswahili now acquired an additional instrumental dimension as the language of white collar employment. Tanzanians were encouraged to heighten their proficiency in the language partly because it widened their own economic opportunities in the society.

In terms of post-colonial language policy, the first decade of Kenya's independence witnessed very little change from the old imperial British pattern. The English language continued to be the primary official language except perhaps in broadcasting. The Voice of Kenya led the way in popularizing the image that Kiswahili was the national language while English was the official language.

It was not until 1974, more than ten years after independence, that the government took the major step of introducing Kiswahili into parliament. Today, even though legislation continues to come before parliament written in the English language, both English and Kiswahili enjoy equal status as the languages of parliamentary debate.[2] Parliamentary candidates are required to be proficient in both English and Kiswahili.

In addition to its role in broadcasting, Kiswahili also has a strong presence in Kenya's press, in book publishing, and in the lower courts of law. In 1983, with the introduction of a new educational system, Kiswahili also became a compulsory subject in primary and secondary education. This move has increased tremendously the number of university students willing to major in Kiswahili.[3]

In the area of nation building in Tanzania and Kenya, politicians have used Kiswahili in both sentimental and instrumental terms. This is in contrast to English, which has had purely instrumental value in nation building. As intimated earlier, there was a time when in Kenya, outside the coast where it is a native language, Kiswahili had limited sentimental value in spite of its pronounced instrumental value. But since independence Kiswahili has been progressively augmenting its sentimental value.

Some of the reasons for the enhanced sentimental status of Kiswahili in Kenya include, first, the enlarged national constituency of the language (with more and more people speaking it); second, the improved proficiency of Kiswahili outside the coast due to the standardizing influence of the media and the school; third, the political decline of African adversaries of Kiswahili such as the former Minister of Justice, Charles Njonjo; and fourth, changes in Kenya's educational philosophy in favour of Kiswahili.

The situation in Uganda has been different. Until the soldiers first captured power in January 1972, Kiswahili was more a language of economic than of political participation. Kiswahili helped expand the modern wage sector of the economy and facilitated the emergence of a modern working class. But in practice the language was hardly utilized in national politics between independence in 1962 and the military takeover in 1971. Almost by definition, the military takeover was a reduction of political participation by the masses. Parliament and political parties were abolished, and even student politics gradually ground to a standstill.

And yet, paradoxically, this 'shrinking of the political arena' in Uganda (Kasfir, 1976) was accompanied by an expansion of the use of Kiswahili in national life. As indicated earlier, Kiswahili was already a language of the military in Uganda, as it was in Kenya and Tanzania. Military rule, therefore, increased Kiswahili's chances of participation in Uganda's national life. Radio and television employees were ordered to use Kiswahili for the first time as one of their languages, and the government formally conferred upon the language the status of a national language. The soldiers, meanwhile, precisely because they were in power, increased the use of Kiswahili in their own contacts with the general public.

But the return to civilian politics in the 1980s, while expanding the arena of popular participation, reduced Kiswahili's role in national political life. The restriction of the military to the barracks also reduced Kiswahili's contact with society at large. The victory of Yoweri Museveni's National Resistance Army (NRA) against the government of Milton Obote in 1986, however, gave Kiswahili a new impetus in Uganda's national life. The NRA, too, came to rely heavily on Kiswahili in facilitating communication between its multi-ethnic, though mainly Bantu-speaking, members. As the editorial of the *Weekly Topic* of 1 October 1986 aptly put it, 'Faced with a practical problem of communication and unity while in the bush, the NRA was bailed out by Swahili.' In fact, not long after its victory, the NRA declared Kiswahili as its official language. Again, contact between army personnel and the general public has consolidated the use of Kiswahili in Uganda's national life.

The question which remains is whether, when Uganda returns fully to civilian rule, Kiswahili's role in national life will be allowed to expand. The debates that went on in Uganda just prior to the adoption of the present constitution would seem to suggest that such a development is unlikely. Part of the explanation lies in the power politics between Kiswahili, a lingua franca, Luganda, an ethnic language, and English, the imperial language.

Kiswahili has a place in national policy in East Africa partly because it is a *preponderant language*. It is used as an additional language by tens of millions of East Africans who outnumber the native speakers of the language by a very wide margin. People who are ethnically Swahili constitute such a small minority in East Africa that they do not seem to be a potentially significant factor in the ethnic power politics of the region.[4] Kiswahili became accepted as a national language in both Kenya and Tanzania, without opposition from any of the other ethnic languages, partly because the Waswahili (the Swahili people) were not numerous enough as an ethnic unit to make a substantial difference in the ethnic power equation in these two countries.

The situation contrasts sharply with that of Hausa in West Africa, for example. Like Kiswahili, Hausa is a transnational lingua franca spoken by tens of millions of West Africans. But those to whom Hausa is a native tongue constitute the largest majority of West Africa's Hausa-speaking population. People who speak Hausa as an additional language are still in a minority. In other words, while Kiswahili's destiny has long ceased to be in the hands of its native speakers, the destiny of Hausa is still primarily determined by the Hausa people themselves. Selecting Hausa as the national language of Nigeria, therefore, would have generated fears of Hausa hegemony in national affairs. In this sense Hausa can be said to be a potentially hegemonic language.

As in Kenya and Tanzania, people who are native speakers of Kiswahili have not been regarded as politically significant in Uganda. But as a second language Kiswahili has come to assume a certain ethnic character. The status of Kiswahili in the armed forces and police in Uganda was originally purely instrumental. Kiswahili was the language of command. The armed forces of Uganda from 1961 to 1986 were at once *multi-ethnic* and largely *uni-regional*. The soldiers were overwhelmingly from the north of the country, but the north itself was multi-ethnic. The multi-ethnic nature of the armed forces created the instrumental need for a lingua franca like Kiswahili. But the uni-regional (northern) nature of the army eventually created sentimental attachment to Kiswahili, virtually as a northern lingua franca. In the cultural divide between the mainly 'Nilotic' northern Uganda and the mainly Bantu southern Uganda, the northerners paradoxically espoused Kiswahili almost as their own language. It fell upon the mainly northern government of Idi Amin Dada to adopt Kiswahili briefly as a national language of Uganda, and seek to spread it as the country's preponderant language.

The ascendancy to power of the NRA in 1986 changed this ethnic-military equation in Uganda. Because the NRA, in the popular consciousness of Ugandans, was a movement intended to end the continued tyranny of Nilotic people, it mostly attracted Bantu speakers to its ranks. For a while, the confrontation between the NRA and the Uganda government's army was seen as an ethnic confrontation between speakers of Bantu and Nilotic languages. And when the NRA became victorious a new ethnic-military equation had emerged in the politics of Uganda.

Precisely because the Bantu speakers are not themselves a homogeneous group, Kiswahili continued to feature as an important language of the new military set-up. Despite this, however, the constitutional debates in Uganda revealed that there is still strong opposition to the choice of Kiswahili as a national language from, especially, the Baganda. Many Baganda, inspired by a strong sense of ethnonationalism, would prefer to see their own language, Luganda, rather than Kiswahili, become the national language of Luganda.

Yet, among Ugandans of non-Baganda origin, Luganda is *potentially* a hegemonic language. Though it has been acquired as an additional language by an increasing number of speakers of other Bantu languages, its demographic might is still located within the confines of Baganda ethnicity.[5] Making Luganda the national language of the country is seen as a linguistic empowerment of the already powerful Baganda at the expense of other ethnic groups. In the most likely case of a stalemate between Kiswahili and Luganda, therefore, English is likely to emerge as the overall winner.

The politics of communication in East Africa, therefore, manifest three different constellations of languages. In both Tanzania and Kenya, Kiswahili has been accepted as the national language without competition from other local languages. Tanzania's socialist ideology, however, raised Kiswahili to a position of supremacy over English. In capitalist Kenya, on the other hand, English has continued to reign supreme as the official language even though Kiswahili, too, has made some substantial gains. In Uganda, however, English has not only been the official language, but is also likely to be the *de facto* national language of the country.

The secularization of Kiswahili has, of course, been part of its universalization. The language's growing instrumental and sentimental value has also strengthened its potential for universalization. Efforts to develop a metalanguage and a scientific limb for Kiswahili have continued. Kiswahili may be one of the first indigenous languages of Africa to acquire a scientific vocabulary.[6] Kiswahili's universalization also includes its expanding use in international broadcasting and its inclusion in programmes of higher education in other parts of the world. And as the language becomes increasingly universalized, it becomes more consolidated and gains greater legitimacy as a preponderant language with immense instrumental and sentimental value to the peoples and nations of East Africa.

Between the imperial and the preponderant

There is an historic dialectic between English as the imperial language and Kiswahili as the preponderant language of East Africa. Almost by definition an imperial language begins from above as a language of power. English in East Africa started as the language of the rulers before it could gradually develop into the language of the people.

Kiswahili, on the other hand, probably began as a language of the people before it became the language of its rulers. Indeed, when the rulers of Zanzibar were Arabs from the Sultanate of Oman, Kiswahili conquered the conquerors. The language of the colonized assimilated the imperial power – just as the Hausa language and culture in Nigeria substantially assimilated the conquering Fulani. In the history of East Africa and its invaders, we might therefore say that Kiswahili was an African language which captured the allegiance of its Arab conquerors. English, on the other hand, was a European language which sought the allegiance of its African subjects.

The Arab immigrants passed on their religion to their African neighbours; the Africans passed on their language to the Arabs. British penetration of East Africa, on the other hand, was far less symmetrical. The European conquerers transmitted both their religion and their language to their African subjects. But the European conquerors accepted neither conversion to African indigenous religions nor assimilation to African languages and cultures.

Yet another characteristic of an imperial language is that its localization begins with élite formation. English became the basis of an alternative African élite in East Africa. Competence in the imperial language became an avenue of upward social mobility for Africans. Traditional credentials for leadership based on ancient custom were being replaced or undermined by the mystique of the new imperial language.

On the other hand, as Kiswahili evolved into a preponderant language, it was linked to the forces of proletarianization and urbanization. As indicated earlier, it became the language of the labour force, the trade union, and the market place. Both Kiswahili and English were slow in capturing the peasantry of East Africa, and Kiswahili was much faster in capturing the emerging proletariat and wage-labourers than English has been. Even in Uganda Kiswahili has been a major factor in proletarianization; English has continued to be a major factor in élite formation and embourgeoisement in all three countries.

Still another characteristic of an imperial language is that, at a certain level, it has to be learned formally. For Africans in East Africa, English initially was over-whelmingly a language to be learned in classroom situations and from books. Some sailors, seaport workers and household workers could learn English in other ways, but as an imperial language, the primary method of acquiring its command was in the classroom or from a formal tutor.

On the other hand, only a tiny minority of those who spoke Kiswahili did so through formal language training. During the colonial period, there were very few schools in Kenya and virtually none in Uganda which taught Kiswahili.[7] In Tanganyika and Zanzibar there was a bigger proportion of schools interested in teaching Kiswahili, but even in those countries most people learned the language by informal means – by socialization rather than by training.

A related characteristic of an imperial language is that it comes across as part of a written civilization. As a result, command of English tends to be associated with being 'literate' and 'educated'. On the other hand, no such presuppositions accompany a command of Kiswahili. Some of the most articulate of Kiswahili speakers may not be literate at all. While the majority of those who speak 'good' English in East Africa, are almost by definition, part of the 'literati', the majority of those who speak 'good' Kiswahili are not 'men and women of letters' at all.

In Kenya modern-day anomalies are the most striking. The language of the constitution (a legal text) is English; the language of practical politics is primarily Kiswahili. The official language of the judiciary is English. The official languages of the law-making body (parliament) are both Kiswahili and the English language. In their capacity as law makers, parliamentarians need their English; in their capacity as national politicians, the members of parliament need their Kiswahili.

As for the presidency, Kenya has now reached a situation in which a president has to be *trilingual.* A Kenyan president has to be competent in the imperial language (English), the preponderant language (Kiswahili), and the language of a major ethnic constituency (Kikuyu, Kalenjin, Luo, or other). A trilingual president in Kenya is a *de facto* requirement.

In Tanzania a president need only be *bilingual* in the preponderant language of Kiswahili and the imperial language of English. An Afro-ethnic language is not a political necessity in Tanzania. Julius Nyerere has such an ethno-language of his own but it was not a political asset. Indeed, it was sometimes a political liability. For Ali Hassan Mwinyi, the succeeding president, who was a native speaker of Kiswahili, an ethnically bounded language was quite irrelevant in any case.

In Uganda the imperial language (English) has been the undisputed qualification for presidency. The Afro-ethnic language has been a political risk in this deeply divided society. On the other hand, the role of Kiswahili as a preponderant language has been more popular among the northerners and the military than among the more numerous southern Bantu. Theoretically a Ugandan president could be unilingual – simply competent or at best brilliant in the English language.

To summarize, Kenyan presidents need to be trilingual to survive. Tanzanian presidents can survive by being bilingual in Kiswahili and English. Theoretically, Ugandan presidents can survive by being only unilingual in the imperial language, just as President Hastings Banda in Malawi was when he first captured power in his country. Ugandan presidents need to belong to a local ethnic group but not necessarily to command a local ethnic language. They may need ethnic support but not necessarily ethno-linguistic proficiency. That was precisely Hastings Banda's trade-off. He had lost his ethnic language in exile, but still retained his ethnic identity. That political equation could work in Uganda. But it cannot work in Tanzania, where a bilingual executive is needed, or in Kenya, where a trilingual president is required.

Paradoxically, the same conditions which have made the Ugandan presidency almost unilingual seem to have made the Ugandan people the most polylingual. Because Uganda was the most fragmented linguistically of the three East African countries, and Kiswahili had less of a role as a lingua franca, Ugandans learned each other's Afro-ethnic languages more readily than did Tanzanians and Kenyans. Particularly widespread was Luganda. The people of Uganda seem to be the most impressively polyglottal of all East Africans: 'African facility in handling different languages is remarkable. The barely literate house-servant at Makerere would speak to her family in Ru Toro, to her neighbours in Luganda, to the traders in Swahili, to her employers in English and to her employer's amazement and near-monoglot embarrassment, to a visitor in fluent French, explaining that her former husband was Rawandais' (Griffiths, 1985: 24). The abundant diversity of languages in so small a country, combined with the weakness of Kiswahili as a lingua franca, fostered a more polyglottal national culture in Uganda. It also favoured the imperial language (English) more decisively than in the other countries.

What the situation did not favour was the development of Luganda as a hegemonic language. Although the Baganda were very influential in the economy, well placed in the liberal professions, and relatively better educated than other ethnic groups, they were not powerful in the armed forces. Their relative demilitarization made them politically vulnerable. They never acquired in Uganda the powerful status enjoyed by the Amhara in Ethiopia. And unlike Amharic, Luganda never developed into a hegemonic language in our sense. Once again, the overall beneficiary of this situation was the language inherited from the colonial order – English.

As the political and economic situation in East Africa continues to favour the spread and consolidation of English, will social conditions eventually prompt the development of this imperial tongue into a preponderant language?

Towards the Africanization of English?

The English language in East Africa is, of course, a product of the British colonial legacy. Expectedly, then, it suffered the handicaps of all European languages in Africa in their earlier phases – a low level of sentimental value among the indigenous population, alongside a high imperial instrumental value. It is true that the French language has enjoyed greater sentimental value in former French colonies than the English language has in former British colonies. French colonial policies of cultural assimilation, combined with the linguistic nationalism inherent in French culture itself, transmitted to the colonial subjects a greater 'feel' for the French language than other imperial languages have commanded among colonial subjects elsewhere.

Like Kiswahili, the history of English in East Africa can be divided into four stages. These have been, first, as a *language of immigrant European traders*; second, as a *language of imperial control* when the British were in power; third, as *a language of post-colonial governance* in Kenya, Uganda and, to a lesser extent, Tanzania; and fourth, as a potential *Eurafrican language* if and when the language becomes indigenized. The English language in East Africa is historically now in its third phase, a language of post-colonial governance. What, then, are the chances that one day English will be fully 'Africanized' as a first stage in its development into a preponderant language?

The consolidation of English in East Africa specifically is, in a sense, part of its more general trend towards globalization. In this regard English can again be contrasted with the French language. France intended to disseminate its language across the globe. Its policy of assimilation was not only designed to make people French, but also to make the French language and culture supreme on a global scale. But partly because the British empire was larger than the French, and partly because France never produced a linguistic equivalent of the United States – a child bigger than the mother which began to contribute even more than the mother to the spread of the shared language – French began to lose out to English.

The English, on the other hand, were less keen to spread their language. On the contrary, where conditions permitted, they preferred language policies that would limit the dissemination of their language among their colonial subjects. Under the pretext of an enlightened colonialism intended to keep Africans African and the English language exclusive, colonial administrators were sometimes disturbed by attempts to teach the 'native' English at an early age. In the words of Lord Lugard, a leading British colonial administrator, 'The premature teaching of English ... inevitably leads to utter disrespect for British and native ideals alike and to a denationalized and disorganized population' (cited by James S. Coleman, 1958: 136–7).

In spite of these influential reservations about the 'reckless' spreading of the English language, however, it gained its own momentum and rapidly outstripped French both in the number of countries in the world that adopted it as a major national medium, and in the number of speakers. The British, who did not want their language to become a universal medium, have been dealt precisely that fate, while the French have had to embark on a determined attempt to stop their language from receding in importance.

Today it is the United States that has become particularly influential in the spread of English. It keeps gaining new ground across the seas partly because of American pre-eminence in the global economy, in science, aviation, films and so forth. Already by 1966 it was reported that 70 per cent of the world's mail, an even bigger percentage of cable transmissions and 60 per cent of the world's broadcasts were in English; and 'when a Russian pilot seeks to land at an airport in Athens, Cairo or New Delhi, he talks to the control tower in English' (*Reporter*, August 1966: 13).

As English expands geographically it may also be consolidating itself demographically. Politically significant populations of black native speakers of English on the African continent are still restricted to Liberia and, perhaps, Sierra Leone in West Africa. But an increasing number of Africans are growing up bilingual in English and in their own ethnic languages. Hitherto, African ethnic languages have been regarded as predominant in the household domain. To a very large extent this is still true today. In urban Tanzania the African lingua franca, Kiswahili, has often replaced Afro-ethnic languages as a household medium.[8] In many parts of Africa, however, there is a growing tendency for highly educated parents to use English in the home to communicate with each other as well as with their children. To these children, then, English may be as important a medium in the home and the community as their ethnic languages.

Yet it would be possible for English to be spoken by all the inhabitants of the continent of Africa and still be regarded as a foreign language by Africans themselves. What factors, then, may lead to the eventual indigenization of this ex-colonial language? One possible factor is the emergence of a politically significant group of Africans in individual nation-states who acquire English as a 'first' language in three senses of the term.

English may be considered a first language in a functional sense. There is a growing number of Africans whose lives are virtually dominated by the English language in meeting their communication needs. Many members of the African élite, critically placed in the destinies of their nations, have come to rely on English in public interaction as well as in their private lives. In the future the size of this section of the African élite is likely to grow rather than to dwindle.

English may also be a first language in a chronological sense. We have already indicated that there is an increasing number of Africans who are growing up bilingual in English and their respective Afro-ethnic languages. But because the children are exposed to the ethnic language only in the home, while they get English both at home and in school, English begins to gain the upper hand. This functional primacy of English may also lead to its chronological primacy among the élite. Though bilingual, they may end up regarding English as more of their first language than their ethnic languages.

The third sense of English as a 'first' language relates to its role as a lingua franca, as a medium of inter-ethnic communication especially among members of the élite. Inter-ethnic marriages among educated Africans seem to be on the increase. If they do not have a common African medium of communication, spouses in such marriages come to rely almost exclusively on English as the language of the home. Children of such marriages, therefore, are likely to grow up speaking English as the first language. These Africans to whom English is a native language we have termed Afro-Saxons.[9]

The growing functional and chronological primacy of the English language in many parts of Africa is already casting doubt about the extent to which the language can continue to be regarded as 'foreign'. During a 1989 UNESCO seminar held in Lagos, Nigeria, on the role of languages of minority groups as media of instruction, participants concluded that 'English in Nigeria is no longer a foreign language but is rather a *second language*' (Van Dyken, 1990: 41). In some senses it is also increasingly becoming a first language to some Nigerians.

Another factor that may contribute to the indigenization of English is its linguistic localization. While British standard English continues to be regarded as the linguistic norm of many Africans, there are prominent African writers such as Ezekiel Mphahlele and Chinua Achebe who seem to believe that the outlines of a peculiarly African brand of English are already in formation (Egejuru, 1980: 44–50). As African English deviates from the British norm in a linguistically discernible manner, it may be regarded less and less as a foreign language and more and more as an African tongue.

The above considerations, which apply to English-speaking Africa in general, also apply to the particular East African region with which we are concerned. Bilingualism in English and Afro-ethnic languages, the emergence of Afro-Saxons, the functional supremacy of English, the rise of local variants of English, are all growing phenomena in East Africa, especially in Kenya and Uganda.

But it is not the social dynamics among members of the upper classes alone that may be helping the indigenization of the English language in Africa. Most Africans are willing to invest in the acquisition of the English language because of the socio-economic benefits instrumentally accruing to it. But, in this regard, African economies are also finding it increasingly difficult to deliver. There is a growing number of educated Africans who, finding it difficult to secure 'white collar' jobs, are being forced to accept more 'menial' jobs which, until recently, were taken only by the uneducated. This new class of Africans is gradually extending the realm of Western languages from the office to the marketplace. English is reaching the proletariat.

It is not only in the homes of the highly educated that English is acquired at a fairly young age. In the educational sphere too, especially in Kenya, children are increasingly exposed to English at a much younger age than was the case a couple of decades ago. In major cities like Nairobi and Mombasa, English is introduced into the school system as early as the nursery and kindergarten levels. During the colonial period there were some serious attempts to pursue the goal of mother tongue education in which students' first languages featured as the media of instruction in early primary education. But except in Tanzania, where Kiswahili is the only medium of instruction in primary schools, the ideal of mother tongue education in African languages is increasingly capitulating to the silent demand for English in both urban Kenya and Uganda.

But even in Tanzania there are signs that a new linguistic balance is in the making. As indicated earlier, Kiswahili was installed as the official language of Tanzania after its declared move to the left. The ultimate goal was to achieve complete Swahilization of the entire pre-university educational system after a decade or so. By design in post-primary education, and by default in many white collar jobs, English continued to retain its value to some degree. But there is no doubt that with the Arusha Declaration of 1967 English began to decline, as Kiswahili began to rise in value. By design, knowledge of Kiswahili now became increasingly necessary for an increasing number of vocations in Tanzania.

Because of the uncertainties of Tanzania's post-colonial economy, however, there were some members of the élite who were not particularly enthusiastic about the idea of total Swahilization of the educational system. These people perhaps saw the economic fortunes of their children in transnational terms. Placed in key decision-making positions, they are said to have done little to support Tanzania's Kiswahili policy, and in some cases have even 'subverted' it (Massamba, 1989: 72–3; Mulokozi, 1991: 13).

As the economic situation in Tanzania, as elsewhere in Africa, has been deteriorating, the value of English has been increasing. Today more and more Tanzanians look beyond Tanzania's borders for employment and business opportunities in areas which favour the knowledge of English. Increasing dependence on international tourism and greater Americanization of world culture in general are also boosting the value of English in this East African country. As in Kenya and Uganda, this rise in the value of English in Tanzania may be prompting its spread downwards to the 'common man'. In sum, then, the deteriorating economic situation in Tanzania, and the country's increasing abandonment of socialist ideals, are gradually tilting the linguistic balance back in favour of English, though not necessarily at the expense of Kiswahili.

Conclusion

The histories of English and Kiswahili in East Africa, then, have had a remarkable dialectical relationship. English was identified soon after arrival in East Africa with the new Western civilization of science and technology. There was an initial period, of course, when the language also evoked strong Christian associations, but this tendency was quickly overshadowed by the language's role as a medium of scientific discourse. Kiswahili, on the other hand, was identified originally with the religion of Islam. The benefits of English have begun to 'trickle down' from the pinnacles of science to ordinary people. And the benefits of Kiswahili have spread from the fountain of religion to secular domains.

In their respective phases, the two languages both scored high in instrumentality, but English scored high in scientific instrumentality and Kiswahili scored high initially in religious instrumentality. At some point the instrumental value of the languages was also profession-specific, with English being strongly tied to the civil service and Kiswahili to military service. The most important collective instrumental value of both languages in Kenya has been the quest for national integration. Both languages have been used as a means of nation building. But both languages have also had individual instrumental value in terms of promoting the aspirations and goals of individual users.

As a language, English arrived in East Africa when it had already acquired universalist credentials. In East Africa the question has been: when will English ever become a genuinely local language? On the other hand, Kiswahili began as a local language. At its most ambitious, the question has been when and whether Kiswahili will be the first African language to have anything approaching a universalist role. For English in East Africa the struggle for legitimacy has been from the universal to the local. For Kiswahili, the struggle for international vindication has been from the local to the universal.

But precisely because this sociolinguistic dialectic is still unfolding, the social pressures have been towards the development and maintenance of English-Kiswahili bilingualism for the purpose of fulfilling both individual needs and collective concerns. These two trans-ethnic languages, then, are likely to be locked in a relationship of complementarity and competition, within the repertories of individual speakers and in the society at large, for quite some time to come.

To understand the constellation of languages in East Africa, however, we must place the phenomenon of English-Kiswahili bilingualism within a wider socio-linguistic matrix. In addition to the trans-ethnic English and Kiswahili, there are approximately 200 Afro-ethnic languages in the East African nations of Kenya, Tanzania and Uganda. Except in border areas, virtually all these languages are subnational in the sense of being used by populations, mostly of native speakers, that are restricted to particular regions within each nation-state. Relatively few of these languages, such as Gikuyu and Luo in Kenya, Luganda and Lwo in Uganda, and Chagga and Sukuma in Tanzania, are spoken by people whose numbers are in millions, though still well below the ten million mark. The majority, however, are spoken by much smaller populations, many of no more than a few thousand.

Against the background of East Africa's present politico-economic dynamics, this immense linguistic heterogeneity naturally tends to favour a polylingual configuration. In this regard, the 3 ± 1 equation, proposed by David Laitin (1989) for India, may also describe the linguistic situation in East Africa. Native speakers of Kiswahili would normally add just one other language, and that language is likely to be English. Non-native speakers of Kiswahili may acquire an additional Afro-ethnic language and/or Kiswahili and English. We must also bear in mind, however, that there is an increasing number of East Africans who may be acquiring English as a first language in a functional and/or chronological sense. These, too, would normally acquire an ethnic language and/or Kiswahili to meet their vertical communication needs. The norm in East Africa, then, continues to be one of bilingualism or polylingualism.

For polylingualism to attain a degree of stability over a long time, however, the languages involved would normally have to maintain some degree of functional complementarity. For some time the East African countries seemed to provide the social conditions for stable polylingualism, with ethnic languages serving as the media of intra-ethnic communication and solidarity; Kiswahili as a language of inter-ethnic communication, blue collar vocations and national identity; and English as the instrument of administration, white collar vocations, and inter-national communication.

But, as we have tried to demonstrate, this situation is still fluid and complex as the social dynamics force the different languages to encroach on each other's domains and overlap in function. Economic conditions, political considerations, and forces of urbanization and industrialization are constantly interacting and serving as agents for the diffusion of some languages at the expense of others. Hegemonic and preponderant languages are especially expansionist. It is therefore not at all surprising that code-mixing and code-switching, pidginization and creolization, linguistic divergence and linguistic convergence have become fairly pervasive phenomena in Africa. In the words of H. S. Bhola, 'A significant thing is happening to languages all over the world as also in Africa. Through a process of cultural accretion, interethnic marriages and intense social interactions, linguistic pluralism is being reduced at least in the urban areas. Many of the languages are merging into each other and disappearing not as does a river in the sand, but as do small streams into a larger river' (1990: 8).

There is yet another reason why the sociolinguistic situation continues to be somewhat fluid. On average there is much less linguistic nationalism in Africa than there is in Asia. Strong Jewish nationalism has led to the revival of, and shift towards, Hebrew in Israel. A strong sense of linguistic nationalism has led to determined efforts to design language policies that could ensure the maintenance of local languages in many parts of Asia. But successful language maintenance and language shift motivated purely by considerations of nationalism are quite rare in Africa. Pragmatic rather than ideological factors, instrumentality rather than sentiment, seem to be the overwhelming motive forces behind the complex patterns of language maintenance and language shift in Africa.

Notes

1. There are no comprehensive statistics on the demographic distribution of English and Kiswahili in East Africa, but it appears that the number of users of both languages is increasing proportionately throughout the region.

    In Uganda, by 1971, about 35 per cent of the population could hold a conversation in Kiswahili, and 21 per cent in English (Ladefoged, Glick and Criper (1972: 25).

    In Kenya, by 1980, over 65 per cent of the population was estimated to have acquired Kiswahili as a second language (Heine, 1980: 6). Whitely (1974a: 321–3), on the other hand, reported that over 70 per cent of Kenya's rural population claimed competence in Kiswahili at some level, compared with over 40 per cent for English. The figures for both languages are likely to be higher in favour of Kiswahili.

    In the case of Tanzania, Edgar Polome (1980) has shown that by 1970 Kiswahili had far surpassed English both in terms of the proportion of speakers and the frequency of use. Since then, the sociolinguistic situation has developed progressively in favour of Kiswahili.
2. An impressionistic survey of a small sample of the National Assembly debates indicates that English is used far more frequently than Kiswahili as a language of parliamentary discourse (Republic of Kenya, 1987).
3. According to Mr. O. Ogutu, the marketing Manager of East African Educational Publishers (Kenya) Ltd., for example, the sale of individual Kiswahili titles to the University of Nairobi and Kenyatta University, has increased ten-fold over the last few years partly as a result of the increase in enrollment figures of students majoring in Kiswahili.
4. According to the 1979 census, for example, people who can be considered ethnically Swahili constitute less than 1 per cent of the total population of the country.
5. By 1971 Luganda was spoken by 39 per cent and Kiswahili by 35 per cent of the population. However, the largest percentage of those who spoke Luganda were, in fact, ethnically Baganda. Kiswahili, on the other hand, tended to be more multi- ethnic (Ladefoged, Glick and Criper 1972: 25).
6. The Institute of Kiswahili Research of the University of Dar-es-Salaam has already produced a comprehensive English–Kiswahili dictionary of biology, physics and chemistry (*Taasisi ya Uchunguzi wa Kiswahili*, 1990).
7. Interestingly, in Uganda where Kiswahili was squeezed out of the educational system in colonial days, knowledge of the language has been noted to increase with education, though the increase for English is much greater still (Ladefoged, Glick and Criper, 1972: 27). In Kenya, the average number of years for people claiming monolingualism in an ethnic language, bilingualism in Kiswahili and an ethnic language, and bilingualism in English and an ethnic language, are, respectively, 0, 2–3, and 7 (computed from Whitely, 1947b: 39–41).
8. Polome (1980: 102) provides figures indicating that by 1970 the Tanzanian 'vernaculars' were already losing ground to Kiswahili in various informal domains of discourse.
9. Much of the preceding discussion on the geographic and demographic expansion of English in Africa is based on Ali A. Mazrui's study on the place of language in the black experience and the emergence of a world culture (1974: 82–110).

10

A Tale
of Two Englishes

The Imperial Language
in Post-Colonial Kenya & Uganda

An imperial language can be defined as one which has acquired a dominant role in a given society as a direct result of conquest or colonization by another power (see Chapter 9). It is a language, originally imposed by the conquering power, which remains dominant without being the mother tongue of those who were conquered. It is in this sense that English can be considered an imperial language in both Kenya and Uganda.

Although next-door neighbours, Uganda and Kenya provide striking contrasts in many other respects. The British found in Uganda relatively centralized indigenous societies, complete with monarchies. Some of the earliest students of the English language and of British culture were in fact Bantu princes and sons of aristocrats in southern Uganda.

The British found in Kenya (outside the Coast) relatively decentralized African communities, basically stateless societies. There were no hereditary kings and princes beyond the Kenya Coast. The first students of the English language were sons and daughters of ordinary peasants and workers. While in Uganda the learning of the English language and British culture made little difference to stratification in such kingdoms as Buganda and Bunyoro, in most of Kenya anglicization was a process of restratification. While in Buganda the most impeccable English was (by the 1940s) spoken by the Kabaka himself (Mutesa II spoke English entirely without an accent – he sounded entirely British), in Kenya English was creating new élites in competition with the more traditional leaders. In the Uganda kingdoms anglicization helped to consolidate the traditional hierarchy. In Kenya anglicization helped to modernize lines of traditional authority.

Another major contrast between Uganda and Kenya was the fact that Kenya was deliberately developed as a 'white settler colony' – whereas Uganda was 'protected' by the British to remain a primarily black colony. Paradoxically, the presence of large numbers of European settlers in Kenya initially hurt rather than helped the spread of English among Africans. As compared with Uganda, African education in Kenya was slow to take off. Many European settlers regarded the teaching of the English language to 'natives' as a potentially subversive force. Social distance between master and subject had to be maintained through linguistic distance. And many European employers insisted on speaking 'broken Swahili' (ki-Settla, meaning the settlers' version of the language) to their African employees even if the African's command of English was a little better than the European's command of Kiswahili. It is safe to say that the presence of a significant English-speaking white population in Kenya from the 1920s to the 1940s was often more of a liability than an asset to the spread of the English language in the country. Uganda produced an English-speaking black élite faster than did Kenya.

In subsequent years the proximity of a sizable white population began to help the fortunes of the English language in the larger society. African education in Kenya became less and less subject to settler lobbying within the country and more subject to the wider imperial policies of Britain after the Second World War. The capacity of the white settlers to inhibit the spread of English among Africans declined. On the other hand, their presence as a major English-speaking economic force in the country began at last to have a demonstration impact favourable to the spread of English.

But behind the basic contrasts between Uganda and Kenya as colonies there remained the basic sameness of the imperial power, Great Britain, with its own distinctive policies and designs. It is to this basic interaction between Britain and her two East African colonies that we must now turn.

British policy before the Second World War

Kenya and Uganda are among the East African countries which, after the Berlin conference of 1884–5, came under British colonial rule until the early 1960s. Kenya attained its independence in 1963, and Uganda a year earlier. Though this African encounter with colonialism lasted for less than a century, its impact, in certain cultural spheres like language and religion, was relatively profound and seemingly more permanent. Indeed, the English language today is perhaps one of the most enduring legacies of Africa's experience with British colonialism.

This consolidation of English in Kenya and Uganda had its origins in colonial language policies which were often informed by a combination of ideological and pragmatic considerations. As demonstrated in Chapter 1, imperial powers differed significantly in their cultural attitudes on the issue of language. At one extreme, the Germans once believed that no African was good enough to speak the German language. At the other extreme, the French believed that no African was good enough unless he or she spoke French. German arrogance wanted to maintain the cultural distance between the 'natives' and their rulers, between German culture and African culture. On the other hand, French arrogance denied legitimacy to native culture and permitted cultural cooptation through French assimilation.

Somewhere between German policies of cultural distance and French policies of cultural assimilation lay the unique if untidy British variation. The British agreed that no African was good enough to become English, but there was some virtue in being minimally anglicized. Like German colonial rule before the end of the First World War, the British encouraged the learning of some African languages – though British motives were different from German ones.

The British respected African cultures and languages to a greater extent than did either the Germans or the French – although all three European imperial nations had regarded African cultures and languages as inferior to European ones. The British committed greater time and resources to the codification and promotion of such languages as Kiswahili, Luganda, and Hausa. Publications appeared in those languages under British rule, and indigenous languages generally had a place in the curriculum of colonial schools, if only as media of instruction in the lower classes.

This paternalistic linguistic ideology of the British was in conformity with the notion of the 'dual mandate' as conceived by Lord Lugard, perhaps the most influential British administrator in colonial Africa. The dual mandate advocated, in part, that the British had a duty to facilitate the 'civilization' and 'modernization' of Africans while, at the same time, safeguarding the integrity of their cultures and identities. In the linguistic realm, this meant providing the African access to the English language in such a regulated manner as not to endanger political stability or impede the development and growth of more local tongues.

This linguistic dimension of the dual mandate came to find its most explicit expression in the 1925 report of the Phelps-Stokes Commission. The report argued that while 'natives' should not be denied the opportunity to acquire the English language, they have an inherent and inalienable right to their mother tongues (Jones, 1925). This, in fact, is the linguistic philosophy that held sway in many British colonial settings until the end of the Second World War.

Until 1945, therefore, the situation in both Kenya and Uganda was one in which English as well as local African languages maintained a certain degree of complementarity in official institutions of the state. If the English language dominated the higher levels of colonial administration, it is the African languages which prevailed in the lower administrative echelons. As a result, demonstrated knowledge of African languages often became one of the requirements for the appointment and promotion of British colonial officers seeking to work in Africa. Again, English was the only official language of the higher courts; but the lower and 'native' courts were almost the exclusive preserve of local languages. If the body that made the law, the Legislative Council, was the domain of the English language, the institutions charged with the enforcement of the law, like the police, the prisons and the army, were heavily dependent on the local lingua franca, Kiswahili.

The most extensive discussions of British colonial linguistic policies probably centred on the place of language in education. And here, too, the linguistic implications of Lugard's ideology of the 'dual mandate' came to prevail. In Kenya, a 1949 report of the Department of Education noted that the language of early primary education was the 'vernacular', but that from grade four onwards, Kiswahili became the medium of instruction; English, on the other hand, was introduced as a subject at this stage and assumed the role of an instructional medium in secondary schools (Gorman, 1974a: 428).

With regard to Uganda, a 1948 report of the Department of Education noted that there were six local languages, Kiswahili being one of them, which had been recognized as regional vernaculars and were used as media of instruction in primary schools. English was introduced as a subject in grade five, and in secondary schools it replaced the local languages as instructional media (Ladefoged, Glick and Criper, 1972: 91).

In short, then, in the period up to the end of the Second World War African languages enjoyed a favourable political climate while English was introduced with relative caution. Indeed Lord Lugard himself was of the belief that 'the premature teaching of English … inevitably leads to utter disrespect for British and native ideals alike and to a denationalized and disorganized population' (cited by Coleman, 1958: 136–7). As a result, the inter-war period turned out to be the golden age for African languages as far as their development and promotion by the colonial administration was concerned.

In Kenya, the presence of a strong British settler community was initially a curse rather than a blessing to the spread of English. Some settler leaders, like Major E. J. Grogan, could not imagine 'a more desperate happening than introducing English to Africans whose main vocation should be to work in the fields' (cited by Gorman, 1974a; 417). So, while the colonial administration in Kenya experienced a lot of opposition from the British settlers in its modest programme to expose Africans to some English, the colonial administration in Uganda was able to proceed with its English language agenda without this settler 'impediment'. Unlike Kenya, Uganda was not intended to be a settler colony – a fact that, ironically, initially favoured the expansion of English in that country.

British policy after the Second World War

In the period after the Second World War, however, a shift in British colonial policy with regard to language and education began to take place. The first victim of this post-war mood was Kiswahili, hitherto recognized officially as the inter-territorial lingua franca of East Africa. It was at this juncture that the colonial Advisory Council on African Education in Kenya adopted the recommendations of the Beecher Report on the teaching of languages in African schools to the effect that 'more emphasis should be on the teaching of vernacular languages, and that English should take the place of [Ki]Swahili as the colony's lingua franca in as short a time as practicable' (cited by Gorman, 1974a: 427). This led to the gradual replacement of Kiswahili by English as the medium of instruction in the educational system. And in Uganda, Kiswahili lost its status as one of the regional 'vernaculars' of the country, and was eventually phased out of the school system altogether (Ladefoged, Glick and Criper, 1972: 93).

These efforts to eliminate Kiswahili as a significant player in the educational process, and the introduction of English at earlier stages in the primary school, was explained in terms of Kiswahili's adverse effects on the learning of both English and the 'vernacular' (Marshad, 1984: 37). But considering that these efforts were most intense in the post-war period when there was growing resistance to British colonial rule, a leading Ugandan sociologist and historian, Tarsis B. Kabwegyere, has suggested that the move was in fact intended to minimize intra-African contact at the level of 'the masses' as a way or weakening the nationalist struggle against colonialism (1974: 218–19).

As the nationalist resistance kept growing, however, and independence from colonial rule appeared imminent in both Kenya and Uganda, the British became concerned about creating a new élite, both economically through land redistribution, and culturally through the educational process. In the cultural domain, the Drogheda Report recommended that the first essential step in the creation of a Westernized élite was to increase knowledge of the English language (Marshad, 1984: 56). Subsequent to this, the British Information Service supposedly intensified its political and propaganda efforts in the area of language, aiming specifically at this emergent élite (Whiteley, 1971). Against this political backdrop, then, efforts to consolidate the position of English kept mounting, and by 1953 it had been made a compulsory subject in the national examination in the final year of primary education, and the main subject of the curriculum in African intermediate schools in Kenya (Gorman, 1974a: 432).

In Uganda, too, the promotion of English in the school system was pursued with some zeal. The deBunsen Report of 1952, for example, advocated the wider use of English in the primary schools, recommending that English be taught as a subject from the second grade as teachers and materials became more readily available. The report also mentioned the need to train teachers of English and for a detailed study of the content and methods of English teaching in schools and training colleges (Ladefoged, Glick and Criper, 1972: 92). In both Kenya and Uganda the supposed lack of instructional materials in the local languages was used as an additional argument to justify the use of English as a teaching medium from even earlier phases of the educational structure.

Indeed the only factor that seemed to deter the colonial education authorities from proceeding any faster in the establishment of English education was the lack of sufficient teachers of the language. It was often feared that introducing English 'too rapidly' without the availability of a large enough corpus of competent teachers could only lead to the acquisition of a bad smattering of the language which the English found objectionable (Marshad, 1984: 52).

Ironically, British interest in spreading their language in East Africa found tremendous support in African nationalist demands for 'more English'. The colonial education office found itself pressured by African nationalists to move faster than it was prepared to do in the introduction of English in schools (Gorman, 1974a: 430–1).

In an essay on English and the origins of African nationalism, one of the authors of this chapter, Ali Mazrui, argued that the English language in Africa facilitated the development of certain notions of self-determination and the growth of anti-colonialism in Africa itself (1975: 47). Some of these notions expressed themselves in terms of equality of rights, freedoms and opportunities. English had become the language of white collar employment and wider economic opportunities. Nationalists thus regarded Africans as underprivileged when Europeans and, to a lesser extent, Asians were accorded greater access to the language than Africans in the racially divided school structure. The nationalist demand for 'more English', then, was part of the wider demand for equality of opportunity.

Capitalizing on this nationalist mood, the colonial government continued to push for its dual agenda of promoting English and marginalizing Kiswahili in the educational system. The East African Royal Commission Report of 1955, for example, regarded 'the teaching of Swahili as a second language to children whose early education has been in other vernaculars as a complete waste of time and effort'. On the other hand, it described English as a gateway to a new world which the people of East Africa are very keen on entering. The Commission, therefore, recommended that the 'teaching of English should begin in as low a class as possible, and should become the medium of instruction as early as it can be followed by pupils' (cited by Gorman, 1974a: 434).

While efforts were in progress to introduce English as rapidly as possible in African schools, the new African élite became the target of experimentation with all-English medium schools. In Uganda, for example, a multiracial primary school was established in 1956 in the capital city of the time, Entebbe, partly for the purpose of providing places for children of African ministers who came to Entebbe from all parts of the country. Admission to the school was based on fluency in the English language, and parents were charged with the responsibility of providing their children with private tutoring in the language to prepare them for entry into this school (Ladefoged, Glick and Criper, 1972: 93). The objective of creating a highly anglicized African élite, therefore, was now in place, paradoxically supported by the nationalist momentum.

But as indicated in the introduction, linguistic anglicization had less effect on restratification in Uganda than it did in Kenya. The fact that Uganda had a highly developed class of traditional élites who were the first to appropriate the English language as a class symbol, tended to reinforce rather than undermine the pre-existing social hierarchy. In Kenya, on the other hand, the acquisition of the language by children of peasants and the semi-proletariat from the outset became a significant factor in *new* élite formation almost outside the more traditional social structure.

In the meantime, there was some concern in British colonial circles that the switch in instructional medium from the local languages to English was a drawback in the learning process since this change supposedly took place when the subject matter itself was becoming more considerable (Curtis, 1965:31). Partly in an attempt to investigate this problem the Special Centre was set up in Nairobi in 1957 with the express aim of alleviating difficulties arising out of multilingualism in Asian schools. There were European schools always using English as a medium, African schools with English being used as a medium from grade 5, and Asian schools which used Gujerati, Punjabi and Hindi/Urdu for the first three years of schooling with English taking over from grade 4. It is this latter population of Asian students that the Special Centre was initially established to serve.

The Special Centre began its work in 1958 by experimenting with English as the exclusive medium of instruction from the first grade in select Asian schools in Nairobi. In the meantime, the Nairobi Centre helped set up another special centre at Nakawa, in Uganda, which was also 'to experiment with the use of English as a medium of instruction for the lower classes of schools in Kampala' (Ladefoged, Glick and Criper, 1972:95), and it was immediately recommended that more schools, both Asian and African, which are located in the urban areas of Nairobi and Kampala, adopt the English language instructional model – now advocated under the name of the New Primary Approach. In both countries, therefore, the course was adapted for African schools from about 1961. As a result, the programme grew in leaps and bounds. In Kenya, for example, 'the number of English medium classes in African primary schools rose from 14 in 1962 to 290 in 1963' (Gorman, 1974a: 437). In private schools, on the other hand, early English medium instruction quickly became the norm in the urban areas. This was presumably in response to public demand for 'more English'.

Outside the main cities, the ideal of using local languages as educational media continued to be pursued to one degree or another. But partly because education in the local languages was not integrated into teacher training courses, and partly because there were no real efforts and investments in developing appropriate material, instruction in these languages was left to the skills, abilities and resourcefulness of the individual teacher. These limitations created conditions in which English took the place of the local languages as early as grade 1 throughout the region. And, in the urban areas, English began to be introduced as early as the kindergarten and the nursery school.

The situation after Independence

English as a medium of instruction

After Kenya became independent in 1963, the Ministry of Education appointed a commission under the chairmanship of Professor S. H. Ominde to advise the government on issues of educational policy and, subsequently, to recommend reforms which would express the aspirations and cultural values of an independent African country and contribute to the unity of the nation. On the question of language policy, in particular, the commission noted that the sentiments and popular wishes of the great majority of witnesses were in favour of English being used as the medium of instruction from the first grade of primary school. The commission then proceeded to declare its support for these sentiments on grounds that English would expedite learning in all subjects, partly by avoiding the difficult transition from the 'vernaculars', and partly because of the language's own intrinsic resources (Republic of Kenya, 1964: 60).

This report gave further impetus to the national momentum to introduce English medium instruction at an earlier phase in the educational pyramid than the British themselves had done. The so-called New Primary Approach (NPA) spread like wild fire. By 1966, half the primary schools in Kenya were reportedly being taught in English under the NPA (Republic of Kenya, 1967: 5).

Witnesses interviewed by the Ominde Commission, however, also expressed the need to promote Kiswahili in education for purposes of national and pan-African unity. Kiswahili thus came to be offered as a compulsory subject in Kenya's primary schools. But it was not to become an examinable subject – that is, it did not become a mandatory subject of the national examination – until the 1980s.

Despite this introduction of Kiswahili in the syllabus, however, English has continued to enjoy tremendous support in terms of human and material resources. After the release of the Ominde Commission Report, the Kenya and British governments began to work closely together in the area of English-based education, investing large amounts of resources to ensure the success of the NPA and other supplementary projects. The period after 1965, in particular, 'saw a heavy investment in English language teaching by the governments of Kenya and United Kingdom at different levels, including technical assistance for curriculum development (at the Kenya Institute of Education), pre-service teacher training (in teacher's colleges and universities) and a cadre of OSAS English teachers in secondary schools' (Republic of Kenya, 1992: 4). The Overseas Development Administration (ODA) of the government of Britain also provided funds and personnel to set up English communication skills units in the various universities in Kenya.

In Uganda, on the other hand, the government continued to demonstrate some commitment to the ideal of 'vernacular' medium education in the years immediately after independence. But, as Livingston Walusimbi (1972) shows, education in local languages in Uganda was faced with such myriad problems, both practical and attitudinal, that it gradually broadened the path for the ascendancy of the English language. By the end of the civil war in the late 1980s, English seemed to have emerged as the only medium of instruction in virtually all subjects in the curriculum (Mukiibi, 1991: 40). The infrastructural destruction wrought by the war severely undermined the demographic expansion of English in the country as a whole. But, in the process, the 'vernaculars' were squeezed out of the educational system almost completely, leaving English with little competition as a medium of instruction.

As in Kenya, the government of Uganda received substantial assistance from foreign governments and agencies in its efforts to promote English in schools. Much of this assistance was targeted at the training of teachers and was provided mainly by the US Agency for International Development (USAID), ODA and the Canadian government (Ladefoged, Glick and Criper, 1972: 122). Many of these efforts and projects, however, were suspended or terminated altogether after the rise to power of Idi Amin in 1971 and the subsequent civil conflicts that followed his misrule.

In the aftermath of the civil war, however, and since 1988, in particular, there has been a revival of active involvement of foreign agencies in English language education projects. The British Council, for example, is currently involved 'in efforts to uplift the standards of teaching and use of English. Expatriate teachers of English are in schools in substantial numbers again and experienced trainers of teachers of English are now available to the teacher training colleges and Makerere University on either direct British Council sponsorship or through programmes arranged by it. It has also started funding in-service courses of English' (Mukama, 1991: 336).

Education and English language proficiency

In spite of this extensive spread of English to the earliest possible levels of education, and in spite of the tremendous resources invested in its promotion, there have been numerous claims of 'falling standards' of English in the educational institutions as well as in the society at large. Catherine Mukiibi notes that, in Uganda, there has been 'an outcry from different corners, the media for one, and even from the Uganda National Examination Board (UNEB), at the gradual falling standards of English generally' (1991: 40). Mukiibi attributes this trend to the growing number of students in individual classrooms, lack of teaching materials and supposedly insufficient time allocated to English in school timetables. In addition to being the only medium of instruction, then, it is now deemed necessary to accord English more time *as a subject*.

In Kenya too, the fear of falling standards of English has been a recurrent issue in government reports and the media. A 1993 report of the Kenya National Examination Council, for example, notes that 'the standard of English has been falling while that of Kiswahili has shown improvement since it was made a compulsory subject in the 8-4-4 system of education'. The report goes on to state that students cannot follow basic instructions in English and end up giving irrelevant answers in examinations (*Daily Nation*, 14 August 1993).

But perhaps the most alarming statement on the falling standards of English in Kenya came from Professor J. Kiptoon, the vice-chancellor of Egerton University. Kiptoon claimed that many undergradate students in Kenya's public universities are functionally illiterate in English and could not even write a simple application for a job in the language. Kiptoon went on to claim that 'a good number of employers have complained that many graduates cannot communicate effectively in English which is the official medium of instruction right from primary to university level' (*Daily Nation*, 5 June 1993). Kiptoon's revelation triggered a long newspaper debate about the possible causes of this supposed decline in the standards of the English language.

One recurrent issue in this debate is how the problem of the quality of English as an instructional medium is leading to poor performance in other subjects. The impression is thus created that the whole of education in Kenya is virtually in a state of crisis, and that the only possible way to save the situation is to invest immensely more resources in raising students' English proficiency. The Primary Education Strengthening Project and the Secondary English Language Project, both sponsored by the British government, have in fact been launched partly to redress this academic 'problem' (*Daily Nation*, 5 June 1993).

Particularly noteworthy in this entire debate is the total absence of voices even mildly suggesting that, perhaps, the policy of English medium instruction from Primary 1 deserves another look altogether. The question that preoccupied the

British colonial administration, as to which language was more suited to learning in early childhood education has not featured at all in the recurrent Ugandan and Kenyan debate on English as a medium of instruction and its implications for the acquisition of knowledge in other subjects in general.

The demand for 'more' and 'better' English in the educational system in both Kenya and Uganda has led, predictably, to increasing involvement of, dependence on, and investment by foreign governments and agencies. This is particularly true of the British government through its ODA and the British Council. Whether or not this external involvement in the promotion of English is part of a grand conspiracy to foster the spread of English for the overall economic and political interest of the West, as suggested by Phillipson (1992), is difficult to determine. But there is little doubt that both these British bodies have been particularly active in initiating and administering a chain of projects intended to strengthen the position of English, at least in Kenya.

A demographic profile of English

Not only has the English language dominated the entire educational structure in Kenya and Uganda, its use in the society at large has also been expanding. There is, first, a growing number of people whose lives are virtually dominated by the English language in meeting their communication needs. Many members of the educated African élite have come to rely on English in public interaction as well as in their private lives.

In serving as a medium of inter-ethnic communication among members of the élite, English comes to have special implications for the linguistic destiny of the offspring of inter-ethnic marriages. In the absence of a common African medium of communication, spouses in such marriages come to rely almost exclusively on English as the language of the home. Children of these marriages, therefore, are likely to grow up acquiring English first before any other language. These are the Africans who have sometimes been described as the 'Afro-Saxons' (Ali Mazrui, 1975: 9–16).

There is also an increasing number of Kenyans and Ugandans who are growing up bilingual in English and one or more ethnic languages. In Kenya for instance there is a growing

> ... number if high cost private and international schools where many of the teachers are expatriate native speakers of English. Children who go to these expensive schools come from rich, western educated élite families, normally with both wife and husband possessing high competence in the English language.... The children live in exclusive and expensive multinational suburbs where the primary language of the playground, shopping center, schools, places of entertaniment, churches, and hospitals is English. (Abdulaziz, 1991: 397)

And because the children are exposed to the ethnic language only in the home, while they get English both at home and outside, English gains the upper hand in terms of functional primacy.

It has been observed that there is a gradual shift from local languages to English in general in Kenya (Gorman, 1975b: 361), especially among middle and upper class children in urban areas. And this teenage variety of English, according to Abdulaziz, is becoming increasingly Americaninzed due to the influence of American pop music, films and video movies (1991: 398).

In Uganda the country's political instability has ironically stabilized the

Britishness of its English – at least compared with Kenya's. Because Uganda has had less exposure to American television programmes, videos, films, and other aspects of American culture, the British imperial version of English has faced less competition even among young Ugandans.

The pace of Americanization in Kenya has also been facilitated by international tourism, which is almost dead in Uganda, and by the periodic traffic of American naval forces in Mombasa, a factor wholly inapplicable to Uganda. Tourism in Kenya is , in most years, one of the foremost foreign-exchange earners in the country. It brings in hundreds of thousands of Westerners, most of whom are serviced in the English language. Local motivation to learn English in order to make money out of the tourists has become a fact of life in big cities and resort centres. By contrast, tourism in Uganda has been almost completely wiped out by the civil strife and the high security risks to person and property.

The impact of cultural 'coca-colonization' is, therefore, significantly greater in Kenya than in Uganda. The linguistic consequences include the emergence of Americanisms in the lexicon of young semi-Westernized Kenyans, and the beginnings of American pronunciation. The English of semi-Westernized Ugandans (while sometimes bearing the stamp of Ugandan languages) remains more loyal to the British model. In any case, there is evidence to suggest that the élites in the kingdom of Buganda (restored as monarchies by President Yoweri Museveni in 1993) have been more profoundly Anglophile since the colonial days, and would prefer their speech to approximate British English.

But the spread of English in the society as a whole is by no means limited to the middle and upper classes. In a 1987 study on language and community formation among the urban poor in the Nairobi slum of Kibera, 235 out of 485 respondents claimed some proficiency in the English language, even though among these only 13 claimed to use the language extensively in their homes (Alamin Mazrui, 1988: 185).

There are still no comprehensive statistics on the demographic distribution of English in Kenya and Uganda. But impressionistically it is clear that the number of users of the language is increasing at a rapid rate throughout the region. The latest figures for Uganda are those provided by Ladefoged, Glick and Criper, suggesting that 21 per cent of Ugandans could hold a conversation in English. These writers also show that this percentage falls as people get older and school is left further behind (1972: 25). The civil war in Uganda, however, is likely to have disrupted this demographic development of English language seriously in ways that are yet to be determined.

For Kenya, Whiteley (1974a: 37–45) provides figures of respondents, based on a multi-ethnic and predominantly rural sample of 848, claiming some competence in English. If one computes the national average from his results, which are broken down by district and ethnic group, we see that the largest number of respondents who claim competence in English are trilingual in the mother tongue, Kiswahili as a second language and English. This group constitutes about 32 per cent of the total sample, a figure proportionately higher than that of respondents claiming competence in the mother tongue and Kiswahili alone. Those who claim competence in English and one or two 'vernaculars', without any competence in Kiswahili, constitute less than 6 per cent of the sample.

In discussing patterns of language use in rural Kenya, Whiteley observes that while English, Kiswahili and one or more ethnic languages, as additional languages, may have comparable instrumental value at the homestead, 'English has a higher "prestige" rating and is more frequently cited as being used in the home "to help the children", "to discuss current affairs" and so on' (1974b: 330). Whiteley also shows that while Kiswahili has a virtual monopoly in the area of small-scale trade, it is experiencing increasing competition from English in the domain of the church (1974b: 332–6) and in communication with friends and acquaintances (1974b: 334-5).

Gorman, on the other hand, demonstrates that the extent of English usage depends not only on domain, but also on topic, interlocutor and channel. Written communication to an elder sibling on a subject related to life in school, for example, is likely to be in English, whereas oral conversation with a younger sibling on a traditional ceremony will, most likely, be in a local language (1974b: 379).

If by 1974 the spread of English was already so extensive in the rural areas of Kenya as Whiteley's figures seem to suggest, then its impact on the urban population is likely to be even deeper. Due to the greater concentration of schools as well as of speakers of English as a first or additional language, and the greater availability of radio, television, films, magazines and other entertainment in English, the urban population generally has greater access to the English language than the rural population. And the international status of Kenya's capital, Nairobi, has intensified the importance of English in the country as a whole and the quest for its acquisition.

An equally important factor in the accessibility of English is gender. In absolute as well as proportional terms, in both Kenya and Uganda, there are more men than women who can speak English. Monolingualism in a local language in Kenya, for example, is described by Whiteley as 'a feature of the older generation and women rather than men' (1974a: 48). In the 1969 Uganda Language Survey, 13 per cent of women respondents, in contrast to 28 per cent of male respondents, claimed they could hold a conversation in English (Ladefoged, Glick and Criper 1972: 25).

This gender difference in English proficiency may be attributed partly to the educational factor. The English language is still acquired primarily in school (Gorman, 1974b: 358). But in spite of the increasing number of girls who are getting absorbed into the educational system, access to the school continues to be biased in favour of boys. In addition to being an instrument of class formation, therefore, the English language has sometimes served to maintain the gulf of privilege between men and women.

Language and the mass media

The advent of the politics of pluralism and the opening up of political space in general in the 1990s has also been marked by a significant increase in the proportion of English newspapers and magazines in Kenya relative to those printed in Kiswahili. Until recently Kenya had three English-language dailies, the *Daily Nation* and the *Standard* (which are privately owned), and the *Kenya Times* (which is government owned), and two Kiswahili dailies, the *Taifa Leo* (a sister paper to the *Daily Nation*) and *Kenya Leo* (a sister paper to *Kenya Times*). Virtually the only weekly news magazine that appeared regularly was the *Weekly Review*.

Over the last few years, however, there have appeared on the Kenyan scene at least six English-language weekly newspapers, *The People*, the *Weekend Mail*, the *Nairobi Weekly*, *The Guardian*, *The East African* and the *Target*. The growth of the magazine industry, all in English, has been even more startling. The expansion has not only been in news magazines like *Society*, *Finance*, *Monthly Review*, *Economic Review* and the *Nairobi Law Monthly* but also in magazines catering for women and mothers, teenagers, business executives, motorists and so forth, even though most of these are available only in major cities like Nairobi and Mombasa.

In Uganda, the printing industry generally has been less developed than in Kenya and the print media came to a virtual standstill during the civil war and its immediate aftermath. It was only after the National Resistance Movement of Yoweri Museveni came to power in 1986 that the gradual revival of the print mass media began. At present the only daily that comes out regularly is the government-owned English newspaper, the *New Vision*. There are also a couple of weeklies, like the *Weekly Topic, The Star,* and *The Monitor,* which tend to be irregular. Ugandans also get a regular supply of Kenya's more established dailies as well as the *Weekly Review* magazine. There are also a few irregular weekly papers in Luganda, like the *Taifa Uganda Empya* and *Ngabo,* which are mainly available in Kampala.

Unlike the print media, the electronic mass media in both Kenya and Uganda are mainly under government control. Radio Uganda used to broadcast in English and, secondarily, in some 16 local languages until Idi Amin ordered that the local lingua franca, Kiswahili, be given some air time. Kenya, on the other hand, has maintained two radio services, the National Service in Kiswahili and the General Service in English. In addition, there are short programmes daily in 14 other local languages.

Uganda's television is also dominated by English-language programmes, even though Luganda and Kiswahili also play a small role in news transmissions for a few minutes each evening. Kenya's government-owned Kenya Broadcasting Corporation (KBC) television is divided almost equally between English and Kiswahili programmes. Since Kenya changed its laws in 1990 to allow for private television companies, however, there have been additional television channels like the Kenya Television Network (KTN). All of KTN's programmes are in English, and the company relies heavily on American programmes, from CNN headline news to American soap operas for entertainment. In its style of delivery, too, it seeks to emulate American television. At present KTN is available only in Nairobi but its programmes are immensely more popular in middle-class homes than those of the KBC.

Language use in creative literature

In theatre, while English plays are quite common, there is strong competition from Luganda theatre in Uganda, and from Kiswahili and, increasingly, Gikuyu theatre in Kenya. In fact, it seems that theatre in local languages tends to attract much larger African audiences than theatre in English.

If the English language is facing competition from some local languages in the performing arts, however, its status in the written creative arts is definitely more secure. The readership interested in reading novels, plays or poems in Kiswahili or Luganda, for example, seems rather narrow. English literature in general seems to enjoy a much wider readership than literature in local languages. According to Onyango Ogutu, the marketing manager of East African Educational Publishers, Kenya, sales of literary titles in local languages other than Kiswahili are very limited (personal interview, 15 July 1993).

More interesting, however, is the possibility that popular literature from the West, from the writings of James Hadley Chase and Harold Robbins to those of Sidney Sheldon and Danielle Steele, are in much higher demand than the 'more serious' English works of African creative writers like Ngugi wa Thiong'o and Chinua Achebe. Literary works by African writers, whether in English or in local languages, seem to be read mainly when they are set texts in school syllabuses.

It is this seeming appeal of popular literarure from the West that may have prompted Kenyan writers like Charles Mangua and David Maillu to experiment with local versions of this sub-genre. Their works became an instant success, leading to a rapid growth of the popular tradition in Kenya which now includes series from 'Afromance', 'Crime Series', 'Drumbeat Series', 'Pace Setters', 'Spear Books' among others. All these are writings which appear very popular with young people throughout the East African region.

The book publishing industry in general, in both Kenya and Uganda, has come to depend heavily on an English readership. The most important market zone for publishing companies is the school. And since English is the medium of instruction for virtually all subjects throughout the entire school system, publishers concentrate on producing English titles to tap this population. But since 1984 when Kiswahili became a compulsory and examinable subject in Kenya, the sale of Kiswahili titles has also increased tremendously (Onyango Ogutu, personal interview, 15 July 1993).

Language attitudes

The consolidation of English in Kenya and Uganda, however, is due not only to the educational, political and socio-economic dynamics in the region. It is also aided by social attitudes towards the language and its perceived value in society. Unfortunately, there has been little research on language attitudes in East Africa, and the little that is available is primarily impressionistic.

In her study on the choice of a lingua franca in Kampala, Scotton shows that in Uganda English is considered a language of socio-economic ascent and 'is valued as useful because a high economic status is equated with being able to speak English well. If one speaks English well, he is educated and has a good job' (1972: 82–93). In terms of prestige value, Mukama agrees that while local languages are loved and clung to, it is English that is admired and respected in Uganda (1991: 342).

The attitudes towards English noted in Uganda are no less prevalent in Kenya. In the words of Abdulaziz:

> The use of English in Kenya is a marker of good education and modernity. The level of competence and style of use of English helps to identify a person's level of education.... It also marks the speaker's degree of modernization and westernization – often, these days, regardless of the speaker's manner of dress. (1991: 400)

According to Abdulaziz, such attitudes are important in determining who speaks how to whom (1991: 401).

An important study on language attitudes in Kenya is that of Kembo Sure (1991). Sure shows that while attitudes towards both English and Kiswahili are sufficiently positive to allow for balanced bilingualism in the country, the substance of the attitudes towards these languages differs. The positive attitudes towards English are, by and large, 'instrumentally' motivated: 75 per cent of primary school students and 67.9 per cent of secondary school students felt that English would take one further in life than Kiswahili.

The favourable attitudes towards Kiswahili, on the other hand, are said to be 'integratively' motivated. While only 36.7 per cent of the student respondents felt that Kiswahili is a linguistic advantage in the job market, over 80 per cent regarded the language as essential for full participation in the 'national life' of the country.

Finally, Sure demonstrates that language attitudes change with age and level of education. More primary than secondary school students, for example, felt that English is a beautiful language, and would take one further in life than Kiswahili. In this regard Sure concludes that 'the secondary school pupils seem to want to downplay any attributes of English that may, even slightly, suggest that it is a superior language to Kiswahili', the national language of the country (1991: 23).

Language and national consciousness

The seemingly more nationalistic attitudes of secondary school pupils towards Kiswahili naturally bring us to the whole question of language and national consciousness. The absence of strong and generalized opposition to European languages, on one hand, and the apparent lack of strong commitment to promote local languages, on the other, have led some observers to suggest that in many parts of Africa there is less linguistic nationalism than has been observed in places like Malaysia, India and Bangladesh (Mazrui and Tidy, 1984: 299). And, as we argued earlier, during the colonial period nationalism actually led to demands for more rather than less English among the emergent middle class as part of the struggle for equality of opportunity in the educational sphere.

Nonetheless, nationalistic feelings that have sometimes challenged the hegemony of the English language in society have not been altogether absent. Perhaps the earliest expression of a political desire to reduce the role of English in Kenya came from the newly elected first president of the country, Mzee Jomo Kenyatta. After delivering a prepared speech in English to the first parliamentary congregation of the new republic, Kenyatta concluded by urging the house to free itself from 'linguistic slavery' by adopting Kiswahili as its language of official business (Republic of Kenya, 1965: column 8).

In fact Kenyatta was eager to see Kiswahili serve not only as the language of parliament, but also as the national language of the country in general. In this objective, he had the full backing of the ruling party, the Kenya African National Union (*East African Standard*, 7 April 1970). But these sentiments were obviously not shared by everyone. There was a small but influential group of politicians, led by the then attorney general of the country, Charles Njonjo, who were obviously not in favour of reducing the role of English in parliament or in the society at large (see, for example, Republic of Kenya, 1969: columns 2517–25).

After some ten years of recurrent debate, in and outside parliament, however, it was the nationalist position of Jomo Kenyatta that prevailed. In 1974, Kiswahili was declared the national language and, for the first time, English had to share the parliamentary platform with a local language. There has been no evidence, however, of any substantial investment on the part of the government to prepare Kiswahili for this onerous task. As a result, English has remained the primary language of parliament, and is probably slowly acquiring national credentials in competition with Kiswahili.

This emerging image of English as one of the possible national languages of the country may be due partly to its seeming linguistic localization. An East African, and perhaps even a Kenyan, brand of English may be in the making (Schmied, 1988). Sure is of the opinion that in Kenya 'nationalist attitudes are growing against English, especially among the youth, and these are working against the learning of the 'standard forms' of the language.... There is thus a distinct non-native form emerging that could be described as Kenyan English' (1991: 24).

But the more empirical section of Sure's own study demonstrates that, in fact, there are no antagonistic attitudes towards English among the youth. A local variety of English, therefore, may be emerging independently of any presumed sentiments of hostility towards the language. Once formed, that local variety may take English closer to other local languages in its acceptability as a 'Kenyan language'.

Nationalistic feelings in favour of a local language that would offer some challenge to the dominance of English in the political domains of the affairs of the country have also been expressed repeatedly in Uganda. On the eve of independence, for example, the ruling Uganda People's Congress (UPC) showed an early awareness of the need for a local alternative to English as a language of Ugandan politics. As a result, at its Annual Conference immediately after the country's attainment of independence, the UPC passed a resolution urging that Kiswahili be taught in Ugandan schools (Mazrui and Mazrui, 1995).

But the Uganda government of Milton Obote continued to drag its feet over the matter until the military took over power in 1971. It was a military dictator, then, Idi Amin Dada, who eventually declared Kiswahili the national language of Uganda and decreed its use on Uganda radio and television (Mazrui and Mazrui, 1995: 113). The peasant and proletarian background of its rank and file has made the military in Uganda generally more hostile than civilian governments to English. But, again, as in the case of Kenya, little else was done in terms of concrete investment to strengthen the position of Kiswahili as a national language.

In the turbulent years following Idi Amin's ouster from power, there was little change in language policy. After the National Resistance Movement came to power in January 1986, however, the issue of a local national language for the country surfaced once again. President Yoweri Museveni, himself a fluent speaker of Kiswahili, is said to be in favour of giving the language a more prominent role in Ugandan society and of reintroducing it in the school system:

> The government of President Yoweri Museveni has introduced the idea of developing Kiswahili in schools as part of the reforms envisaged in the Educational White Paper under debate. Education Minister Amanya Mushega said: 'We are going to have Kiswahili taught. What is wrong with people speaking Kiswahili ... and English at the same time?' (*The Standard*, 26 June 1993).

In this statement and in its tone the Minister of Education was reacting to opposition aroused by the government proposal to introduce Kiswahili in schools and elevate it to the status of a national language. As indicated in earlier chapters, this opposition to Kiswahili in Uganda goes back to the colonial days and has come mainly from the Baganda, the single largest ethnic group in the country. Strong Baganda ethno-nationalism has always been in favour of promoting Luganda as the national language of the country.

Among Ugandans of non-Baganda origin, however, Luganda is potentially a hegemonic language. Though it has been acquired as an additional language by an increasing number of speakers (of, mainly, other Bantu languages), its demographic might is still located within the confines of Baganda ethnicity. Making Luganda the national language of the country would be seen as a linguistic empowerment of the already powerful Baganda at the expense of other ethnic groups. This continuing tug-of-war between advocates of Kiswahili, on the one hand, and advocates of Luganda, on the other, creates a political climate in favour of the further consolidation of the English language.

The Luganda situation in Uganda may be contrasted with that of Gikuyu in Kenya. Both of these are *heartland ethnic languages*. A heartland ethnic language combines two characteristics: It is the language of the largest ethnic group in the country and is the primary ethnic language of the capital city. It is in that sense that Luganda is the heartland ethnic language of Uganda, and Gikuyu the heartland ethnic language of Kenya.

Luganda has generated more ethno-linguistic nationalism among its speakers than Gikuyu has done. While Luganda-speakers (the Baganda) have been the most implacable foes of any pro-Kiswahili policy in Uganda, Gikuyu-speakers have been in the vanguard of *promoting* Kiswahili in Kenya. Jomo Kenyatta combined an attachment to his native Gikuyu *culture* with an attachment to the Swahili *language* (or Kiswahili); Kenya's leading novelist, Ngugi wa Thiong'o, is a champion of the Gikuyu language as a vehicle of culture and the Swahili language as a vehicle of national and international politics.

The Baganda's hostility towards Kiswahili in Uganda has favoured the fortunes of the English language in the country. The Gikuyu's acceptance of at least the instrumental value of Kiswahili for national purposes has sometimes harmed the fortunes of the English language in Kenya. The Baganda's linguistic nationalism is anti-Kiswahili but pro-English. The Gikuyu are less nationalistic on the issue of language, but in any case their leaders have sometimes promoted Kiswahili even at the expense of English.

Kiswahili as a national language has also been caught up in the politics of class conciousness in the two countries. Partly because the heartland 'tribe' of Uganda was a monarchy before and during colonial rule, and partly because the British gave the Baganda a privileged position in the national hierarchy during colonial rule, class consciousness among the Baganda is more sharply hierarchical than among the Gikuyu. On the contrary, the Gikuyu had been a relatively egalitarian society before colonial rule, and suffered the main brunt of white settler oppression during colonial rule. These differences in the fortunes of the two heartland 'tribes' had repercussions on linguistic attitudes.

The Baganda élite have regarded Kiswahili openly as the language of 'the lower classes' (*Bakopi*, Luganda for peasants) since Kiswahili was the language of the workplace and the market, and the language of soldiers from the barracks. Less openly, some Baganda aristocrats have also regarded Kiswahili as the language of 'lesser breeds' in the ethnic sense, the northern ethnic groups despised by such haughty aristocrats.

This negative proletarianization of the image of Kiswahili in Uganda has helped the cause of the English language. The Baganda have opposed pro-Kiswahili policies in Uganda both because they regarded them as a threat to Buganda and Luganda, but also because the Baganda's hierarchical status conciousness has demoted Kiswahili into a lumpen-language.

In Kenya, on the other hand, the image of Kiswahili is more class-neutral. It was once the language of 'sultans' at the Coast. It later became the preferred political language of independent Kenya's founder-president, Jomo Kenyatta. But it has always been the language of the market, the workplace and, in parts of the country, the language of the family and the home. The heartland 'tribe' social egalitarianism contributed towards making Kiswahili in Kenya class-neutral – a factor which helped Kiswahili's national image and might at times have militated against the interest of the English language in Kenya. Language nationalists in Kenya have sometimes opposed English partly because of its presumed class status as a medium of the élite, and have advocated Kiswahili partly because of its seeming relative class neutrality.

In addition to politicians, poets and other creative writers have sought to counter-balance the pervasiveness of English with local languages. Perhaps the most prominent and most influential figure has been Ngugi wa Thiong'o, the Kenyan writer now working and residing in the United States. Assuming a quasi-Whorfian position, Ngugi has accused the English language of being intrinsically racist and imperialistic, of devaluing the 'others' and controlling their mental universe (1986). He himself turned increasingly to using his mother tongue, Gikuyu, in his creative writing, And it is due to this supposed imperialistic role of Western languages in Africa that Ngugi decided to wage a campaign against them in favour of Kiswahili as a world language (1991).

The sentiments of poets and politicians notwithstanding, however, there is little doubt that the social, economic and technological developments and dynamics in the region, as well as globally, are gradually leading to the consolidation of English in East African society, 'nativizing' it in the process while at the same time giving it a more global outlook.

A tale of two Englishes: a conclusion

Despite the many areas of convergence, Kenya and Uganda also manifest several features of divergence in their experiences with the English language. We began this study by referring to the special advantages which the English language had enjoyed in the colonial period in Uganda – the language of kings and aristocrats in southern Uganda, in a colony which was protected against a white settler invasion. We also referred to the disadvantages suffered by the English language in the earlier years of settler rule in Kenya, without influential African aristocrats to plead the African case at Westminster or the Colonial Office.

After independence the advantages and disadvantages were switched around, but for reasons which seemed at first to be unconnected with the colonial factors. The English language sustained a number of reverses in Uganda, arising out of the horrendous instability of the country after the mid-1960s. On the other hand, the English language enjoyed a number of windfalls in post-colonial Kenya as the country became at once one of the most stable and most internationalized in Africa from 1963 into the early 1990s.

The first crisis of stability in Uganda occurred in 1966 and was partially linked to precisely the influence of those Uganda monarchies which had once favoured the fortunes of English. A confrontation between the kingdom of Buganda and the central government of Uganda in 1966 led to an attack on the king's palace and his flight into exile in Britain. The central government put Buganda under a state of emergency indefinitely, and abolished all the monarchies of Uganda in 1967.

The kingdoms that had once favoured the fortunes of the English languge in Uganda were now either under occupation or otherwise in decline. The Baganda especially had been the vanguard of the English-speaking élite of the country – dominating most of the modern liberal professions. The 1966 crisis put them in eclipse.

In 1969 Mutesa II died in exile in London under mysterious circumstances. He was a symbol of how anglicized the king of the Baganda had become. Indeed, in 1939, the elders had chosen him (among his father's sons) partly because he had a stronger command of the English language and was more anglicized. His death in 1969 re-emphasized the decline of the Baganda not only as a monarchical people but also as the vanguard of Uganda's English-speaking élite.

Then came Idi Amin's military coup in January 1971. His decade in power (1971–9) was a further setback to the English language. The new rulers had a limited command of the imperial language and were often hostile to the Westernized intelligentsia. Thousands of intellectuals were either killed or fled into exile.

In addition, Idi Amin's government elevated Kiswahili to the status of one of the national languages of Uganda, pushed it as a broadcasting language on radio and television, and was hoping to promote it in the educational system. The Amin years were, in this sense, the golden years of Kiswahili in Uganda, and to that extent a setback to the supremacy of the English language.

In 1979 Idi Amin invaded Tanzania and provoked a counter-attack by the Tanzanian army, all the way to Kampala, forcing the Ugandan ruler into exile. There followed a few short years of the semi-occupation by Tanzanian armed forces (1979–82). They were basically speakers of Kiswahili. The streets of the major cities of Uganda echoed with a more sophisticated Kiswahili than had been heard in the country on such a scale before. More Ugandans learned Kiswahili for pragmatic and security reasons. In some cases this may have been at the expense of trying to improve their English. At any rate, the supremacy of the English language seemed more questionable when Uganda was under partial Tanzanian occupation.

The second Obote administration in Uganda (1980–5) overlapped with this Tanzanian phase. But the return of Milton Obote brought an additional setback to the fortunes of the English language. The country plunged deeper and deeper into a civil war which destroyed many schools and caused great damage to the entire educational system – and thus to the teaching and learning of the English language.

In 1986 Yoweri Museveni's rival army at last captured power. The country has made considerable progress in pacification and stabilization under Museveni. But there remain some questions relevant to the fortunes of the English language. First, how fast will Uganda's educational infrastructure continue to recover after two decades of chaos and tyranny? Second, will Yoweri Museveni leave the supremacy of the English language unchallenged? There are signs that he would like to improve the status of Kiswahili in the country. His own command of Kiswahili may be better than that of any Ugandan president since the country's independence in 1962. He also shows signs of being more pan-Africanist than almost any of his previous seven predecessors as presidents of Uganda. These factors may eventually incline him towards challenging the supremacy of English as the national language of Uganda.

If Uganda was a case of colonial advantages and post-colonial setbacks for English, Kenya is a reverse case of colonial disadvantages and post-colonial windfalls for this imperial language. One windfall has been the rise of Nairobi as arguably Africa's leading international centre. It houses the United Nations Environmental Programme (UNEP), the first UN Agency ever to be located outside of the Western world. Nairobi has also been the headquarters of the All-Africa Conference of Churches, and the regional capital of a number of inter-African and pan-African enterprises. Nairobi has also become the favourite venue in sub-Saharan Africa for world congresses – including the UN Conference on Women in 1985, major UNESCO meetings, one important World Bank–International Monetary Fund meeting, and such academic congresses as the World Conference of Philosophy in 1991. The internationalization of Nairobi has favoured the fortunes of the English language not only within the city itself but in the country as a whole. Kampala fares less favourably by comparison.

Yet another windfall for the English language in post-colonial Kenya is the pro-Western foreign policy which the Kenya government under both President Jomo Kenyatta and President Daniel Arap Moi decided to follow. This policy encouraged a constant flow of English-speaking experts and expertise into Kenya, including books and international magazines. In contrast Uganda under Milton Obote's 'Move to the Left' (1969–71) alienated many Westerners, while Idi Amin's expulsion of British Asians in 1972, and his record of brutal rule, drastically curtailed interaction with the Western world. The subsequent general instability of the country kept many Westerners at arm's length even under Obote's second administration, when he tried to mend his fences with the West. In short, foreign policy has implications for the fortunes of the English language. Kenya's foreign policy favoured English; Uganda's fluctuating policies did not.

The fortunes of the English language in post-colonial Kenya were also helped by the fact that Kenya's rulers remained civilian. Civilian rulers in most of Africa tend to be better educated and more Westernized than their military counterparts. The civilians therefore have a better command of the imperial language and usually a vested interest in it. Kenya's stability under civilian administrations therefore favoured the consolidation of the English language in the country. Uganda's military rulers were sometimes hostile to the imperial language, partly because they themselves were less well educated than were the civilian rulers they had over-thrown.

Another bonus for the English language in post-colonial Kenya is the publishing infrastructure of the country. Kenya has the most flourishing publishing industry in sub-Saharan African after South Africa and Nigeria. Varied publications in English, as well as Kiswahili, appear almost every day in Nairobi. There is also, as we indicated, a significant range of newspapers and magazines in English published in Kenya.

By contrast, publishing in Uganda – always more limited than in Kenya – has shrunk dramatically as a result of the many severe economic and political problems since 1971. Because of foreign exchange constraints, fewer books are being imported into Uganda from abroad, and yet the local capacity to publish alternatives in Kampala is weaker than ever.

And so the saga of contrasts between Uganda and Kenya continues. Seldom have two African countries so geographically close to each other, and once ruled by the same imperial power, manifested sharper contrasting characteristics in the domain of language and political culture. In those very contradictions lie major insights into the interplay between precolonial continuities (such as monarchies), colonial legacies (such as the English language) and the dynamics of post-colonial societies.

11
Roots of Kiswahili

Colonialism, Nationalism & the Dual Heritage

Kiswahili is one if the most successful indigenous lingua francas in Africa. Next to Arabic it is perhaps the most pan-African in terms of its transnational scope, with a growing population of speakers estimated to be in the tens of millions. With a tradition of writing that goes back centuries before European colonial rule, it has one of the richest literary heritages on the continent. It is known to have served as an important instrument of mass mobilization in the struggle against colonialism in both German and British East Africa. In addition, the language has fostered vertical and horizontal integration, nationally as well as regionally, and has functioned as a medium of trade, religion, education, civil administration, practical politics and collective bargaining throughout the East African region. Increasingly, too, Kiswahili has consolidated its potential as a language of science and technology.

Partly because of these achievements of the language, it quickly came to acquire a sentimental value in addition to its older instrumental value. Many Africans developed strong nationalist sentiments towards Kiswahili, seeing it as a language of national sovereignty, as a possible symbol of transnational and continental unity, and as a reminder of the common origins of people of African descent now scattered throughout the globe.

At the more local level, we have the case of Kiswahili being declared the national language of Kenya and Tanzania. In both these countries, citizenship is constitutionally defined, in part, in terms of some degree of proficiency in Kiswahili. At the transnational level is Kiswahili's role not only as a language of intercourse and integration across national boundaries in East Africa, but also as a potential symbol of continental pan-Africanism. Kiswahili today is taught as a subject not only in its original home in East Africa, but also in universities on the opposite side of the continent, in countries like Ghana and Nigeria. Prominent writers like Wole Soyinka and Ngugi wa Thiong'o have sometimes campaigned for Kiswahili as a language of Africa. Finally, at the transcontinental level, it is the African language that is in highest demand in the African diaspora, especially among African Americans. From the ethno-nationalist confines of its native speakers on the narrow strip of the coast of East Africa, therefore, Kiswahili has stretched its wings outward to become, albeit with some exaggeration, the language of pan-African nationalism on a global scale.

The kind of political consciousness that I have termed 'nationalism', however, is often a reaction to the politics of the 'other'. And the 'other' that Africans have often reacted to in nationalistic terms in the twentieth century has tended to be the European 'other', primarily because of the brutal and humiliating experiences of enslavement and colonization. As a result, the nationalist sentiments towards Kiswahili were bound to involve a rejection of any seemingly negative projection of the language which may have been engendered by colonial discourse.

African nationalism and linguistic purism

One important dimension of this colonial projection was Kiswahili's presumed 'dual nature', part 'African' and part 'Arab'. Kiswahili was often defined, sometimes quite pejoratively, as a hybrid child (Whiteley, 1969: 7) of a union between the languages of Africans and Arabs – or the 'highest of animals' i.e. Africans, and the 'lowest of human beings', i.e. Arabs (Captain Stigand, 1912: 130). Half-baked ethnographic ideas from Europe thus went on to create the impression that the achievements of Kiswahili would not have been possible without its presumed 'more human' Arab parentage.

In reaction to this colonial, sub-humanizing, sociolinguistic conception, therefore, African nationalists rejected not only the suggestion that Africans were less than human, but also the thesis that Kiswahili was less than wholly African. Kiswahili and its achievements now came to be presented as the product of the collective genius of the African people themselves who, at the maximum, just borrowed items from Arabic – as English borrowed from French, for example – to meet certain functional needs in their expanding world. Mohammed Hyder, for example, assumed this typically nationalist position when he commented:

> many people have held the view believed to be originally from the Rev. Canon Hellier that Swahili is a hybrid of Bantu and Arab origin. The author does not share this view.... In biological terminology, one would say that the so called hybridization is not and never has been a genetic process which affects the form and structure of the language, but a phenotypic manifestation related to function. (1966: 81)

In reaction to the colonial stance, therefore, African nationalists generally have been inclined towards a quasi-purist position with regard to the origins of Kiswahili. Kiswahili is regarded as having evolved 'purely' from an African foundation on a Bantu base. And the supposedly 'later' contributions to the language from Arabic and other languages are of a nature that has left Kiswahili's Africanity completely intact, both in form and structure.

One of the problems of this nationalist position, however, is the basic assumption that Arabic is *not* an African language at all. Nationalists have reacted to the thesis of Kiswahili's dual heritage partly because they have regarded Arabic as alien to Africa. If Kiswahili was a linguistic fusion of, say, Chigiryama (a Bantu language of the Kenya Coast) and Orominya (a Cushitic language of southern Ethiopia), both believed to be fundamentally and unambiguously African, the claims of a hybrid origin of the language would probably not have raised any nationalist hostility. But precisely because Arabic is deemed foreign to Africa, and a language belonging to the 'other', suggestions of its formative role in the evolution of Kiswahili are seen to be in disharmony with the position of the nationalists.

Arabic: African or Arabian?

But how un-African, in fact, is the Arabic language? We may determine the Africanness, or otherwise, of a particular language in terms of the demography of its speakers and/or its historical-linguistic origins. If the language is spoken as a native tongue by a significant population of people indigenous to Africa, then there is a case for regarding it as an African language. If English, for example, were to be spoken as a mother tongue by sections of the Ibo, Zulu, and Gikuyu people, then we could claim that English is an African language in a demographic sense. This, of course, would not preclude the fact that English is, at the same time, an American language, a Caribbean language, or a European language. A language could conceivably belong to a number of regions or continents at the same time.

With regard to Arabic, specifically, over 70 per cent of the lands in which it is spoken as a native tongue, and a larger proportion of those who speak it as a mother tongue are, in fact, in Africa. In addition, the majority of these African speakers of Arabic are not migrants from the Arabian peninsula; rather, they are indigenous to the continent of Africa. They are a people who, in a sense, became Arabized by a process of linguistic assimilation. There is an ethno-linguistic principle among the Arabs that anyone to whom Arabic is a first language is automatically Arab regardless of his/her national or 'racial' origin. Through this linguistic conversion many people became Arab to a point where Arab identity today has become a truly 'multiracial' and 'multinational' phenomenon. As Erskine Childers put it:

> The Arab world ... comprises very many widely varying races or historical groups. The short list is bewildering, and distinguishing racial definitions are themselves treacherous. From west to east, the list must include Berbers, Carthaginians, Romans, Vandals, Arabians, Turkomans, Egyptians, Nubians, Haemites, Greeks, Armenians, Circassians, Assyrians, Babylonians, Hittites, Sumarians, Kurds, Persians, and a small host of ancient migratory infusions who it is safer to describe simply as Semitic. (1960: 17)

The acquisition of Arabic as a native tongue by Egyptians, Berbers, Nubians, Tuaregs and Sudanese, therefore, constitutes one important credential that makes Arabic an African language.

It is possible, of course, to go a step further by questioning the very boundaries of the continent we call Africa. There is no reason why Africa should end at the Red Sea and not at the Arabian Gulf, given that the Arabian Peninsula itself formed part of a common land mass with Africa before the great rift. As Ali Mazrui reminds us, the decision to make Africa end at the Red Sea rather than at the Arabian/Persian Gulf was made neither by Africans nor by Arabs, but by European map makers and cartographers (1986: 23). Even geologically, it has been argued that there is good reason to regard the Arabian Peninsula as part of the continent of Africa. In the words of Paul Bohannan, 'Geologically, the whole of the Arabian Peninsula must be considered as unitary with the African continent' (1966: 42).

In the final analysis, however, we are now all bound by these boundaries imposed by Eurocentricists for mainly imperialistic reasons. Nonetheless, the possibility alluded to by Ali Mazrui and Paul Bohannan does lead us more naturally to the proposition that Arabic may be an African language in an historical-linguistic sense, in addition to being one in a demographic sense of the word. And it is to this historical parameter of Africanity that we must now turn.

Arabic belongs to a group of languages classified as Semitic and long regarded as Asiatic in origin. The supposed Asiatic roots of Semitic languages, however, may be a thesis that was, initially, inspired by the Eurocentric conception that equated language with 'race'. Semitic languages were seen as belonging to lighter-skinned races in Asia which had no 'genetic' links with the darker 'Negroid' peoples of Africa. This racial classification of languages served well to reinforce the Eurocentric tendency to claim for itself the achievements of others. Ancient Egyptians were once 'white-washed' so that their achievements could be appropriated as part of a putative European heritage. In the words of Martin Bernal:

> For 18th- and 19th- century [European] Romanticists and racists it was simply intolerable for Greece, which was seen not merely as the epitome of Europe but also as its pure childhood, to have been the result of the mixture of native Europeans and colonizing Africans and Semites. Therefore the Ancient model had to be overthrown and replaced by something more acceptable. (1987: 1)

In a similar way, European racists may now have found the racial differentiation of Arabic speakers from the darker-skinned and accursed 'Nigritic' speaking peoples of Africa necessary in order to come to terms with the Arab contribution to world civilization in the more recent era of Islam. It is the politics of racism, then, that may have led to the persistence of a Eurocentric tradition that regards Arabic as fundamentally non-African.

By the turn of the twentieth century some linguists had begun to reject this equation of language with race. It was not until Joseph Greenberg (1963) came up with a new 'family tree' of African languages, however, that the racial paradigm of language classification in Africa was challenged altogether. In particular, Greenberg posited an Afro-Asiatic family which subsumed Ancient Egyptian, Berber, Chadic, Cushitic and Semitic groups of languages. For the first time, therefore, the Semitic languages of Asia, like Arabic and Hebrew, were seen to have some linguistic affinity not only with the Semitic languages of Africa, like Amharic, Gurage, Tigre, and Tigrinya – which happen to be significantly greater in number than those in Asia – but also with the almost two hundred non-Semitic African languages of the Afro-Asiatic family. Greenberg's work, complemented by other evidence, ultimately led some linguists to speculate that Semitic languages may originally have spread from the African continent, adding that 'the unity of the Afro-Asiatic language family does not support any theory of Asian influence on Africa in historic times' (Curtin *et al.*, 1978:121).

If this thesis about the origins of Semitic languages is correct, therefore, we would have some historical reasons for regarding Arabic as an African language. In addition to the demographic characteristic of having the majority of its lands and native speakers situated in Africa, Arabic would also qualify as an African language on the basis of its historical-linguistic links with the continent.

Proceeding, then, from the possibility that Africa is where Semitic languages were founded, Asia can be regarded as a continent where they became sacralized. With regard to Arabic, in particular, the advent of Islam marked the beginnings of its transformation into a sacred language of the religion. Arabic now became intrinsically religious not only because it is the chosen language of Islamic ritual, but, more importantly, because it is regarded by Muslims as the language in which Allah revealed the holy Qur'an to the Prophet Muhammad. Reading the Qur'an in

Arabic, even when one does not understand its meaning, is considered an act of piety in its own right. That is why the Qur'an is perhaps the most widely read book in its original form in human history.

Having sacralized the language, Islam then gave Arabic a new momentum of spread. As the religion continued to expand in Asia and across a large section of Africa, it carried with it the Arabic language. And the encounter between this language of Islam and other African languages ultimately gave rise to what may be described as Afro-Islamic languages like Kiswahili, Nubi and Somali in East Africa, as well as Hausa, Fulfulde, Kanuri and Mandinka in West Africa.

Afro-Islamic languages may be defined as those whose native speakers are predominantly Muslim and whose vocabulary, especially its religious idiom, is influenced heavily by Arabic. Ethnic groups bound by Afro-Islamic languages are virtually all neo-Islamic in a *cultural* sense. This does not mean that their individual members are necessarily Muslim in religious faith; but it does mean that they have a strong Islamic orientation in their cultural ethos. Not all Arabs in Lebanon, for example, are Muslim in faith. But even the country's Christian Arab population betrays a strong Islamic inclination in its cultural predisposition. It is in this cultural sense, then, that ethnic groups like the Hausa, the Mandinka and the Swahili, for example, can be said to be neo-Islamic. And it is partly this deep-rooted culture of Islam which has rendered their languages Afro-Islamic by our definition.

Kiswahili's duality: the imperial connection

Within colonial discourse, however, the conception of the Swahili language as an African-Arab mixture of a sort may not have been unrelated to the politics of the time. As we have learnt from the African colonial experience in general, colonial military invasions and subsequent rule were often preceded by a series of Christian missionary ventures. Christian missionary enterprises were almost indispensable in laying the ideological foundations of colonialism. The civilizing mission was initially based on the Europeanization of Christianity, on the myth that Christianity was European and Euro-Christians themselves were the bearers of human civilization. Before administrative colonialism could be established securely, therefore, the primitiveness and barbarity of the 'native' had to be tamed by the divine power of the gospel. The education of the 'native' was thus inseparable from the attempted Christian saving of 'heathen' souls.

But communication with the indigenous population proved problematic for the missionary establishment. The 'natives' were not familiar with European languages, and the Christian initiation of the population through the spiritual transportation of Jesus to the 'dark continent' certainly could not be made to wait until the African had acquired a foreign language. The solution was to get the bearers of the biblical word to learn the languages of the Africans, a linguistic task that they assumed with characteristic missionary zeal. One of the results of this policy was the codification of several African languages – the introduction of writing in the Latin script and some degree of standardization.

This linguistic policy of the missionary establishment, however, did not always solve the problem of spiritual communication. Apart from the question of which African language or set of languages to select from the multitude for missionary work, there was consideration of what language would be most effective in spreading the Christian word. A section of missionaries, inspired by David

Livingstone, believed that the best way of reaching the African spiritually was through his 'tribal' milieu and medium. Missionary acquisition of all and every possible African language, therefore, was encouraged, again as a matter of policy.

Other missionaries, however, were highly suspicious of many of the African languages. They feared that a majority of these languages were so infused with idolatrous and animistic concepts that their use in African Christianity was bound to corrupt the Christian message. To these missionaries only European languages could impart the true Christian message; and if Christianity was to be truly consummated in Africa, there was no satisfactory alternative to teaching European languages. But God could not be made to wait, and hence an interim linguistic arrangement had to be forged. It was a section of these missionaries who became inclined towards Kiswahili, which, in their opinion, had virtually lost its 'idolatrous' and 'animistic' content due to its long exposure to the outside world and to monotheism. The fact that Kiswahili was already a language of wider communication added to its credentials, and soon Kiswahili was to become the major language of East African Christianity. Just as Kiswahili came to aid the spread of Christianity, the Christian church in turn came to aid the further spread of Kiswahili.

Kiswahili as a language of Christianity, however, was not without its adversaries. Some missionaries were suspicious of the kind of monotheism supposedly inherent in the Kiswahili language. To these missionaries the monotheistic content of Kiswahili was essentially Islamic, and thus wholly objectionable and antithetical to Christianity. They sustained this argument by pointing to the Arabic elements in Kiswahili. Capitalizing on the Eurocentric equation that Islam was as Arab as Christianity was European, they argued that Arabisms in Kiswahili necessarily carried the substance and spirit of Islam. To these people, then, the 'Arabness' of Kiswahili discredited it as a possible language of Christianity; and so the Christian campaign against Islam was also extended to Kiswahili language.

This tendency to associate Kiswahili with Islam was by no means restricted to Kenya. In German East Africa, or what was later to become Tanganyika, the same fears were expressed. Wright, for example, notes:

> In Germany, Director Buchner proved to be an unrelenting foe of Swahili, going so far in a speech before the Kolonialrat in 1905 as to declare that it was so irredeemably mixed with Islam that every expedient ought to be employed to obstruct their joint penetration … Buchner's opposition to Swahili was adopted and expanded by Julius Richter, a member of the Berlin Committee. Richter delivered a diatribe during the Kolonial Kongress in 1905 against the pernicious influence of Islam everywhere in Africa. Isolating East Africa as the scene of the worst danger, he envisaged a mosque alongside every coastman's hut, and took the official support for Swahili to be blatantly pro-Islamic.(1971: 113)

Naturally this fear of Islam led to the tendency to give undue prominence to the Arabness of Kiswahili language.

From pidgin to Bantu?

As intimated earlier, a debate has long raged about the origins of Kiswahili that has pitted nationalist scholarship against colonial scholarship. While colonial scholarship, based mainly on ethnographic methods, tended to promote the theory of the 'dual nature' of Kiswahili's roots, nationalists have insisted on its exclusively Bantu origins.

The more advanced methods of linguistics, in contrast to those of ethnography, however, came to challenge the idea that Kiswahili is a linguistic hybrid. Historical linguists argued that the language was African, and specifically Bantu, in form and origin, and that its supposed Arabness was merely a product of linguistic borrowing, a phenomenon that is no more an attribute of Kiswahili than it is of any other language.

Where historical linguists and some nationalists seem to part ways is on the question of the longevity of Kiswahili. In addition to establishing the Bantu origins of Kiswahili, linguists also tried, less successfully perhaps, to put a date on its historical point of emergence as an independent language. The idea is that there existed a hypothetical (reconstructed) parent language, so to speak, which together with other hypothetical 'parents' and 'grandparents' belonged to a hypothetical family of Eastern Bantu languages. These hypothetical linguistic parents, or proto-languages as linguists would call them, were more like amoebas than humans. The amoeba would reproduce essentially by splitting into two. Each of these parts would now have a life of its own, grow, and eventually reproduce, again by splitting into two. The same principle applies to linguistic reproduction, and a language is said to have come into being at the point at which its parent splits into two or more independent languages.

For historical linguists, then, the task was one of determining at exactly what point Kiswahili, Pokomo, Mijikenda and others separated from a hypothetical umbrella Sabaki parent to become independent languages. According to Ohly (1973) the language originated at some time before the tenth century. Somewhat in agreement with Ohly, Nurse and Spear place the birth of Kiswahili after AD 500 and proceed to suggest that by the ninth century 'an early form of Swahili was probably spoken in these coastal settlements, not merely in the north but at least as far South as Kilwa' (1985: 49).

Swahili nationalists, however, are bothered by this 'Eurocentric' tendency to ignore oral sources from the traditions of the Swahili society itself in connection with the history of their language – and, of course, their people. To them, this is tantamount to European appropriation of Swahili history. Chiraghdin (1974), for example, recounts the local version of the history of Kiswahili as having originated from a pre-existing Kingozi supposedly spoken at one time around the Lamu archipelago on the northern coast of Kenya. Using arguments based on observations contained in the second century document *Periplus of the Erythraean* Sea, Chiraghdin further suggests that there is no reason to believe that 'Kiswahili' could not have existed prior to the second century of the Christian era.

Chiraghdin's arguments are certainly not based on any scientific data; they are merely based on scientific reasoning. And partly in support of this claim of an earlier beginning in the evolution of Kiswahili Mazrui and Shariff (1994: 64–9) have suggested that the language may have once originated as a pidgin, later developing into a creole and culminating in a phenomenon that has sometimes been described as decreolization. Let us look briefly at what all this means..

A *pidgin* is essentially an auxiliary language which develops to fulfil a narrow range of linguistic functions. It arises in a situation in which there are several linguistic groups of people who need to communicate with each other for reasons of trade, for example, but lack a common medium of communication. Precisely because of its limited functions which usually do not involve the necessity of expressing abstract and/or complex thought, a pidgin would have a small range of vocabulary drawn, to a very large extent, from one language. Its grammatical structure would also be somewhat 'simpler' and would be based, to a large extent, on some universal features of the grammar of human languages.

In time, a pidgin may acquire extended functions as areas of interaction between peoples from different linguistic groups increase. Slavery, the emergence of new administrative structures in a community, a high incidence of intermarriages among members of different ethnic groups – these are some examples of the human experiences which could diversify the functions of a pidgin. This functional diversification not seldom leads to the gradual acquisition of a pidgin as a first, and sometimes the only, language by a significant group of people. Eventually it may become a first language to members of an entire society. Once this happens, once a pidgin becomes the first language of a speech community, then it is said to have become a *creole*. There is evidence, for example, that what is today called Nigerian Pidgin is already becoming a creole as an increasing number of Nigerian children are growing up speaking it as their first language.

The central difference, then, between a *pidgin* and a *creole* is that the latter has what we may call native speakers, while the former does not. The vocabulary and structure of a pidgin are generally carried over into a creole. But because a creole is expected to perform many more functions than a pidgin it gradually acquires an expanded lexicon and a more elaborate grammar. In such cases the languages that exist within the immediate environment of the creole, become the main source of its elaborated lexicon and grammatical system. In lexis, however, a creole, like any other language, may continue to borrow from various other sources.

This process may not stop here. A creole may now be *decreolized*. It may draw more and more from one or more of its surrounding languages to eventually acquire all the features, all the complexities, the depth and breadth, of other human languages. In essence a decreolized language will have lost virtually all traces of its pidgin and creole genesis.

The question that Mazrui and Shariff raise, therefore, is whether Kiswahili could have begun as a pidgin of Arabic as early as 100 AD or so, when the author of the *Periplus of the Erythraean Sea* travelled to East Africa. Is it possible that this pidgin later developed into a creole as more and more people on the East African coast acquired it as their first and only language? And could this creole tongue eventually have been decreolized, gradually taking on the structural features of one or more of the Bantu languages around it, in time becoming fully 'Bantuized'?

Nurse and Spear (1985) classify Kiswahili as a Sabaki language belonging, with many other languages like Pokomo, Zigula, Pare and Zaramo, to the North-eastern Coast Group of the Eastern Bantu Family. Descriptive linguistics has also demonstrated that Kiswahili, like virtually any other language, is divided into regional dialects like Chimiini, Kibajuni, Kisiu, Kipate, Kiamu, Kimvita, Kivumba, Kiunguja and so forth, all of which are, to one degree or another, mutually intelligible. Could this Bantu classification of Kiswahili be the end result of a long evolutionary process that began with an East African pidgin Arabic many centuries ago?

Building on an earlier study by himself and Derek Nurse, Thomas Hinnebusch offers an excellent critique of the Mazrui and Shariff hypothesis. In so doing, he also provides compelling arguments against positing pidgin Arabic roots for Kiswahili and in favour of an exclusively Bantu origin of the language (Hinnebusch, 1996). In spite of this linguistic evidence, however, which seems to support the nationalist position on the origin of Kiswahili, the professional perspective of historical linguists falls short of satisfying some of the nationalists on the question of the historical longevity of the language.

Conclusion

We have seen how, as a result of the colonial and neocolonial experiences, Kiswahili became entrapped in a Eurocentric racial equation that posits a 'two-nature theory' of the language, polarized between its supposed 'Arabness' and supposed 'Africanness'. Arabic is said to belong to a Semitic race, other African languages are said to belong to a 'Negroid' race, and by implication Kiswahili, because of its duality, is seen as *sui generis*, neither Semitic nor African.

Fully accepting the proposition that Arabic is foreign to Africa, African nationalists were quickly inclined to the other extreme of linguistic purism, denying 'external' contributions to the formation of the language. While this nationalist position ultimately received the support of historical linguistics, its sentiments of 'purism' betray what are essentially Eurocentric terms of reference. Furthermore, these African beginnings are sometimes claimed, especially by some nationalists who are ethnically Swahili, to go back to a more distant past than the present linguistic evidence seems to support. The European racist fixation with 'Western' civilization as purely European and ancient in origin, was now counteracted with an African nationalist fixation with origins of 'African' achievements as 'purely' African and historically deep. Following in the footsteps of European racists, African nationalists now also came to trek the dangerous path of ethnocentricism in quest of 'racial' and linguistic purity and longevity.

12

The Secularization
of an Afro-Islamic Language

Church, State & Marketplace
in the Spread of Kiswahili

The most important indigenous language in Africa is Kiswahili, otherwise known as 'Swahili'. It belongs to the Bantu family of African tongues, which range from Luganda on Lake Victoria to the Zulu tongue in South Africa. What is distinctive about Kiswahili is that it is at once the most idiomatically Islamic of all the Bantu languages and the most geographically successful in terms of spread. Let us first examine this Islamic genesis.

The Islamic origins

Much of the debate about the origins of Kiswahili has focused on whether it is a product of the interaction between the Arabic language and Bantu languages. In this chapter we focus on the 'parenting role' not of Arabic but of Islam as a civilization. Languages do not spring only from other languages; they often evolve out of whole cultures or civilizations. The impact of Arabic upon the development of Kiswahili is part of the wider impact of Islam. It is not accidental that classical Swahili poetry is at once part of the heritage of Africa and part of the universal legacy of Islam.

This is therefore not another case of denying Africa credit for one of its own achievements – comparable to the old theories which wrongly traced the origins of the stone structures of Great Zimbabwe to the Phoenicians. The influence of Islam on Kiswahili is similar to the impact of the Normans upon the evolution of the English language.

In any case, Kiswahili is one arena of *mutual* penetration between Islamic civilization and Africa. Just as many Arabic expressions are part of Islam's contribution to Kiswahili, so the great Swahili states and culture were part of Africa's contribution to the wider civilization of Islam. Some of the great classical Swahili poems constitute both African and Islamic literary achievements.

The Islamic origins of Kiswahili partly lie in its readiness to borrow concepts, words, and idioms from the Arabic language and from Islamic civilization. Although its structure is completely Bantu and not remotely Semitic, Kiswahili has borrowed a higher proportion of its vocabulary from Arabic than English has from

Latin. Sometimes there is almost a 'balancing act' in vocabulary between Bantu and Arabic. The words for north and south are probably Bantu (*kusini* and *kaskazini*), whereas the words for east and west are Arabic-derived (*mashariki* and *magharibi*). The word for economics is Bantu (*uchumi*) whereas the word for politics is Arabic-derived (*siasa*). The word for monarchy is probably Bantu (*ufalume*) whereas the word for republic is Arabic-derived (*jamuhuri*). The word for God is Bantu (*Mungu*) whereas the word for angel is Arabic-derived (*malaika*).

Basic sociological words not only for religion (*dini*) but also for language (*lugha*), trade (*biashara*), and kinship (*umajaa*) are Arabic-derived. The name of the language is widely regarded as Arabic-derived, denoting the language of coastal people. By a strange linguistic destiny, Swahili and the geographical region of the Sahel in West Africa probably have the same Arabic derivation.

In addition to its links with Arabic, Kiswahili has other Islamic connections. Those to whom Kiswahili has been the mother tongue have been overwhelmingly Muslim. As a linguistic group called the Waswahili, they are distributed mainly along the coastlines of Kenya, Tanzania, and northern Mozambique. The native speakers of the language, however, are only a small minority of the total number of users, the great majority of whom speak it as a second language – after their own ethnic ('tribal') language. These fifty million people who speak Kiswahili as a second language are multi-religious in composition. It is the Waswahili proper who are overwhelmingly Muslim.

To this latter Islamic group *Uswahili* is a whole distinctive culture, and not merely a language. *Uswahili* includes, as well as the language, traditions of special lifestyle, dress, architecture, kinship patterns, marriage customs, distinctive music and song, and a Swahili cuisine. Underlying all aspects of this Swahili civilization has been the influence of Islam.

The third reason why the Swahili language is Islamic in origin concerns its links with the Sultanate of Zanzibar. As we shall demonstrate, it was the European rulers of East Africa who decided which of the various dialects of Kiswahili would form the basis of standard Kiswahili. European power finally opted to make the dialect of Zanzibar the basis of standardizing the language. Under British rule in East Africa *Ki-Unguja*, the Zanzibari dialect, became the language of Swahili classes in schools, the medium of government business, and increasingly of books, newspapers, and other domains of the written word. Since Zanzibar was an Arab imperial system, the dialect of that island kingdom was already deeply Arabized – perhaps more so than the rival dialect of *Ki-Mvita* of Mombasa, which has stronger Bantu foundations but is slightly weaker in Arabisms. The British preference for *Ki-Unguja* of Zanzibar over *Ki-Mvita* of Mombasa enhanced the Arab content of standard Kiswahili in imagery and range of sounds.

The fourth factor in the Islamic origins of Kiswahili concerns its original alphabet. Kiswahili has been a *written* language for at least five hundred years. Until the twentieth century the script was based on the Arabic alphabet with such modifications as were necessitated by the more elaborate sound system of the cross-cultural language of East Africa. It was under European colonial rule in this century that the Roman alphabet gained the ascendancy in written Kiswahili. Today very few people even among the Waswahili themselves or other East African Muslims any longer use the Arabic alphabet for the Swahili language. The Latinization of the Swahili alphabet seems irreversible. Although the language has given up the Arabic alphabet, however, it continues to borrow more and more Arabic words.

The fifth factor in the Islamic origins of Kiswahili concerns the classical poetry of the language. The oldest poetry of Kiswahili is strongly Islamic in content, mood and orientation. Some would argue that the greatest poetry of the language comes from before the twentieth century – and all pre-twentieth century Kiswahili literature was strongly Islamic. (Some would argue, too, that the greatest English poetry also comes from before our times – Shakespeare, Milton, etc.) Long Swahili poems like *Al-Inkishafi*, *The Song of Mwana Kupona* and the general poetry of Muyaka are steeped in Islamic tradition and imagery. The poems were also originally written in the revised Arabic alphabet and preserved for posterity through that medium.

Between ecumenical and secular processes

Although Kiswahili thus began as an Afro-Islamic language, it has increasingly become the heritage of Africa as a whole. The great impact of Arabic in loan words is as irreversible as the impact of Latin on the English language. But Kiswahili is becoming less Islamic and more African because of its very success. Two trends have made it less Islamized. One is its evolution into an *ecumenical* language – a medium of worship and theology for Christianity and indigenous African religion, as well as Islam. Kiswahili is now the language of a Christian hymn, of an Islamic sermon, and of funeral rites in African traditional creeds. Swahili religious concepts which were originally intended only for Muslim discourse have now penetrated the vocabulary of the Bible and of African initiation rites. The ecumenicalization of Kiswahili is part and parcel of its universalization.

Then there is the secularization of Kiswahili. This is an even more wide-ranging process. It has involved the increasing use of Kiswahili in areas of African life which are no longer as deeply affected by religion as they once were. In colonial and post-colonial contexts, the secularization of Kiswahili has encompassed its use for administrative, economic and political purposes. Kiswahili has become one of East Africa's most important instruments of nation building and economic development.

As for the relationship between Kiswahili and the West's impact on East Africa, this has been a process full of contradictions. The West's impact arrested the spread of the Islamic religion but fostered the spread of this particular Afro-Islamic language. The religious part of Islamic civilization suffered, but the linguistic side of Islamic civilization gained. Both the Germans until 1918 and the British afterwards contributed significantly to the triumph of Kiswahili as a region-wide lingua franca. European missionaries generally promoted Christianity and constrained the spread of Islam: ironically, they often used the Afro-Islamic language of Kiswahili to spread the Gospel of Jesus.

British rule forced Kiswahili to give up the Arabic script in favour of the Roman. And yet today Kiswahili is the most serious challenger to the English language itself in East Africa. Kiswahili was forced by the British to *de-Arabize* its script. Today Kiswahili, in turn, is helping East Africa to reduce the European content of its post-colonial culture. In Tanzania and Kenya the spread of Kiswahili in public life and political processes is often at the expense of English.

Let us look more closely at those complex ways in which Kiswahili has been transformed from a relatively provincial Islamic language into the most important indigenous language that Africa has produced. How has the language been ecumenicalized? How has it been secularized? In what ways is it becoming universalized?

How the language spread

The spread of Kiswahili in East and Central Africa has taken place against the background of interaction between church and state and between economics and politics. Missionaries, merchants and administrators, politicians as well as educators, have all played a part.

We shall argue further that the role of Kiswahili as an economic medium is, in some regards, older than its role as either a political or religious medium, though many of the traders were themselves Muslim. After all, the language initially spread as a result of expansion of trade in East Africa, often under Muslim leadership. We hope to demonstrate that the role of Kiswahili as an economic medium has been the most spontaneous and the most natural of its three historic functions, and the least dependent on formal education and lessons in schools. Where Kiswahili is needed purely for purposes of trade, marketing, and employment, the language has not fired the imagination of educators. Certainly in Uganda in the last sixty years, Kiswahili has played a major role in important sectors of the economy, but this role has not persuaded successive Ugandan educational authorities to introduce the language formally in schools on any significant scale. Yet the economic role of Kiswahili has been important in horizontal national integration, fostering contacts across ethnic groups at grassroots levels. The political role of Kiswahili, on the other hand, has promoted vertical integration, creating links between the élite and the masses.

It is when Kiswahili is needed for political or religious purposes that educational policy makers become inspired, and governments or missionaries move with dispatch towards giving the language a role in the formal structures of training and socialization.

Let us now look more closely at these different dimensions.

Pre-colonial trade and early Kiswahili

The language itself goes back at least to the fifteenth century, possibly the twelfth. G. S. P. Freeman-Greenville has argued that Kiswahili was probably the ordinary tongue of Kilwa and the rest of the East African coast by the thirteenth century (1963: 168). But the bulk of the evidence seems to demonstrate that the language remained overwhelmingly a coastal phenomenon until two hundred years ago. The beginnings of trade into the interior by the coastal inhabitants have been traced to the last quarter of the eighteenth century. It was not until Seyyid Said bin Sultan established full residence in Zanzibar in 1832 and consolidated the el-Bussaidy sultanate on the islands that trade with the interior of the continent developed more substantially. The momentum of this trade was also a momentum of linguistic spread.

There were obstacles to internal trade which in turn served as obstacles to the further spread of Kiswahili. In some parts of East Africa militantly protective communities acquired the reputation of ruthless hostility to foreigners, and were thus able to keep away many an enterprising merchant from the coast. The Maasai in both Kenya and Tanganyika had such a reputation and hindered both the expansion of trade and the spread of Kiswahili, especially in Kenya.

A third factor concerned economic anthropology *per se*. There were communities in East Africa that were not interested in economic exchange, or any kind of entrepreneurship. Resistance to entrepreneurial activities was sometimes primordial, derived substantially from ancestral beliefs and values. There were communities in East Africa that relied on herding their own cattle, and augmenting them through raids rather than trade. There were other communities that were minimally based on subsistence, cultivating their own ground, without feeling the impulse for surplus and exchange. Even the Gikuyu, who quite early showed signs of considerable entrepreneurial skill in their relationships with their neighbours – even before colonization – were some time hostile or uncooperative in their relations with traders from afar. Muslim merchants from the coast found Gikuyuland inhospitable for either trade bases, marketing, recruitment of porters or replenishment of supplies. The Kamba, on the other hand, were actively trading far from their own homes in the same period, and for a while appeared to be far more entrepreneurial than the Gikuyu, and among the most enterprising of all the Bantu communities of this part of the continent.

As the nineteenth century unfolded, trade expanded. Settlements inhabited by large numbers of people drawn from different linguistic groups increased, and the need for a lingua franca also arose.

> By the eighteen-sixties traders, principally from Pangani, had penetrated the Lake regions from the south and by the eighteen-seventies they had reached Mount Elgon. A route from Taveta to Ngong was also developed. In the last decades of the century, as trade increased, a number of centres of influence were established at Mumia's and at Kitoto's, for example, but ... these were never comparable in size or number or in importance to the major settlements in the south. (Gorman, 1974: 388)

The slave trade, especially in the second half of the eighteenth and much of the nineteenth century, also played a part in the dissemination of Kiswahili. In this part of the continent the Arabs were particularly active in the slave trade and had their own African agents in different parts of the region. As this trade was regarded simply as an additional area of economic activity, it ought to be seen as part of the total impact of economic considerations on the spread of Kiswahili. Those who used Kiswahili for purposes of trade and commerce ranged from the Kamba to the Mijikenda, from the Nyamwezi to newly arrived Muslim immigrants from the Persian Gulf. All these are instances of economic spontaneity affecting linguistic spread. These were the days when the language could claim no special hold on the imagination of educators.

An orthography based on the Arabic script had already come into being among the Arabs and the Mijikenda of the coast. Kiswahili poetry goes back several centuries, and had used this orthography previously. But while many studied these poems as works of art in East Africa, and others knew them as media of religious instruction, actual preoccupation with the teaching of the language as such was something awaiting fulfilment in the future.

The Islamic poets and the religious instructors in the mosques played an important role in enriching the language, but at this stage it was still pre-eminently the merchants and traders who spread the language. Its dissemination entailed to some extent dilution as the distance grew between its place of origin and its new locale of economic function. The Swahili culture remained overwhelmingly a Muslim phenomenon of the coastal areas, but Kiswahili as a language found more purely technical functions in the marketplace. The spread of Kiswahili at this stage must therefore be seen as a phenomenon almost entirely independent of schools and other structures of training and education.

Church and state in linguistic spread

Apart from Coast Qur'anic schools, the entry of Kiswahili into the mainstream of formal education in East Africa on any significant scale did not come until European countries colonized this region, and missionaries infiltrated African societies. The great debate then got under way about media of instruction for Africans: the comparative merits of Kiswahili as against what were called 'vernacular languages' and as against the English language. The debates which began at the turn of the century continue today. The great competition on one side was between English and Kiswahili as the regional lingua franca; and on the other side between Kiswahili and more localized, indigenous, ethnic African languages. This debate, especially when it touched upon the fundamental issues of educational policy, quite often became an issue between church and state in a colonial situation. It is to the ramifications of this grand dialogue, half-religious and half-political, that we must now turn.

A rather simplistic but nevertheless suggestive distinction needs to be made in this regard, namely between, on one hand, training the mind of the colonized African and, on the other, converting his soul. Colonial policy makers in the administrative field, at their most enlightened, viewed education as a medium for the training of the African mind; the Christian missionaries viewed education as a method of winning the African soul. In reality, there was a good deal of overlap between these two concepts, and in practice they were rarely sharply differentiated. But it is still true to say that the European missionaries in those early days were especially concerned about 'spiritual transformation', the elimination of 'heathen tendencies', and the spread of the Gospel itself. The secular colonial policy makers, on the other hand, were beginning to be interested in producing some levels of indigenous human power for some of the practical tasks of here and now. The European policy makers were also interested in legitimizing colonial rule itself in the eyes of the outside world, by providing education as an instrument of modernization rather than an aid for spiritualization. Kiswahili became involved in this debate between the soul and the mind, between the spiritually oriented missionary activist and the modernizing colonial administrator. The ecumenical role of Kiswahili was in competition with its secular role.

Because Kiswahili developed within an Islamic culture, and borrowed many Arabic words, the language initially carried considerable Islamic association. Many of the individual loan words from Arabic were inevitably influenced by these prior associations. Many terms connected with religious experience, ranging from the concept of the hereafter to the idea of praying, carried overtones or undertones derived ultimately from Islamic practice and thought.

In the earliest days of European colonization and evangelism, this association of Kiswahili with Islam was not held against Kiswahili by the Christian missionaries. On the contrary, quite a number felt that since both Islam and Christianity were monotheistic religions drawn from the same Middle Eastern ancestry, and shared a considerable number of spiritual concepts and values, Kiswahili would serve well for the conversion of indigenous Africans to Christianity – precisely because Kiswahili could already cope with the conceptual universe of Islam. By contrast, 'vernacular languages' like Luganda or Luo were too saturated with associations and connotations drawn from an indigenous religious experience much further removed from Christianity than Islam was. The utilization of 'vernacular languages' for Christian proselytism carried the risk of conceptual distortion greater than that posed by Islam. In the words of Bishop E. Steere: 'Neither is there any way by which we can make ourselves so readily intelligible or by which the Gospel can be preached as soon or so well than by means of the language of Zanzibar' (1870: Preface).

Bishop Steere, the Reverend Krapf and Father Sacleux are among the missionaries who not only championed the use of Kiswahili for the Christian Gospel, but also made substantial contributions towards the systematic study of the language. (Whiteley, 1969: 15–17). In Uganda, Bishop A. Mackay records for November 1878:

> Fortunately Swahili is widely understood, and I am pretty much at home in that tongue, while I have many portions of the old and new Testament in Swahili. I am thus able to read frequently to the King and the whole court [of Buganda] the word of God. (1898: 103)

There was also a feeling of using Kiswahili as at least a transitional medium for the Christian Gospel, linking European Christian vocabulary with African 'vernacular'. O'Flaherty records translating tales and the like, and teaching many Baganda catechumens the skill and art of translating from Kiswahili into Luganda. Other Christian missionaries also record their use of both Kiswahili and Luganda for devotional purposes. This was certainly the great transitional period, using Kiswahili as a lingusitic medium which would gradually modify and influence the religious vocabulary of 'vernaculars', and bridge the conceptual gap between European theological language and the indigenous spiritual universe in Africa. Kiswahili was assuming its complex role as an ecumenical language.

For a brief while Christianity came to be identified partly with a knowledge of Kiswahili and the ability to read in that language. But as this identification began to get under way, a new swing of opinion was also becoming discernible. Certainly in Uganda a movement to replace Kiswahili altogether with Luganda became quite strong. The old Swahiliphile views of Mackay were coming under increasing challenge, and the ancient association of Kiswahili with Islam was now regarded as *ipso facto* dysfunctional to Christianity. In the words of Bishop Tucker in Uganda:

> Mackay ... was very desirous of hastening the time when one language should dominate Central Africa, and that language, he hoped and believed, would be Swahili.... That there should be one language for Central Africa is a consummation devoutly to be wished, but God forbid that it should be Swahili. English? Yes! But Swahili never. The one means the Bible and Protestant Christianity – the other Mohammedanism ... sensuality, moral and physical degradation and ruin.... [Swahili is too closely related to Mohammedanism] to be welcome in any mission field in Central Africa. (Mackay, 1908: 215)

In fact, Tucker's support for the English language was hedged with a number of reservations, and these reservations were widely shared by other missionaries. As far as the missionaries in Uganda were concerned, Kiswahili was deficient for spiritual purposes as compared with the 'vernaculars'. On the other hand, as far as colonial administrators were concerned, Kiswahili was deficient when compared with the English language, but richer when compared with 'vernaculars'.

Among some European missionaries, the so-called 'Livingstonian principle' began to hold sway. This was the principle that in the final analysis each African community could be consolidated in its Christianity by the efforts of its own indigenous members and by using the conceptual tools of its own indigenous cultures. Kiswahili became suspect precisely because it had developed into a lingua franca. A lingua franca was 'unfitted to reach the innermost thoughts of those understanding the conversions to Christianity'. There was also the argument that a child should in any case be educated initially in its own language – 'one of the chief means of preserving whatever is good in native customs, ideas, and ideals, and therefore preserving … self-respect'. And underlying both the educational and the religious factors as perceived by missionaries was the question of how best to handle the business of winning souls (Whiteley, 1969: 55).

Westermann's educational theories exerted a considerable influence at that time. He advanced the following thesis:

> Mental life has evolved in each people in an individual shape and proper mode of expression; in this sense we speak of the soul of a people and the most immediate, the most adequate exponent of the soul of a people is its language. By taking away a people's language we cripple or destroy its soul and kill its mental individuality…. And educational work which does not take into consideration the inseparable unity between African language and African thinking is based on false principle and must lead to the alienation of the individual from his own self, his past, his tradition, and his people. (cited by Gorman, 1974: 436)

For a while longer there were still administrators willing to put up a strong fight in defence of Kiswahili. From the colonial state's point of view, there were indeed significant advantages to be had from a lingua franca. Administration could be facilitated, regulations would be available in fewer languages, and district officers and commissioners could be moved to different parts of the country without having to learn the local 'vernacular' in each case.

In Tanganyika, that is what the Germans, after some hesitation, proceeded to do. They promoted Kiswahili on a vigorous scale because it afforded considerable administrative convenience. The impact of the period of German rule in Tanganyika upon the fortunes of the language in that country was considerable. The fact that education in the German colonies was much more controlled by the state and less dominated by the missionaries than education in the British colonies in those days was itself a factor facilitating the spread of Kiswahili in German-ruled Tanganyika. The position of missionaries there, in favour of 'vernacular' languages, though humoured to some extent, did not prevail. There were times when the missionaries even resolved not to accept subsidies from the German administration for education unless they were assured that the education would be given in the 'vernacular'. On balance, however, administrative convenience prevailed over spiritual ease:

> in areas controlled by Britain … the policy of leaving the control of education to the missionary order was more marked than was the case in French colonial territories, for example, or more relevantly, in Tanganyika during the period of German occupation. Indeed, the relative success of the German government in establishing government schools at which future members of the administrative service were educated in Swahili in Tanganyika as the language of adminis-tration and as the lingua franca…. (Gorman, 1974: 392)

But in British East Africa also there were, for a while, strong voices championing the administrative virtues of a lingua franca like Kiswahili. Particularly noteworthy was Governor W. F. Gowers of Uganda who submitted an incisive memorandum to the Secretary of State for the Colonies:

Kiswahili should be adopted as the *Lingua Franca* throughout a considerable portion of this Protectorate for the purpose of native education in elementary schools, and on the lines adopted in Tanganyika ... Kiswahili is the only vernacular language in East Africa which can prove in the long run anything but an educational cul-de-sac, in Uganda, as in Kenya and Tanganyika ....

Governor Gowers compared the arguments for Luganda, Kiswahili, and English as educational and administrative media and concluded that, in the Bantu-speaking districts of Uganda, proper 'Kiswahili would be introduced as an extra subject in lieu of English'.

In the same memorandum he had argued earlier against the suggestion that English should be utilized as the lingua franca and against the contention that English could be learned as easily by non-Bantu tribes as could a Bantu language. Gowers feared 'the dissemination of a barbarous jargon of English', and asserted that 'for mutual comprehension between Europeans and Africans ... inter-communication should be in an African vernacular [that is, Kiswahili], even if it is not the local tribal dialect rather than in so-called English'(Gowers, 1927).

A year later, in 1928, the Colonial Report included reference to measures which had been adopted to introduce Kiswahili 'as the dominant language for educational and administrative purposes throughout a considerable area of the Protectorate'. The Annual Report of the education department for 1929 also confirmed the vigour with which the new policy was being implemented.

But champions of Kiswahili in Uganda underestimated the opposition which would soon be released. Kabaka Sir Daudi Chwa, hereditary guardian of the cultural heritage of the Baganda, inevitably felt bound to oppose the introduction of Kiswahili as the official native language of Buganda. The Baganda, in alliance with the European missionaries and their belief in 'conversion through the vernacular', began to organize opposition against the pro-Swahili policies. In spite of the establishment in 1930 of an Interterritorial (Swahili) Language Committee, the Ugandan bishops, both Protestant and Roman Catholic, submitted a long and weighty memorandum to the Colonial Secretary in London through the Governor of Uganda. The burden of the memorandum was to demolish the arguments for Kiswahili as the official native language, and put a strong case for Luganda. Was Kiswahili to be denied an ecumenical role in Uganda?

The colonial education department included in its 1931 Annual Report a rebuttal of the bishop's memorandum. Controversy grew. Then a Joint Committee on Closer Union in East Africa was set up, and evidence was taken on language matters, as well as other things.

Curiously, the Baganda were suspicious of Kiswahili partly because they were suspicious of the white settlers of Kenya. The very arguments by administrators in favour of Kiswahili as a lingua franca created in the minds of many Baganda the fear of being incorporated more fully into an East African protectorate encompassing Kenya as well as Uganda. They began to feel that the Swahilization of their country would be part of the political process of its Kenyanization, and power in Kenya lay in the hands of the European settlers. When the Baganda gave evidence to the Imperial Joint Committee on Closer Union in East Africa, their opposition to Kiswahili formed part of their opposition to closer union in the region. In fact, the only people who gave evidence in London to the Joint Committee were Luganda speakers. The views of the country were not sought on an ethnically representative basis.

It was out of the Joint Committee's report and verdict that Uganda's language policy evolved. At the formal level of administrative and educational use, the Luganda language had won against Kiswahili. The Baganda themselves were employed widely as administrators in areas other than their own, and their language often used as a medium of instruction not only in Buganda but also, for a time, in some of the other Bantu areas.

In terms of the broader policy making, however, the missionaries had succeeded by and large in making the 'vernaculars' in both Kenya and Uganda the medium of elementary education except on the coast. Those administrators in favour of a lingua franca had lost that round. At least in Kenya and Uganda, Kiswahili was to depend less and less on educational policy for its spread.

After a time, both missionaries and administrators came to agree on the importance of using and promoting English at the higher levels of education. The administrators now saw in English a more effective medium for 'training the African mind' than Kiswahili, just as the missionaries had found 'vernacular languages' better instruments of 'cultivating the African soul' than Kiswahili. Except along the Kenyan coast, the educational system seemed to be by-passing Kiswahili. But, just as its ecumenical and educational roles were on the defensive, a new secular role was on the horizon – trans-ethnic and anti-colonial. Kiswahili was becoming secularized and at the same time more politicized.

The British administration's enthusiasm for Kiswahili as a lingua franca waned further when the growth of national consciousness and anti-colonialism in East Africa began to benefit from Kiswahili as a trans-ethnic, grassroots language of mobilization. Political consciousness was now regarded by Britain as a dangerous 'post-war epidemic' extending from the Gold Coast to Uganda and Kenya. British educational policy makers in the East African region moved more decisively against 'over-promoting Swahili'. In the words of the Ugandan scholar, Tarsis B. Kabwegyere:

> In the light of ... the African awakening in the post-war period, it is not unreasonable to assert that the stopping of Kiswahili was a strategy to minimise intra-African conflict. In addition, intensive anglicization followed and East African peoples remained separated from each other by a language barrier.... What this shows is that whatever interaction was officially encouraged remained at the top official level and not at the level of the African populations. That the existence of one common language at the level of the masses would have hastened the overthrowal of colonial domination is obvious. The withdrawal of official support for a common African language was meant to keep the post-war 'epidemic' from spreading. (1974: 218–9)

Kabwegyere's observations bring us back decisively to the whole problem of national integration. It is to this process that we should now return.

Kiswahili and economic integration

Despite being given the cold shoulder by educational and language policies in up-country Kenya and Uganda, the language spread in these areas. One of the major processes involved concerned the role of the language as a medium of economic relationships in the fields of employment, trade and general urbanization in contemporary East Africa. The secularization of Kiswahili gathered momentum in the marketplace.

Class formation in the region touched upon the whole competition between

Kiswahili and English as national media. The English language in the region was still a medium to be acquired at school. The prestige of the imperial language converted it into a resource relevant to class formation. As East Africa approached independence, and both colonial policy makers and missionary paternalists sought to facilitate the emergence of an educated élite, the balance of influence and power was beginning to tilt significantly in favour of those who had acquired the cultural symbols and educational skills derived from the imported metropolitan civilization. Included among these candidates for the élite were products of Christian missionary schools.

Opportunities for the educated and the semi-educated were disproportionately located in the urban areas. The relationship between the English language and urbanization was therefore different from the relationship between Kiswahili and urbanization. Rural boys educated enough to speak and write English were moved to the cities in order to capitalize on their new skills. It might even be argued that the boys joined the migration to the urban centres because they were already equipped with the potentially profitable English language.

On the other hand, not so well-educated rural boys who sought employment in the cities as porters or domestic servants, proceeded to acquire some competence in Kiswahili in order to facilitate their own individual urbanization. To some extent this was a reversal of cause and effect. The educated ones went to the cities, motivated by having already acquired English; the less educated ones wanting to move to the cities acquired Kiswahili in order to do so.

This is, of course, an over-simplification of a set of phenomena which were and continue to be sociologically complex. But the distinction being made is still defensible if we think of the educated class as rural misfits being forced by their very qualifications at times to migrate to the cities, whereas the less educated with a smattering of Kiswahili began as urban misfits, improving their Kiswahili as part of the process of adjustment. Curiously enough, one word for 'civilization' in Kiswahili is linked to both urbanization and Arab etymology. The word is *utamaduni*.

The educated are deemed to be rural misfits sometimes by their own families. Many parents go to considerable trouble and sacrifice to put their children through school: fees have to be paid, books acquired, in some cases uniforms purchased. Rural families, otherwise deeply deprived, nevertheless put their trust in the future, and proceed to make sacrifices for their children's education. The last thing such parents would welcome when graduation day comes is to see their sons still on their own little plot of land, seeking a living in rural areas in ancestral ways, instead of exploring wider opportunities beyond the green fields. By the time the youngster has been through school, and articulated that ultimate status symbol of command of the English language, both orally and in writing, his family's expectations are in the direction of office work in urban areas, or at any rate something that could not have been had but for their sacrifices. It is in this sense that the educated in African villages become to some extent rural misfits, and are therefore under social pressure to seek white-collar respectability far from home.

But the less educated, too, sometimes feel the pressure to seek to improve their lot in the urban areas. Sometimes there are too many sons to have adequate land for cultivation in the rural areas; sometimes there are too many women who would be underemployed unless the men went to the cities to earn and supplement the income of the extended family. Many an African husband works in a town, while his wife cultivates their land in the village. The movement towards those urban centres increased the need for a lingua franca among the diverse groups. Kiswahili, even in parts of East Africa where it was completely ignored by the educational system, found its own momentum of spread partly under the impact of these processes of urbanization.

Although no adequate comparative work has been done, it seems probable that East African cities are by now more multilingual, given their relatively small sizes, than West African cities. There are large urban centres in West Africa, constituting points of demographic congregation for large ethnic communities – sometimes numbering several million – that are overwhelmingly unilingual. But East Africa, by contrast, has both fewer and smaller urban centres, and smaller ethnic communities. The few towns and cities, once communications improve enough, begin to draw from a larger range of linguistic groups than would be the case in, say, Eastern or Western Nigeria.

In the case of some of the East African cities, communications with the rural areas are still so modest and rudimentary as to retard the full realization of linguistic diversity. But as these communications improve, the tendency will be towards greater multi-ethnic diversity in East African cities than in comparable urban areas on the west coast of the continent. It may already be true that, once we allow for the difference in size, there is greater ethnic and linguistic diversity in Jinja (Uganda) than in Ibadan (Nigeria), in Mombasa (Kenya) than in Accra (Ghana). All these are approximations which have not as yet been computed, nor have adequate comparative studies been undertaken. Nevertheless, the combination of smaller linguistic groups in East Africa and fewer towns and cities would surely indicate a *trend* towards greater linguistic diversity in East African towns than in West African ones.

If such a trend is correct, the case for a trans-ethnic medium in East African cities is proportionately stronger. Part of the triumph of Kiswahili in East Africa lies precisely in the fact that the great majority of East African communities are so small. Only the Baganda, the Gikuyu and the Luo top the three to five million mark in population, whereas language groups in West Africa in some cases have ten or twenty million people. West Africa, therefore, has been less successful than East Africa in evolving an adequate lingua franca apart from the English language.

Hausa (another Afro-Islamic language) is to some extent a lingua franca in West Africa, but suffers the handicap of being the native language of a Muslim group already large and powerful enough to be feared by others. Its acceptability as a lingua franca is therefore retarded precisely because those who speak it as a first language are already so numerous. There are, besides, rival groups almost comparable in size and with languages and cultures of their own rich enough to be regarded as the true equals of Hausa. In Nigeria the Hausa language is distrusted by Christian Nigerians partly because it is associated with a major Islamic presence in the country.

That only a small number of Muslims speak Kiswahili as a mother tongue improves its chances of being accepted by others. Of Kenya's over 20 million people, less than a quarter of a million speak Kiswahili as a first language. The small number of native speakers, and the small size of most other linguistic groups in the country, have interacted to give Kiswahili an expanding role in the life of the nation.

In Uganda the privileges of the Baganda during the colonial period, and the fact that they were the largest group in the country, contributed to the spread of Luganda beyond the immediate confines of the kingdom. In spite of this factor, the increasing indifference of colonial and educational policy makers towards Kiswahili, and the continuing inertia with regard to language policy during the two post-colonial Obote administrations, Kiswahili spread fairly widely in Uganda under the impetus of urbanization and migrant labour. These two latter phenomena, though closely related, were not identical. Urbanization included deruralization, the severance of ties with their ancestral rural roots among some sectors of the urban populations. Migrant labour, on the other hand, could at times represent merely a case of the rural–urban continuum – husbands labouring in towns, wives cultivating the land – in which some maintained spiritual and economic links with their villages. Kiswahili received a new lease of life, in the face of the hostilities of the missionaries and the Baganda, as a result of these twin processes of the growth of towns and cities and the mobility of the workforce.

The political economy of Kiswahili in Uganda has resulted in its being disproportionately a language of men rather than women. Kiswahili and Luganda competed in the great marketplace of human communication. While 52 per cent of Ugandan men are able to hold a conversation in Kiswahili, only 18 per cent of women can. Indeed, more Ugandan men can conduct a conversation in Kiswahili than are competent in Luganda. Yet the percentage of Ugandans of both sexes who can conduct a conversation in Luganda is higher than that of Kiswahili speakers. Luganda speakers include a high proportion of female native speakers. Of course, many more men than women learn languages, in any case. In the case of both Kiswahili and English in Uganda, the number of male speakers of each is well over twice the number of female speakers. In the case of Luganda, however, the number of male speakers, though considerably higher than that of female speakers, is nevertheless significantly less than double. This is because, of the three languages, only Luganda has a large number of native female speakers (Ladefoged, Glick and Criper, 1972: 24–5).

The growth of trade unionism in East Africa added a new and important secularizing role for Kiswahili, independently of educational policy. The wage sector of the economy of each East African country was expanding, and the workers after the Second World War began to experiment with collective bargaining. In Uganda a significant proportion of the workforce came from Kenya, and trade unionism in Uganda was, for a while, partially led and controlled by Kenyan immigrants. The importance of Kiswahili was enhanced in a situation where the workforce was not only multi-ethnic and multi-religious, but also international. So closely associated with workers and the beginnings of proletarian organization was Kiswahili in Uganda that the social prestige of the language among the more aristocratic Baganda declined even further. The language was deemed to be one for 'lower classes' of society, and for the migrant proletarian. The social prestige which Kiswahili enjoyed in Tanzania, with all the associations of a complex culture and political status, was conspicuously absent in Uganda. Many of those who did speak the language did not speak it well. The Kiswahili of Uganda was indeed basically a language for the workers, functionally specific and non-versatile, and for those reasons more limited in scope. Nevertheless, the need for the language as a medium for organizing the workers in these early stages of the growth of trade unionism must be counted as one of the major aspects of the political economy of Kiswahili, and one of the major processes of its secularization.

These new functions of Kiswahili in East African society were integrative at the horizontal level. We define horizontal integration simply in terms of social communication and interaction across geographical, denominational, and ethnic divisions of the society as a whole. We define vertical integration as a process of interaction between different strata of the society, especially between the élite and the masses. To the extent that Kiswahili served as the main language of trade unionism and organized labour, and facilitated social communication between workers and peasants from different ethnic areas and religious groups, the language was performing horizontally integrative functions. To the extent to which these functions were expanding the wage sector of the economy, facilitating the circulation of money across the country as a whole, promoting a consciousness of a national economy, and defining the boundaries of the national marketplace for goods and labour, Kiswahili was involved in the critical process of economic integration within each of the East African countries.

In Kenya, even the shift of the capital from Islamized Mombasa to Christianized Nairobi later enhanced Kiswahili's potential as a mechanism for horizontal economic integration. At first the decision to transfer the capital seemed a blow to the spread of Kiswahili. After all, if Islamic Mombasa was no longer the hub of national life, the impact of Mombasa's language on the rest of the society would be minimal.

By the beginning of the century ... the administrative focus of the East African Protectorate had moved away from the coastal area, Nairobi replacing Mombasa as the headquarters of the Uganda railway in July 1899. In 1907, the capital of the Protectorate was moved from Mombasa to Nairobi and there is no doubt that this transfer diminished the influences on Kenya's development of the coast [Islamized] Swahili culture that became so important in Tanzania's history. (Gorman, 1974: 389)

While it may be true that the spread of Islamized Swahili culture was adversely affected by the shift from Mombasa to Nairobi, it is by no means certain that the spread of Kiswahili as a language suffered with this transfer. On the contrary, it is arguable that the relative centrality of Nairobi increased the spread of the lingua franca on a national level. What happened to many non-Baganda workers in Kampala did not happen to many non-Gikuyu workers in Nairobi. Because the Baganda under the colonial administration had been a privileged group, allowed to retain considerable influence and prestige, their language in turn commanded derivative prestige, and many of the workers who came into the capital of Uganda felt they had to learn Luganda. Indeed, Kiganda culture favoured the linguistic and cultural assimilation of newcomers. In one or two generations many workers who were descended from non-Baganda became, to all intents and purposes, native Luganda speakers and were absorbed into the body politic of Buganda.

The Gikuyu in colonial Kenya, on the other hand, though comparable to the Baganda in size and proximity to the capital, were not a privileged group. On the contrary, they were often the most humiliated and exploited of all groups because of their closeness to the white settlers of Kenya. The Gikuyu also performed some of the most menial tasks even in towns very far from their own areas. These tasks ranged from sweeping the streets of Kisumu to emptying latrine buckets in Mombasa.

For the non-Gikuyu workers pouring into Nairobi there was relatively little incentive to improve familiarity with the Gikuyu language. Many non-Gikuyu workers did indeed learn some Gikuyu, but not for reasons of improving their social status in Nairobi or enhancing their chances of a good job. Kiswahili in Nairobi had an easier time in the competition with the Gikuyu language than it had in the competition with Luganda in Kampala. By the time of independence, very few Gikuyu politicians addressing public audiences in Nairobi regarded it as sensible to use the Gikuyu language. They used Kiswahili or English instead. This was in marked contrast to Baganda politicians addressing public meetings in Kampala, who normally used Luganda in preference to both Kiswahili and English.

Mombasa itself continued to be a Swahili metropolis substantially Islamized, continuing to grow in size and attracting an expanding non-coastal population. Though second in size to Nairobi by the time of independence, Mombasa was nevertheless large enough to be bigger than the capital of either Tanzania or Uganda. Nairobi was linguistically pluralistic, with a widespread use of Gikuyu language and English. But on balance, Kiswahili had been gaining ground at least as the lingua franca for horizontal integration, and increasingly as a medium also for vertical integration in select areas of social change all over Kenya.

What remains remarkable is the extent to which these new secularizing functions of the language in Kenya as a whole evolved in spite of the relative indifference of educational policy makers, and quite often in spite of their actual hostility to Kiswahili. What all this reveals once again is how economic necessity for a particular language in a given sociological situation can generate its spontaneous spread, notwithstanding the formal educational system. The marketplace as an arena of linguistic spread, independent of the classroom, can certainly be decisive. Separation of Kiswahili from missionary schools weakened its ecumenical role – but strengthened its secular role.

The spread of Kiswahili in the former Belgian Congo was also partly linked with economic changes and economic integration. It may not be entirely accidental that Kiswahili prospered best in such major mining areas of the Congo as Shaba, Upper Zaire and Kivu.

A convergence of two historic forces favoured the spread of Kiswahili in the Congo – the movement of Swahili and Arab traders in the earlier centuries and the migration of colonial workers in the twentieth century. Many of those workers were headed for the mines. In many cases a multi-ethnic labour force turned to Kiswahili as a lingua franca. In many homes Kiswahili became more important than the original ethnic language; Kiswahili was thus domesticated – moving from the workplace to the home.

At one level this was a case of regional integration, linguistically linking the Congo and other parts of Eastern Africa. But for a while Kiswahili seemed to reinforce the separate identity of provinces like Shaba (previously Katanga). Indeed, the very name Shaba (meaning 'copper') was a Kiswahili word for the province. Was this provincial separatism detrimental to national integration? Was Kiswahili performing the paradoxical task of helping East African regional integration, on one hand, and harming the internal national integration of Congo, on the other?

Certainly in the 1970s Shaba rebelled twice against the central government of Mobutu Sese Seko. On one of those occasions the Shaba rebellion had to be put down by imported Moroccan troops, aided by French and American logistical support. Were the Shaba rebellions detrimental to national integration or were they pro-democracy revolts?

We now know that Shaba's most famous sons of the twentieth century were Moise Tshombe, who attempted to pull the province out of the Congo in the 1960s, and Laurent Kabila, who embarked on a new effort to reunify the whole country in the 1990s. Moise Tshombe is best remembered in history as a secessionist who contributed to the murder of Patrice Lumumba, the Congo's first post-colonial prime minister. Laurent Kabila wants to be remembered as an integrationist, who completed the national and pan-African mission of Patrice Lumumba. Shaba is the province where Tshombe and Kabila were born, and the province where Patrice Lumumba was murdered.

In 1996 and 1997 Kabila mobilized the Swahili language as the medium of command in a multi-ethnic army of rebellion, aided and abetted by Rwanda, Uganda and Angola (Shiner, 1997). The anti-Mobutu armed rebellion of 1996 started with the Tutsi of Zaire, but escalated not only into multi-ethnic revolt but also into a multi-national movement, with Laurent Kabila as the leader. Kiswahili became increasingly important, not only because many of the fighters who were recruited already had a command of Kiswahili, but also because of the secret participation of training officers and possibly troops from Rwanda and Uganda. The Rwanda Patriotic Front, the basis of the Rwandan army, is mainly Anglophone and Swahili-speaking.

In addition, according to certain Tutsi sources who prefer to remain anonymous, many of the indigenous Zairean Tutsi had for a long time increasingly emphasized the regular use of Kiswahili rather than Kinyarwanda in their own post-colonial homes precisely in order to reduce their being mistaken for Rwandan immigrants. Kiswahili became a kind of linguistic asylum for many Tutsi to reduce their ethnic vulnerability as speakers of 'the language of Rwanda', Kinyarwanda. While they could not entirely conceal their being Tutsi, they could at least de-emphasize it in the face of ethnic prejudice (Duke and Rupert, 1997).

One of the major questions of the post-Mobutu era in Congo is whether it will bring better economic and political relations between the Democratic Republic of the Congo and her neighbours to the east and south-east. Are such regional changes already carrying linguistic consequences? The evidence would seem to suggest that there will be a decline in the Congo's identification with the Francophone community, at least as presently conceived and led by France. Second, there will be a rise in the status of English in the DRC – beginning with Kabila's moves to give English a role in the new orientation of the country. Third, the status of Kiswahili in the Congo, which was recognized officially when Mobutu declared it one of the four national languages of what was then Zaire in the 1970s – the other languages being Lingala, Kikongo and Tchiluba – will now be strengthened even further. There is a chance that Kiswahili will now perform not only the sub-regional tasks it already performed under Mobutu's rule, but will increasingly overshadow Lingala as the language of the politico-military establishment of the new DRC.

Will Kiswahili in Congo replace Lingala as the most important indigenous language for national integration? The trend may have started but the final answer is in the womb of history. At this level economic integration links up with political integration more fully.

Kiswahili and political integration

When a language is needed for vertical integration, especially in the sense of facilitating social communication between the rulers and the ruled, the educational system becomes once again a favoured medium of dissemination.

In Tanzania, the language has also been promoted for reasons of cultural self-reliance and self-development. One governmental area after another has been pronounced as an area in which only Kiswahili is to be used. There has been a definite decline in the use of English in Tanzania, and the beginnings of a decline in general competence in that language. Law courts have increasingly used Kiswahili, and specialist committees have been appointed to work out and develop an adequate legal vocabulary, very often turning to Arabic for loan words. Talks in scientific education on the radio have moved in the direction of disseminating scientific knowledge through Kiswahili. Secularization is becoming 'scientification'. The National Assembly has become unilingual. The political secularization of Kiswahili has also continued.

Tanzania has utilized Kiswahili not only as an expression of the blackness of the Tanzanian people but also as an expression of their being Tanzanian. Kiswahili in this case becomes part of Tanzania's patriotism proper, and is called upon to serve functions which would give Tanzania's national identity true expression and fulfilment.

In a cultural-nationalist context, a resource like Kiswahili is given educational roles where possible. The schools rise to the occasion, teaching it as one of the subjects at school, sometimes adopting it as a medium of instruction throughout the educational system. In Tanzania, educational stages below university level have been Swahilized progressively. English still plays a considerable role, but there is little doubt about its decline since independence. The British tried to de-Arabize Kiswahili. Now Kiswahili is helping to de-Anglicize East Africa.

The growing role of Kiswahili in Tanzania has inevitably resulted in a declining role for expatriate teachers. The utilization of technical assistance in the educational system of an African country usually presupposes the continuing acceptance by that country of a major metropolitan language. To the extent that Kenya, for example, uses the English language in much of its education, or to the extent to which Senegal uses the French language, the capacity of Kenya and Senegal to absorb technical assistance in the education system from Britain or France respectively is augmented. The utilization of the American Peace Corps in schools in Africa inevitably depended on the ability of the host countries to utilize people trained either to teach English, or in the case of those Americans who found their way to French-speaking Africa, equipped with a special competence in the French language.

In contrast, as Tanzania has continued to Swahilize its educational system, it has increased its own burden of producing its own teachers. Linguistic self-reliance implies educational self-reliance. The Swahilization of the educational system reduces not only the role of British and American teachers, but also of Swedish, Hungarian and other European teachers who can teach Tanzanian children more easily in English than in Kiswahili. This Afro-Islamic language has helped East Africa's struggle against dependence.

There are a few cases of expatriate teachers arriving in Tanzania equipped to participate in the educational system in Kiswahili. These have included Chinese teachers for physical training. On the whole, however, the era of technical assistance in the educational system of Tanzania is coming to an end. Cultural nationalism has been mobilized to serve the purposes of Tanzania's Arusha Declaration as an assertion of self-reliance.

Cultural nationalism, with regard to Kiswahili, has sometimes gone beyond immediate national boundaries, making it a most important symbol of pan-East Africanism. East Africans looking for areas of solidarity have sometimes sought it in race, sometimes in a shared history which created shared institutions linking Kenya, Uganda and Tanzania, and sometimes in a shared culture, where Kiswahili has particularly strong credentials. When, at long last, Uganda under military rule adopted Kiswahili as the national language, General Idi Amin emphasized the value of the language from a pan-African viewpoint. Speaking to the nation, he said:

On the advice of the entire people of Uganda, it has been decided that the National Language shall be Kiswahili. As you all know, Kiswahili is the lingua franca of East and Central Africa, and it is a unifying factor in our quest for total unity in Africa. (*Voice of Uganda*, 10 October 1973)

Some Ugandans have been aware of the potential of Kiswahili not only for communication between Kenya, Uganda and Tanzania, but also for communication with countries like the Democratic Republic of the Congo and Rwanda, whose own official language is French. The adoption by different African countries of either French or English, depending on the colonizer, has often created great communication barriers. Among at least some sections of the population of East Africa, this imperial cleavage created by the dichotomy between English and French has been mitigated by the availability of Kiswahili. President Idi Amin himself, though he spoke not a single word of French, did over the years enjoy many a conversation with Zairian dignitaries in Kiswahili. The imperial language of Zaire was French; the imperial language of Uganda was English. Kiswahili was the bridge.

But by the time Uganda adopted Kiswahili as a national language the country was already short of teachers in other fields as a result of Amin's expulsion of the Asians and his fluctuating harassment of the British. The adoption of Kiswahili by Uganda as a national language in October 1973 required that the language be introduced speedily into schools, and after a while given the role of medium of instruction. But the exodus of Asian and other expatriate teachers made the Ministry of Education circumspect about any linguistic experiment at the time. Further, uneasy relations between Uganda and Tanzania after Amin's military coup, and the killing of a number of Tanzanians in Uganda during the period, made it very difficult for Amin's Uganda to recruit Tanzanian teachers to teach Kiswahili in Ugandan schools. The capacity to recruit from Kenya was likewise circumscribed by the security situation in Amin's Uganda. On balance, therefore, the adoption of Kiswahili as a national language, though necessarily carrying educational implications, did not immediately have educational consequences. President Idi Amin saw the necessity of at least a temporary continuation of the previous linguistic policies. As he said in his address to the nation:

It must be emphasized that English shall for the time being remain the official language until Kiswahili is developed to a degree that warrants national usage. Other foreign languages shall continue to be taught in our schools. Vernacular languages shall continue to be developed. (*Voice of Uganda*, 10 October 1973)

Idi Amin's administration was Muslim-led. In some ways his eight years in power were the golden age of Kiswahili in post-colonial Uganda. The language was extensively utilized on radio and television. Even the proud Baganda often thought it prudent to improve their command of Kiswahili as political insurance. Ironically, Idi Amin's regime was overthrown by Swahili-speaking Tanzanians with an even better command of the language. Uganda under a partial Tanzanian occupation (1979–81) extended its honeymoon with the Swahili language a little longer. As for cultural nationalism in relation to class, Kiswahili is clearly much more of a language of the common man than English. Certainly its appeal to someone like Idi Amin, himself only semi-educated and with his roots in the countryside, was partly connected with the proletarian associations of Kiswahili in Uganda.

In Tanzania, the fact that the language was widespread, and spoken by many more people in the country than English, increased its utility as a medium for socialist egalitarianism. In Tanzania, the recruitment of party officials, appointment of administrators, election of parliamentarians and nomination of ministers no longer require competence in English. Political and élite recruitment in Tanzania has therefore been democratized substantially precisely because Kiswahili has permitted the utilization of a larger pool of talent than might otherwise have been available if English had remained a *sine qua non* of political office.

The educational implications of the class factor can be complex. The fact that Kiswahili has become a language of the masses can have an impact on the educational system when the policy makers are egalitarian and socialistic or are themselves drawn from the less privileged strata. In Tanzania, President Nyerere was highly educated but also strongly egalitarian. In Uganda, on the other hand, Idi Amin was someone of far more modest educational qualifications. He was more nearly a peasant than Julius Nyerere, and far less egalitarian. In the Ugandan case, the man at the top would not necessarily favour Kiswahili for the purpose of creating an egalitarian society; but he might favour it for the purpose of reversing the allocation of power in his society. This policy with Kiswahili, very superficially egalitarian, might be perfectly compatible with simply turning the previous class structure upside-down, so that the privileged of yesterday become the under-privileged of today and vice versa. Amin's policies were not precisely that, but they were in the direction of status reversal rather than equality. Nyerere's position, on the other hand, was more clearly egalitarian. Both positions carried great potential for the promotion of Kiswahili in those two countries as a language with a greater role in the affairs of the nation and a clear position in the schools. Tanzania has managed to implement those policies; Uganda, even since Amin, has only just started at best. The future of Kiswahili in the two countries should provide fascinating comparative insights into the interaction between language, ethnicity, race, territorial affinity, and social stratification. Yoweri Museveni became president of Uganda in 1986. By a strange coincidence Museveni is the most fluent Swahili-speaking President the country has ever had. The main reason is that Museveni lived for so long in Tanzania in his earlier years.

In Kenya, on 4 July 1974, the Governing Council of the ruling party, the Kenya African National Union, unanimously resolved to make Kiswahili the national language. President Kenyatta then decreed that the National Assembly should switch to Kiswahili, on an experimental basis, until the clause of the constitution which made English the legislative language was changed, the Hansard recording facilities modified, and other technical problems of transition solved (*The Standard*, 5 July 1974).

The Kenyan government was at last formally recognizing Kiswahili as a potentially vital medium for vertical as well as horizontal integration. The fact that Kiswahili was adopted as the official language on the eve of a general election raised questions about the likely composition of the next parliament. Would there be members fluent in Kiswahili but without any competence in English? Would other candidates previously eligible on the strength of their English now be disqualified because they lacked Kiswahili? Would the composition of the National Assembly be altered significantly by this dramatic change in the linguistic qualifications of parliamentary candidates?

In the Kenyan situation there was a case for a transitional bilingual legislature, using both English and Kiswahili. Members could then speak either English or Kiswahili as they wished. The possibility of installing facilities for simultaneous translation could also have been considered for a five-year period before a final decision was made.

The case for such a bilingual transition in Kenya lay precisely in the educational lag regarding the language. Kiswahili had been demoted even further in the educational system following the declaration of the Mau Mau state of emergency in 1952. This was done in order to reduce political contacts between Africans across 'tribal' lines. This twenty-year educational lag was harmful to the quality of the language spoken outside the coast.

But whatever the final outcome of the fluctuating policies of the Kenya government regarding Kiswahili, the status of the language in the educational system is now in the process of being raised. Once again considerations of political integration are revealing their influence on educational policy making. Bilingual education in Kenya is still in a state of flux, and the government has not yet grappled with the varied implications of such a switch in language policy. But a new phase in the history of Kiswahili in Kenya might well have started.

As Kiswahili is called upon to serve new roles, it has to augment its vocabulary. Much of the new political vocabulary has borrowed either from Bantu sources (like *bunge* for parliament) or from the traditional neo-Islamic sources of Arabic (like *raisi* for president). But English is also becoming a major source of loan words, especially in Kenya, Tanzania and Uganda.

The impact of French on Kiswahili may need to be examined in Burundi, the Democratic Republic of the Congo and Rwanda. Rwanda and Burundi – to the extent to which they are linguistically homogeneous – need Kiswahili less for either vertical or horizontal integration. Kinyarwanda and Kirundi serve both integrative roles well, supported by French as the official language. But in the DRC Kiswahili has been important already in horizontal integration across groups. President Mobutu Sese Seko's policy of 'African authenticity' had moved towards a fundamental re-examination of the language policy of the country. One experiment was the official adoption of four African languages, giving them recognition as *regional* languages, while retaining French for the time being as the official language. The choice of regional African languages included Kiswahili, as well as Lingala. Policy makers consulted Switzerland and India as countries which adopted more than two languages to cope with cultural pluralism and cultural nationalism.

Mobutu's promotion of African authenticity was itself inspired and conditioned by cultural nationalism at both the racial level of black pride and the national level of Zairian self-realization. The impact of Mobutu's 'authenticity' policy on education in the DRC – though still inconclusive – is already manifest.

At the ethnic class levels, cultural nationalism has a rather unsure effect on educational policy makers. But where cultural nationalism becomes necessary for national or racial identification, its translation into concrete educational policies can be speedy and extensive. In relation to Kiswahili, the policies have ranged already from its role in Black Studies in the United States to its propagation as a legislative language in Tanzania.

Religion as a whole seems to have declined as a major factor in the fortunes of Kiswahili. New secular gods now command African loyalties, in addition to those that came with Islam and Christianity. These new secular gods include the quest for greater cultural dignity, the pursuit of racial fulfilment, the forging of territorial identities, the revision of class and status in societies, and the construction of a new Eastern African civilization. Kiswahili first went ecumenical, then secular, and is now exploring the total universe of social experience.

From the crescent to the computer: a conclusion

Four stages in the development of Kiswahili are discernible in the history we have examined: the Afro-Islamic stage, the ecumenical stage, the secular stage, and the nascent universalist stage.

We have sought to demonstrate that the Swahili language began as a fusion of two civilizations – indigenous Bantu and Islamic. The role of Islam in Africa is often studied from a strictly religious perspective. But Islam is a civilization as well as a creed. Its role in Africa is not simply a matter of prayer but also a question of wider human relationships. Islam as a civilization requires much more than the minaret as its symbol – though even the minaret on its own embodies not just worship but also aesthetics, architecture and a sense of geography.

In this study we have focused on a language whose two parents were Africa and Islam. In its infancy the influence of both parents was strong on Swahili. It was a truly Afro-Islamic language. The grammar of the language was indubitably Bantu, but the vocabulary and imagery included strongly Islamic elements. The native speakers of the language (the Waswahili) were overwhelmingly Muslim, many of whom had intermarried with immigrant Arabs. The poetry of Kiswahili was at the time deeply saturated with Islamic metaphors, similes, and Qur'anic illustrations.

By the time the Europeans arrived as colonizers, the most important dialects of Kiswahili were Ki-Amu (the dialect of Lamu), Ki-Unguja (the dialect of Zanzibar) and Ki-Mvita (the dialect of Mombasa). All three coastal settlements – Lamu, Zanzibar, and Mombasa – were major centres of advanced Islamic learning, much of it conducted in Kiswahili. To the present day Lamu and Zanzibar are overwhelmingly Muslim societies, though the population of Mombasa has become more religiously diverse.

When the British decided to promote one of the dialects as standard Kiswahili, the central dilemma was between Ki-Unguja of Zanzibar and Ki-Mvita of Mombasa. The choice of Ki-Unguja was a choice in favour of the more Arabized dialect, though less rich in poetry than either Ki-Mvita or Ki-Amu. The stronger Arabization of the Zanzibar dialect helped to maintain the attractiveness of Arabic as a source of subsequent loan words.

The arrival of Christian missionaries helped to initiate the second phase of the history of Kiswahili – the use of the language for religions other than Islam. The language entered the ecumenical stage of its evolution. The fact that Kiswahili was already a medium of Islamic monotheism, with much of the imagery of the Old Testament, facilitated the use of Kiswahili for Christian purposes as well. Yet the Bantu origins of the language also helped the use of the language for traditional African beliefs.

Words for prayer in Kiswahili include *sala* and *dua* (of Arabic derivation), yet the term for Almighty is *Mwenye-ezi-Mungu*, a compound of both Bantu and Arabic. Moral and ethical vocabulary in Kiswahili is saturated with such Arabic loan words as *udhalimu* (injustice), *murua* (moral behaviour), *dhambi* (sin), *haramu* (taboo) and *halali* (ritually permissible).

But on the whole the balancing act between Bantu and Arabic words is recurrent. The Kiswahili word for no is Arabic (*la*) whereas the word for yes is Bantu (*ndiyo*); the word for clean is Arabic (*safi*) while the word for dirty is Bantu (*chafu*); the word for freedom (*uhuru*) is Arabic-derived whereas the word for slavery (*utumwa*) is Bantu; the word for praise (*sifa*) is Arabic-derived whereas the word for insult (*tukano*) is Bantu; the word for devil (*shetani*) is Arabic-derived whereas the word for God is Bantu (*Mngu* or *Mungu*).

Even when Christian missionaries preferred ethnic ('tribal') languages to Kiswahili, as they did in Buganda, they still looked to Kiswahili for neo-Islamic loan words. For example, the word for *angel* in Luganda is *malaika* (Arabo-Swahili), and one of the words for *taboo* in Luganda is *haramu* (along with the more purely Bantu word *chibi* for *sin*). Thus Kiswahili played an ecumenical role in Eastern Africa. The very word for *religion* in many East African 'tribal' languages, including Luganda, has remained *dini* (Arabic-derived, through Kiswahili).

The ecumenicalization of Kiswahili was, to some extent, the beginning of its secularization. As the language became the medium of worship in diverse religions, it became a medium of communication *across* religions. Its fate in the school curricula of Kenya and Uganda was uneven. As we indicated earlier, educational policy makers sometimes attempted to marginalize Kiswahili. But the language gathered its own momentum in the marketplace rather than the classroom. It fostered trade, facilitated labour migration, and developed into a major cross-ethnic lingua franca.

The role of the language in vertical integration eased the process of class-formation in the wake of colonization. Kiswahili helped social mobility, adding a new complexity to relations between the new élites and the emerging masses in the region. Its role in horizontal integration concerned communication between ethnic groups. Both forms of communication were fundamental to the process of national integration in the new territorial entities created by European colonization. These were some of the central secular roles which the language was called upon to play as it became increasingly indispensable as a medium of regional communication.

Kiswahili became the national language of Tanzania almost immediately after independence. In Kenya it became the language of practical politics, though not yet the legislative language of the constitution (the judicial system still interprets the constitution in its English phraseology). In Kenya Kiswahili spread faster vertically across social strata than horizontally between ethnic groups. It remains the most important single language for national purposes in Kenya.

In Uganda the fortunes of the language have varied according to the regime in power. Although Kiswahili is a Bantu language, it is more popular among non-Bantu Ugandans – especially the Nilotic and Sudanic peoples of the North. Bantu Ugandans like the Baganda have tended to regard Kiswahili as a rival to their own language and culture.

The golden age of Kiswahili in Uganda was when the Muslims under Idi Amin were in control. But it was not Islam which popularized Kiswahili; it was the fact that the regime was northern and military. When Ugandan military forces were primarily non-Bantu in composition, and they were in control of the state, Kiswahili had a powerful political constituency. It featured widely in speech making and broadcasting under Idi Amin. Now the Bantu army which President Yoweri Museveni created is the basis of his power. The paradox of the Ugandan situation since 1986 is that while the country has the most fluent president in Kiswahili since independence in 1962, the regime as a whole is less committed to Kiswahili than any of its predecessors. Even so, since colonial times Kiswahili has spread and consolidated itself in Uganda in spite of succeeding regimes. Today more than half the male population of Uganda can conduct a conversation in Kiswahili, though only a smaller fraction of the women can.

In the Democratic Republic of the Congo the language is already serving regional educational purposes, especially in Shaba and the east. Kiswahili has penetrated educational policy faster in the DRC than in Uganda. In Rwanda, Burundi, northern Mozambique and north-eastern Malawi, Kiswahili is responding to the stimulus of the marketplace and regional proximity, rather than to any direct policy. All this secularization of Kiswahili is part of its universalization. But Kiswahili's universalistic role includes the process of making it a scientific language. Kiswahili in Tanzania and Amharic in Ethiopia may be the fastest indigenous languages of Africa to acquire a scientific vocabulary, and the fastest to be modernized for twentieth century needs. Neither Kiswahili nor Amharic is as yet a language of computer science or nuclear physics – but the two languages are edging their way towards 'scientificity' faster than any other indigenous language in Africa. The computerization of Kiswahili is on the horizon.

The universalization of Kiswahili also includes its expanding use in international broadcasting. Almost invariably, the first African language which external radio systems experiment with in their broadcasting to Africa has been Kiswahili. There are more hours of international broadcasting in Kiswahili than in any other single African medium. Further afield, Kiswahili is included in programmes of higher education in other parts of the world. It features more widely in college curricula overseas than any other African language. There are classes in Kiswahili from Tokyo to Columbus, Ohio; from Copenhagen to Bombay; from Halifax, Nova Scotia, to Port Moresby, Papua New Guinea.

The British once attempted to de-Arabize Kiswahili. Now the language is helping East Africa to de-Anglicize itself. The language has seen itself transformed from a relatively provincial Afro-Islamic tongue into widening circles of overlapping constituencies. The Islamic, the ecumenical, the secular, and now increasingly the universalistic roles of Kiswahili constitute the most astonishing indigenous odyssey of linguistic expansion in the twentieth century. Africa and Islam have once again joined forces to enrich the pool of human civilization.

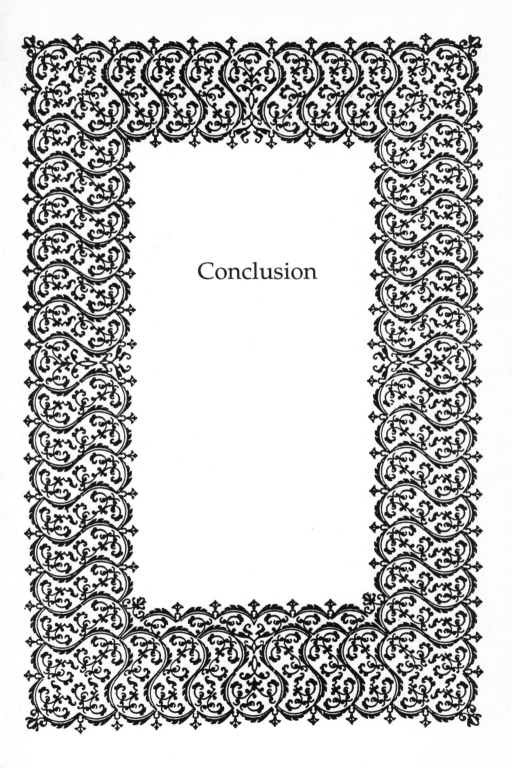

Conclusion

13
The Linguistic Balance Sheet

Post-Cold War, Post-Apartheid
& Beyond Structural Adjustment

For Africa some of the most momentous events of the concluding years of the twentieth century are, first, the end of the Cold War between the North Atlantic Treaty Organization and the Warsaw Pact; second, the triumph of market ideologies in the world system; and third, the end of overt institutionalized racism (though not necessarily the end of other forms of racism). In this final chapter we try to see how these wider changes in the world have impinged upon linguistic trends in Africa.

In a single chapter we can but scratch at the surface of these three big themes. We have to be extremely selective in each case. Our case study for the end of the Cold War will be mainly an evaluation of the fortunes of the French language and its prospects both in Africa and the world.

We shall consider the triumph of market ideologies through the special instance of structural adjustment programmes in Africa as promoted by the World Bank and the International Monetary Fund, and underpinned by bilateral conditionalities between individual Western donors and individual African countries. What are the linguistic implications?

Our topic for studying the effects of the end of overt and institutionalized racism is more obvious. It is nothing less than the demise of apartheid. The end of political apartheid is for the time being the triumph of African nationalism over the old racist claims of Afrikaner nationalism. Open and institutionalized racial discrimination has been dismantled. No more attempts to create racial homelands. No more insistence on separate hotels, schools, residential areas, separate lavatories and separate electoral rolls. But are other forms of racism alive and well? And what are the linguistic implications?

All these three tendencies – post-Cold War, post-apartheid and structural adjustment – have had varied linguistic implications both globally and within the African continent. The Russian language may not be the only one to decline in Africa as a result of the end of the Cold War; this may also be the fate of the French language. The end of apartheid in South Africa has signalled not only the retreat of white racial power, but also the decline of the Afrikaans language. As for structural adjustment, it has had wide-ranging ramifications – from the threat to African higher education to the tensions between the linguistically pluralistic Third World and the linguistically hegemonic United States.

195

Francophone Africa after the Cold War

The end of the Cold War has unleashed a debate in France as to whether France should continue with its traditional role of a special relationship with its former African empire, or whether it should now re-focus its orientation towards East and Central Europe, and become a major economic and diplomatic player among former members of the Warsaw Pact. Russia, Hungary, Poland and Czechoslovakia will never adopt French as their official language – but the Democratic Republic of the Congo, Senegal, Côte d'Ivoire and Guinea (Conakry) already have. Which way should France turn? It is possible to argue that globally the end of the Cold War has partially interrupted the decline of the French language, while in Africa the post-Cold War era may set the stage for a new decline of the language. Let us look at these two trends more closely.

In what sense, if any, can a world language be declining in influence on the global stage? Before the end of the Cold War the decline of the French language was easier to recognize than the decline of English. This was partly because French was, in some cases, losing ground precisely because of the growing importance of English.

Many smaller European countries had decided since the Second World War to give priority to the teaching of English in their schools, often at the expense of French and German. These included Scandinavia (Sweden, Norway and Denmark), the Netherlands, Greece and elsewhere.

In the former French colonial dependencies in the Arab World, Arabic had been gaining ground at the expense of French. This was certainly true of Syria and of some of the former French colonies of North Africa. While the French language was still very strong in Algeria, the Arabicization policies even before the present Islamic conflict had challenged its supremacy.

The collapse or decline of European aristocracies had also reduced the prestige of the French language in the cultural stratification of Europe. In the first half of the twentieth century the nobility of most European countries still used French extensively as the language of status and sophistication. The French revolution of 1789 had helped to destroy the nobility in the whole of Europe – but France thereby helped to weaken the long-term status of the French language in European capitals as well. It was precisely the forces of egalitarianism unleashed in 1789 which subsequently favoured English at the expense of French in much of Europe in the second half of the twentieth century.

The collapse of the USSR and the disintegration of the Warsaw Pact left the United States as the sole undisputed superpower on the world stage. This added to the prestige of the English language as a global means of communication. In some cases this was at the expense of the French language. But was it also opening up new possibilities for the French language? The end of the Cold War may be having complex linguistic consequences. For one thing, the export of the Russian language to Africa has declined sharply. As Eastern Europe has opened up economic possibilities for France, is France likely to invest less in promoting its language and culture in Africa? Will the French language and culture in Africa be compromised in the wake of the end of the Cold War?

Also complex are the fortunes of French in Asia in the post-Cold War era. French colonies in Asia were more linguistically homogeneous than British colonies in Asia. Vietnam, Cambodia and Laos – making up the former French Indo-China – were all linguistically homogeneous. And so, upon the departure of the imperial power, the native national language could assert supremacy more easily, especially when independence was accompanied by militant nationalism and radical socialism. What the end of the Cold War has done is to reduce the militancy of nationalism in Indo-China and deradicalize its socialism. The French language in Vietnam and Cambodia may have a new lease on life – but definitely in the shadow of the English language.

The major British colonies in Asia were linguistically heterogeneous. They therefore needed the imperial language as a lingua franca among the native populations: this applied to India and what later became Pakistan, to Ceylon (Sri Lanka) and, to a lesser extent, to Burma (Myanmar). The greater the indigenous linguistic diversity, the greater the need for the imperial language as a lingua franca. The end of the Cold War has made little difference to this equation. And so English has survived better in India, Pakistan and Sri Lanka than French had in Vietnam, Cambodia and Laos until the post-Cold War era gave it a partial revival.

As the twentieth century comes to a close, the story of the French language globally may be a case of 'decline and rise'. But as the twenty-first century opens, the French language's story in Africa may be a saga of 'rise and decline'. If France stops fighting for its legacy in Africa, the French language will be subject to the challenge of both English and indigenous languages. The linguistic fortune of France is therefore bound to experience a downward trend – for better or for worse. In the remote future will it follow the ominous fate of the German language in Africa which now survives only in Namibia? The triumph of the English-speaking Rwanda Patriotic Front in Rwanda in 1994 was a setback for France. So was the ouster of Mobutu Sese Seko by Laurent Kabila in Zaire (Democratic Republic of Congo) in 1997.

Nationalism is sometimes a combination of culture as identity and culture as communication. When nationalism and the language are either completely or substantially fused, what we get is linguistic nationalism, with its focus on pride in one's language. Among European countries the French are greater linguistic nationalists than the British. Defensively, the French are also greater linguistic purists than the British, on guard against their language being too corrupted or polluted. Part of the crusade has been in schools in Francophone Africa.

But here one may have to distinguish between direct linguistic nationalism and derivative linguistic nationalism. Direct linguistic nationalism is when the central focus is the issue of language in relation to identity, as in the case of separatism in Quebec. France's efforts to promote French in Africa is also a case of direct linguistic nationalism. Derivative linguistic nationalism is when pride in language is part of a wider cultural pride. It is arguable that the French are primarily cultural nationalists – and their linguistic nationalism is part of the wider cultural patriotism, which covers pride in French literature, the French role in history, French cuisine and French civilization. The Arabs are also great linguistic nationalists – but in the derivative sense. They are proud of the Arabic language partly because they are proud of the Arab role in world history, of the Arab impact on world religion, and of Arab civilization through time.

These realities transcended the Cold War while it lasted – and have remained truly resilient now that the Cold War has ended.

In one part of the Arab world linguistic nationalism may be temporarily declining – and the French language is a beneficiary. Curiously enough, while France's commitment to sub-Saharan Africa may have begun to slacken, French commitment to Arab North Africa is on the offensive, at least culturally. In the 1990s the University of Cairo has started offering bachelor's degrees entirely in the French language in the social sciences, alongside more traditional degrees in the Arabic language in those fields. France has so far been funding the French language stream of the Faculty of Economic and Political Science at Cairo University. The Faculty of Law has also embarked on a French language programme. France has invested in that academic venture.

Perhaps a more surprising French investment is the Leopold Senghor University in Alexandria, Egypt, intended for Francophone Africans continent-wide. The surprise is in the location for such a university, considering that the majority of its students are from sub-Saharan Francophone countries.

Of course, the American University in Cairo is an old landmark. It has educated many of the children of the Egyptian élite in the English language – including children of Egyptian presidents. The English language is still used in the teaching of the natural sciences, engineering and medicine in other Egyptian universities as well, including Cairo University.

In the face of the French offensive in the social sciences at Cairo University, Egyptian defenders of the English language have demanded an English language stream in the Faculty of Economic and Political Science alongside the French one. The Anglophone Egyptians are winning the battle. Unfortunately the Egyptians who study the social sciences in the Arabic language are likely to be the least marketable in Egypt after they graduate. Those taught in European languages are more likely to be the élite of the élite.

While Egypt is indeed moving towards partially Westernizing the teaching of the social sciences at the university level, Syria is moving towards Arabizing the teaching of the *natural* sciences. France is culturally losing out in its former occupied territory, Syria, but is gaining in the former British-occupied territory, Egypt.

It is in sub-Saharan Africa that France in the last years of the twentieth century shows its deepest ambivalence. If Hamlet were the Prince of France rather than Denmark, he would still be wringing his hands down Africa's corridors and saying 'To be or not to be; that is the question!' France is unsure whether to try and remain a major cultural and economic presence in Black Africa, in the face of competing opportunities opening up in Eastern and Central Europe.

Market ideologies and structural adjustment

The main title of this book, *The Power of Babel*, properly encapsulates the conviction of the authors that, far from being a divisive force that weakens the bonds of nationhood and wider relations of political identity, linguistic pluralism can be one powerful source of a new humanity within a world of tremendous diversity.

One large question arises: although market ideologies ostensibly favour economic pluralism (or free enterprise), do they also favour cultural and linguistic pluralism? Do they favour diversity in the domain of culture? Let us look more closely at the relationship between capitalism and language, with special reference to experience in Africa and Asia. We shall relate this to structural adjustment as a special instrument for promoting free market economies and the capitalist ethos.

Capitalism has succeeded best where the language of the marketplace has not been too far removed from the language of the classroom. Capitalism has succeeded in those societies where the language of intellectual learning and the language of economic bargaining have not been too distant. In Africa, on the other hand, the language of the marketplace (usually indigenous) and the language of the classroom (usually foreign) are indeed distant. Africa has become the only continent in the world which is attempting a capitalist take-off while having such a massive dependence on foreign languages. Among the contrasts between Africa and East and South-East Asian countries which have been leaving Africa behind in the capitalist race is the linguistic contrast. In Japan, Korea, Taiwan, Hong Kong, China and even Singapore and Malaysia, the language of the marketplace is much closer to the language of the classroom. The Asian élites use indigenous languages much more than do the African élites south of the Sahara. Is it possible that the success of East Asian and South-East Asian efforts in the capitalist game is related to such linguistic considerations? Has more dependence on indigenous languages helped East Asian economies?

Within South-East Asia the Philippines is probably the most dependent on a European language (English) economically and politically. It is also one of the least successful of the South-East Asian capitalist economies. Filipino/a domestic workers are seeking jobs in Hong Kong and Singapore. The Philippines also demonstrates that being Christianized is not necessarily a help in the capitalist game. The Philippines is the only Christian nation in the Association of South East Asian Nations, and also is the least successful economy in the Association.

Africa starts from a disadvantage. Many African policy makers assume that being Westernized in both religion and language improves the chances of 'development'. There is a naïve assumption that Christianity is necessarily a force for modernization, and that European languages are instruments of economic transformation. Not enough attention has been paid to the experiences of countries like Japan, Korea, Taiwan, China, Singapore and Malaysia, where Christianity is minimal and where indigenous languages play a large role in economic transaction and educational policies.

The question arises whether the structural adjustment programmes (SAPs) of the 1980s and 1990s are likely to reduce African naïvete about what is needed for economic transformation. Structural adjustment may have no relevance for choice of religion in Africa, but will it have consequences in the arena of language and other aspects of culture? It is not often realized that SAPs are – in their consequences – also cultural adjustment programmes. The economic changes unleashed by SAPs have repercussions in the field of values, lifestyles and modes of communication. In other words, SAPs have linguistic consequences as well.

African peasants are among the least Westernized of post-colonial Africans. The economic conditions imposed by the World Bank and the IMF on African states are claimed to be farmer-friendly and peasant-friendly. Until the mid-1980s Africa's systems of subsidies were designed to help consumers, mainly in the cities, rather than agricultural producers. This was in stark contrast to Western subsidies to farmers. In 1996 the member countries of the Organization of Economic Cooperation and Development other than the US spent $166 million on agricultural subsidies, while the United States spent over $7 billion in subsidies to cereal producers (Oxfam, 1997).

What Western subsidies to agricultural producers have done over the decades was to create surplus production (the so-called 'mountains of butter'). What African subsidies to consumers did might have helped the city dwellers, but they also reduced the margin of return for African farmers. In some of the worst cases, farming for the domestic market in Africa ceased to be profitable at all in the face of what was being spent on questionable marketing boards and on subsidizing urban consumption patterns.

Conclusion

SAPs sometimes led to the dismantling of unnecessary and expensive marketing boards. They also discouraged all state economic subsidies, which in Africa meant mainly consumer subsidies. Both these moves favoured peasants and farmers – most of whom were among the least Westernized sectors of African populations.

If the incomes of peasants improve, the rural–urban economic gap will begin to narrow – and so, perhaps, will the social distance between Westernized élites (custodians of the Western legacy in Africa) and a revived rural élite (custodians of the indigenous legacy).

Another tendency in SAPs is the demotion of tertiary education as a priority for the state. SAPs view state subsidies to African universities as having been too high and parental responsibility for financing the education of their children too low. Both Western donors and international financial institutions have themselves been less keen on subsidizing African higher education with foreign aid. They have also called upon African governments to get more and more undergraduates to assume responsibility for their university fees either immediately or through a system of loans.

The risks in such a policy include the possibility that university education in Africa will become even more élitist, accessible disproportionately only to the children of well-to-do parents. But will Western disengagement from African higher education also inadvertently help the task of de-Westernizing African universities? If so, this should surely be counted among the gains. For too long African universities have been the ultimate instruments of Westernization in Africa. Their human products were intended to be approximations of graduates of Western institutions. In sub-Saharan Africa the medium of instruction has remained the preserve almost entirely of European languages. Indeed, in only a minority of sub-Saharan universities are African languages taught at all.

If SAPs are demoting the African university, are they not *ipso facto* demoting the highest instrument of Westernization in African societies? The bad news from SAPs is a shrinkage of the pool of educated human power, and the aggravation of élitism in higher education. The good news is the slowing down of the processes of Westernization and of de-Africanization in African societies.

In Africa, SAPs are potentially damaging to the English language, at least in the short run, as higher education suffers. But in the United States, paradoxically, structural adjustment is beneficial to the hegemony of the English language and is detrimental to diversity. In Africa indigenous culture may gain from the reduced rush to Western-style higher education. Structural adjustment may not be an enemy to multiculturalism in Africa, but it may be inimical to diversity in the United States. Let us explore more fully these contradictions of structural adjustment in Africa and the African diaspora in North America.

We regard the resilience of African languages, their will to survive in spite of the destructive offensive of linguistic Eurocentrism, as an important contribution to the world-wide resurgence and growing momentum of pluralism. But precisely because of its potential power, its threat to Eurocentric assimilationism, an array of factors – both overt and covert, direct and indirect, intended and unintended – have sometimes joined forces to undermine the progress of pluralism. One of the most critical of these factors comes in the form of SAPs.

The recent history of African languages in American academia is partly related to superpower rivalries. Area studies, under whose ambit comes the study of African languages, developed in the USA partly in response to the Cold War. It was one of the academic foundations that the US government decided to build in its bid to lay claim to certain regions of the world and 'protect' them from the Communist threat, or to penetrate regions that had already come under Soviet influence. Predictably, then, the end of the Cold War turned area studies into an engagement of relatively low priority in the US government's agenda on foreign relations, as seen in the decreasing funding for international educational and cultural exchange programmes (*Chronicle for Higher Education*, 13 October 1995: A 43). The global shifts that have led to the emergence of the USA as the only superpower, therefore, partly explain decreasing US government commitment to area studies, and by implication to the study of African languages.

Instead, a new policy seems to have developed that seeks to isolate and promote certain 'Third World'languages that the US government regards as 'strategic'for US interests. In Africa, these languages include Xhosa and Zulu in South Africa – reflecting the region's mineral wealth and its potential influence on the politics of sub-Saharan Africa – and Amharic, because of the proximity of the Horn of Africa to the volatile, oil-rich Arabian Peninsula. This is partly the story behind the National Security Education Program (NSEP), formerly known as the 'Boren Bill'. The NSEP, with its direct links to US intelligence agencies and the Pentagon, provides scholarships for undergraduate students to study abroad, fellowships to US students in graduate programmes, and grants to institutes of higher learning, with the aim of promoting the study of specific world regions, languages and cultures determined by the Secretary of Defense (See the undated pamphlet of the Association of Concerned African Scholars entitled *Open Scholarship or Covert Agendas: The Case Against NSEP Funding for the Study of Africa*).

The new situation with regard to African languages has certain historical parallels with the colonial era. British colonial agencies, in particular, sought to promote a few African languages that were regarded as essential to Britain's interests, while marginalizing the majority of the languages of the continent. Politico-economic interests of the West, and of America in particular, in this neo-colonial era may again accord advantage to certain African languages at the expense of others. As in many other respects, therefore, Africa continues to be a mere pawn rather than a significant player in determining the destiny of its own languages, sometimes even within the continent itself.

Important as the end of the Cold War is as a factor in reducing US government support for area studies and African languages, the contribution of the victory of political conservatism in the USA to this academic shift must not be under-estimated, however. And here is where the question of structural adjustment programmes comes in quite clearly. There has been a tendency to regard SAPs as peculiar to Africa or the so-called Third World. But SAPs have also been applied to the USA and to other Western nations by their respective governments, often with similar debilitating effects. In the realm of education in the US for example, student aid increased by 47 per cent in the ten years between 1980 and 1990, while the cost of public education increased by 109 per cent and that of private education by 146 per cent. As in many African countries, the real wages of the average university faculty in the US had dropped below their 1972 level by 1994 (see *The Newsletter for the Committee for Academic Freedom in Africa*, No. 9, 1995: 14). And one can enumerate other policies in American education that actually amount to SAPs in form and effect, if not in name.

SAPs in the USA are also taking their toll on African languages in particular, which, so far, have had the most secure base in American academia. The pendulum of political opinion is increasingly moving towards reduced spending on education, in general, and area studies in particular. Other SAP factors which may threaten the presence of African languages in American universities include: the growing momentum against affirmative action that has provided educational opportunities to many African American students who still constitute the strongest political constituency for African languages in the USA; the rising cost of fees and tuition that is affecting college enrolments, again especially among African Americans; and the increasing focus on number of students in determining the fate of university courses, like those on African languages, which traditionally have had relatively low enrolments, just as the pressure is mounting for less government involvement in subsidizing educational programmes.

This conservative political mood, however, is not only threatening African languages in the USA. It is also a catalyst for the greater consolidation of English precisely at a time when government regulations are being called upon to be more exclusionary against new immigrants, especially those from Africa. The influx of people who are creating a linguistically more diverse USA has sounded once again the alarm bells of assimilation that have constituted the heart of what has come to be known in the US as the 'English Only'movement, a movement that seeks to establish English as the only legitimate official language of the country and obliterate bilingual programmes in American schools altogether.

The connection between immigration and the language question in the USA has been described succintly by Ronald Schmidt in the following words: 'Historically, Anglo Americans have mobilized most frequently on the language question when they have felt most insecure because of mounting numbers of non-English speaking 'newcomers' living and working in 'their' communities' (1993: 75). The English language policy, therefore, becomes in part a way of excluding new immigrants from the job market; but it also serves as a pressure mechanism for rapid linguistic assimilation into the wider Anglo-American world. The paradox thus continues – SAPs threaten the supremacy of English in Africa while trying to assure its hegemony in the United States.

Multiculturalism under threat

The greatest victims of the 'English Only' movement in the USA are likely to be Latino and Asian Americans, for it is from these minority language groups that the largest population increases have been registered over the years. But virtually all minority groups that have a stake in bilingual education, including Native Americans, are facing the challenge of a resurgent conservatism in the USA. Certain politico-economic interests in the USA, then, are increasingly turning against diversity in a nation, ironically, that was founded on diversity.

But to the extent that the English Only movement is also driven by a quest for American national identity, it has implications for African Americans and, therefore, for African languages. Quoting Schmidt once again, advocates of the English Only policy 'appear to feel deeply that the "unity" of the United States is a very fragile thing, and that – given the immense diversity of the population – the English language is one of the very few unifying factors for a national identity for Americans' (1993: 87). This particular question of language and national identity, then, brings us directly to the politics of sameness and difference.

Minorities in the USA came to (re)claim their cultural and linguistic heritages partly because of the realization that the image of America as a 'melting pot' of a sort was merely a myth. The fact of difference thus came to prominence to signal a new national consciousness that America must be accepted as one nation with multiple identities – indeed different but all morally equal. It is partly the gains of this diversity campaign that sustained the African American quest for a reconnection with their African linguistic heritage, leading to their demand, as a matter of civil right, for a permanent place for African languages in American educational institutions.

Now diversity and multiculturalism are being threatened anew. Assimilationists are seeking to make English the *sine qua non* of American nationhood. And those who maintain or attempt to re-establish links with other languages are regarded as less than American, and even as 'traitors' to the ideal of an American nation. Like other minorities, then, African Americans, too, may be under pressure to dissociate themselves from linguistic or other identitiarian connections with Africa. If this trend persists it is likely to have implications for the future of African languages in the USA. Whatever the case, this Anglocentric sense of American nationhood provides one of the political motives for structural adjustment programmes in American academia.

If SAPs pose a danger to African languages in the USA, however, their effects in the African context are probably even more deleterious. African nations have long been the target of SAPs imposed specifically by the World Bank and IMF. It is our contention that the prescriptions of these two institutions essentially function in favour of European languages, in general, and the English language in particular. And, as in the USA, their effects are manifested most clearly in the realm of education. But, in Africa, does structural adjustment facilitate or impede the expansion of European languages?

One of the standard demands of the IMF and the World Bank almost throughout Africa is the reduction of government subsidies in virtually every sphere of society, from health to education. But, given the serious dearth of materials in local African languages – precipitated in part by colonial and in part by post-colonial policies – significant financial support from the government is simply indispensable in the promotion of local languages in African education. Even those African nations that have demonstrated a commitment to (re)centring African languages are increasingly finding themselves with no option but to adopt the imperial languages from the earliest years of their children's education. It was after Tanzania capitulated to IMF and World Bank conditionalities in the 1980s, for example, that the British ODA moved in aggressively to launch the multi-million dollar English Teaching Support Project in 1987. Since then, the Tanzanian government has been back-pedalling on some of its own initial plans to extend instruction in Kiswahili well beyond elementary education. This trend may also be due, however, to the more general deradicalization of the leadership in Tanzania.

SAPs in Africa are also contributing to the consolidation of imperial languages in a more demographic sense. In its attempts to justify its requirement that African governments cut down on educational expenditures and force students to assume part of the educational costs, the World Bank has sometimes argued that the majority of African students can afford to pay for university education. Subsidies to public universities, in particular, are considered not only inefficient educational investment but also regressive social spending, because students enrolled in universities are, supposedly, disproportionately from the upper end of the scale of income distribution (World Bank, 1994:3).

In absolute terms, however, the World Bank figures are unequivocal that the majority of students in African universities – an average of about 60 per cent – come from the ranks of the peasantry, the working class and petty traders who cannot be expected to meet the rising cost of university education. The natural outcome would be an increase in drop-out rates among students from poorer family backgrounds. In Kenya's Moi and Egerton Universities, for example, with their combined population of about 6,000 students, over 2,000 students were deregistered in early May of 1996 over non-payment of tuition fees (*Daily Nation*, 4 May 1996: 18). These tuition defaulters are more likely to have come from lower-class than upper-class families. One of the net effects of SAPs in education, therefore, may be to transform the African university into a 'white-collar' institution in terms of the parental background of its student population. This would make universities more élitist; but will it arrest the pace of Westernization?

This shift in African universities has certain linguistic consequences. The imperial languages in Africa have their strongest demographic base among children of white-collar families. In some African cities, the English language is fast becoming the medium with which middle-class and upper-class children feel most comfortable in virtually all conversational situations and domains. The exclusionary effect that SAPs are likely to have on the children of the poor will give further impetus to the consolidation of the imperial languages in education and, concomitantly, to the greater marginalization of African languages in élite schools. The question still remains, however, whether this arrested Anglicization of the peasantry is a cost or a benefit.

These effects of the SAPs imposed by the World Bank and the IMF fit perfectly well with the expanding role of the English language as a medium of global capitalism – whether or not there is an explicit reference to this connection as part of a broader agenda of the two Bretton Woods institutions. If the forces of capitalism once provided the unparalleled stimulus for the globalization of English, the language has now become critical for the consolidation of capitalism on a global scale. Within the international capitalist context, the centre has virtually been serving as the 'proprietor' while the periphery can be likened more to the labour and consumer dimension of the capitalist equation. And it is the English language which allows the 'proprietor nations' of the centre to have contact with each and every 'consumer nation' of the periphery in a way that leads only to the increasing consolidation of the global capitalist market. As leading representatives of international capitalism, the World Bank and the IMF can be expected to have a vested interest in this interplay between linguistics and economics, to the detriment of African languages. But the unintended consequences of structural adjustment within African countries may in the short term slow down the pace of Westernization by limiting Western culture to a smaller élite.

The picture that emerges from our analysis so far, then, is that the overt pro-English push in the USA has run parallel to the more covert pro-English push globally. And this world-wide, silent promotion of English may be part of the right-wing agenda to bring the world nearer to the 'end of history'. It could be one of the strategies intended to stimulate rapid reorientations which could promote the final victory of capitalism throughout the world under the control of Western imperialism. In the final analysis, then, attempts to (re)centre African languages in Africa itself, and to continue providing them with space in the USA and the West, may require direct engagement in forms of struggle which may contribute to the emergence of a more balanced world order with a multipolar configuration in terms of power relations. Only such a world can guarantee the preservation of multi-culturalism and diversity, of cultural and linguistic pluralism in this world that we all share. Even if we were to believe that the future lies in market ideologies, they have to be tamed and civilized by parity of esteem between languages and cultures.

Language and the apartheid aftermath

Let us now turn to the end of overt and institutionalized racism. What is the effect of the end of political apartheid for Africa as a whole? The struggle against apartheid was a pan-Africanizing experience, creating a sense of solidarity among black people across the continent and between Africa and its diaspora.

Pan-Africanism often flourished, paradoxically, through the unifying force of European languages. Figures like W. E. B. DuBois and Marcus Garvey would never have become founding fathers of trans-Atlantic pan-Africanism without the mediation of the English language. Figures like Aimé Césaire and Léopold Sédar Senghor would not have become founding fathers of Negritude without the role of the French language. Racism and apartheid in South Africa helped to consolidate the solidarity.

But a new contradiction emerged with the end of political apartheid. Governance in South Africa itself was more Africanized almost by definition as Nelson Mandela and the African National Congress assumed control. But across the African continent the end of political apartheid was an experience in dis-pan-Africanization. A major stimulus of solidarity was diffused. Pan-Africanism was wounded by its own success.

And yet narrower forms of African nationalism, less dependent on European languages, began to reassert themselves. Ethnic nationalism among black South Africans and elsewhere became a new manifest destiny. What were its implications for European languages like English?

With the end of political apartheid in South Africa, the English language has made the clearest gains. Although South Africa has declared eleven official languages (theoretically reducing English to one-eleventh of the official status), in reality the new policy demotes Afrikaans – the historic rival to English in South Africa.

Before the 1990s English was officially the co-equal of Afrikaans, but sometimes received fewer resources from the government within the media and within publishing. But the end of political apartheid has raised the question of whether Afrikaans should be regarded in the same light as the nine African indigenous languages. Should Afrikaans be treated as just another 'native vernacular'? The debate is well and truly joined. The distribution of language resources for the media and for education is at stake.

The end of political apartheid in South Africa represents the triumph of a particular kind of African nationalism – the struggle against overt racial oppression and cultural demand. Paradoxically this struggle (but not its triumph) sometimes enhanced the status of the English language among the oppressed. English became not just a language of oppression but also, by a strange destiny, a language of liberation. This was true not just in Africa but also in other parts of the British Empire – from Cairo to Calcutta, from Kingston to Kuala Lumpur.

While on balance the English language has been truly triumphant as a world language, there is a tendency to overlook its setbacks within the grand picture. Let us look more closely at what English has been up against. Sometimes its successes have resulted in its own setbacks. Although French has been a bigger loser than English since the Second World War, there are areas where English has also received setbacks. English has been challenged by the following forces.

Conclusion

Firstly, post-colonial indigenization policies. Some former colonies of Britain have attempted to reduce the role of English in their societies. Originally the Indian Constitution envisaged replacing English completely with Hindi as the official and national language. This ambition was not realized – partly because of objections from Southern India. Nevertheless, India's language policy has increased the roles of Hindi and other Indian languages.

Tanzania has pursued policies of increased Swahilization deliberately at the expense of English in education, the media and politics – even though, as pointed out earlier, English has begun to reassert itself. South Africa after apartheid is experimenting with a policy of eleven official languages. What do they mean as official languages? South Africans are grappling with the problems.

Before July 1997, Hong Kong was a special case where the use of English was declining in spite of Hong Kong's expanding role as one of the major financial markets of Asia, if not the world. Among the main reasons for the decline of English in that society was the prospect of Hong Kong's incorporation into the People's Republic of China in 1997. People began learning the second Chinese language (adding Mandarin to the Hong Kong Cantonese). Hong Kong is now part of the People's Republic of China.

Then there are the post-colonial or post-revolutionary policies of Islamization or Arabization. These policies sometimes result in a reduced role for the imperial language and the promotion of the Arabic language instead. This is what has been happening in the Sudan in the 1990s as the Arabic language has been promoted as the medium of instruction at all levels of education, including most departments at universities. Previously English was the main medium of instruction at the University of Khartoum, for example.

In Iran since the fall of the Shah, English has lost some ground as against the increased use of Persian (Farsi) and Arabic in the reformed syllabuses of education within the post-revolutionary Islamic Republic of Iran. Iran has used English more than any other language, however, in a bid to influence political and diplomatic trends in Africa. Even in its publications for Africa Iran has resorted to the English language more than to any other when it has been attempting to reach fellow Muslim militants. In Islam Arabic is the chosen language of God; but in the politics of the twentieth century English is the chosen language of global diplomacy.

Another setback for English is the rise of the numerate culture (or the culture of numbers). As people communicate in fewer words but more numbers, English and other literate languages pay part of the price. This is partly in the computer world of financial consultations and scientific discourse, where calculations in numbers have more and more 'say'.

Then there is the increased legitimation of pidgin and creole. These languages have reduced the push for standard English in countries like Nigeria, Ghana, Jamaica, Trinidad, and Sierra Leone. While West Africa has evolved its pidgin of English, East Africa and Southern Africa have not. East and Southern Africa's closer approximation to standard English has been helped by the following factors: the stronger presence of white settlers in East and South Africa; the more recent colonization of Eastern Africa (covering only Jomo Kenyatta's lifetime); the more dynamic indigenous cultures of West Africa which have imposed their own personality on English in a manner as yet underdeveloped in Eastern and Southern Africa.

There has also been the increasing recognition of Arabic as an additional international language. It is now an official language in some United Nations meetings; within the Organization of African Unity; within institutions born out of the new

Arab petro-power (OPEC, OPEAC, the Arab Development Bank); within the Organization of the Islamic Conference.

The multicultural movement in the West is another agenda potentially challenging to the English language. The slow acceptance of Spanish as the potential second language of parts of the United States is reducing the supremacy of English. This is what provoked the rearguard action of the 'English Only' movement. The toleration of other languages in Western schools, meanwhile, challenges the old primacy of the English language.

Then there is the phenomenon of former British colonies and the Commonwealth. Countries previously ruled by Britain which have *not* joined the Commonwealth are, on one side, the United States and, on the other, the Arab countries. Former dependencies of Britain in the Arab world include Egypt, Sudan, Iraq and Kuwait. In these countries the English language has lagged far behind. In the United States, on the other hand, the English language has been triumphant.

Why is the United States not part of the Commonwealth? It was independent long before the Commonwealth was born. Later, there were ideological reasons why the United States could not join the Commonwealth, since the British monarch was supposed to be monarch of each member (and later still remained the head of the club, though no longer the head of state of each member). American entry, in any case, would be bound to change the focal point of the Commonwealth, with Washington displacing London. American participation was bound to be opposed both by powerful forces in the US and by influential members within the Commonwealth, especially the British themselves.

But although the United States (unlike Canada) is the grand exception to Commonwealth membership, the United States nevertheless became an even more influential carrier of the English language than Britain by the second half of the twentieth century. People and whole societies wanted to learn English less and less because of Great Britain, and more and more because it was the language which Americans spoke.

With former British dependencies among the Arab countries, on the other hand, English was more marginal than it was in other former British colonies. There were many reasons why these countries (including Egypt, Sudan, and Iraq) declined to join the Commonwealth. Arab nationalism was distrustful of continuing organizational links with the former imperial power, and the Commonwealth was viewed as a rival to the League of Arab States – *Pax Britannica* versus Pan-Arabism. British policies were viewed as pro-Israeli, and the Commonwealth was tarnished as an indirect result. Another reason was religious: the head of the Commonwealth was also the head of the Church of England – always. Thus the Commonwealth (to Muslims) was 'tarnished' indirectly by England's Christian theocracy.

In the case of the Sudan the three-way choice was joining up with Egypt as a confederation; joining the Commonwealth; or remaining a separate independent country. Sudan chose the third. By not joining the Commonwealth, Egypt and Sudan were also making a linguistic decision. They were deciding to be less dependent on the English language in national affairs.

The African impact on world languages

But if European languages have had such a significant impact on the destinies of African languages and societies, have there been cases of the reverse influence of

Africa upon world languages? In Chapter 2 we talked about the presence of Africanisms in one variety of American English, Ebonics, which in turn continues to influence some other varieties of the language. In some of the chapters we alluded to the emergence of local varieties of English in Africa bearing the imprint of African languages in some of their features. Monique Thies (1975) and Raymond Mauny (1975) demonstrate the impact of African languages on French. These and others are instances of African languages playing the role of 'actor', in some cases actually leading to the Africanization of European languages – as discussed in some of the previous chapters of this book and in the following section of this chapter.

The impact of Africa on world languages, however, goes much farther back in history and begins with the factor of genesis. While Europe globalized language, and Asia made language sacred, it was Africa which invented language in the first place. As argued in Chapter Five, since the African continent is, on present scientific evidence, where the human species began, it is also where human linguistic communication and speech originated. Africa's first major impact on world languages is therefore inseparable from the human genesis.

Africa's linguistic influence moves more decisively into history with the birth, development and export of what have sometimes been called Hamito-Semitic languages or Afro-Asiatic languages. The word 'Hamites', of course, has become politically incorrect in some circles. It has been estimated that this family of related languages evolved from a shared 'parent' language which existed about 8000–6000 BC and was located originally in the present-day Sahara. The evidence is based partly on how the languages are distributed. The branches of the Afro-Asiatic family include Berber, Chadic, Cushitic, Egyptian, Omotic and Semitic. It constitutes the main language family of North Africa and south-western Asia, and includes such languages as Arabic, Berber, Hausa, Amharic, Somali and Hebrew (Mann and Dalby, 1987: 11–28).

Of these, by far the most influential globally has been the Semitic branch. The Qur'an has become the most widely read book in its original language, Arabic, in history (the Bible is the most widely read book in translation). The influence of Arabic on the English language includes Arabic-derived words like algebra, tariff, admiral, zero and (ironically) alcohol. Words which the Holy Qur'an shares with modern-day German include surprisingly the word *stratta* (*swirata* in Verse 6, Chapter 1 of the Qur'an, in the sense of highway). The English equivalent, of course, is *street*.

Although the Bible is a scripture mainly in translation, many words from its Hebrew/Aramaic origins have survived into European languages. The words range from *gehenna* to the even more untranslatable *messiah*. The Hebrews have also contributed personal names to Western civilization – from Mary to Peter, from Jacob to James and Moses.

Overlapping with Africa's Semitic contribution to world civilization is the impact of ancient Egypt on neighbouring civilizations in the Mediterranean. Martin Bernal of Cornell University talks of his linguistic odyssey from being a specialist in Chinese, Japanese and Vietnamese languages to a new fascination with Chichewa (a language of Zambia and Malawi), Hebrew, Phoenician, ancient Greek, and ancient Egyptian languages. Bernal tells us:

> I worked … for four years, and became convinced that anything up to a quarter of the Greek vocabulary could be traced to Semitic origins.… [Subsequently] I became convinced that one could find plausible etymologies for a further 20–25

percent of the Greek vocabulary from Egyptian, as well as the names for most Greek gods and many place names. (1987: xiv–xv)

If thought is linked to words, and so much of the vocabulary of ancient Greece was influenced by Africa and the Semites, we may conclude that there was some interplay between Greek thought, Semitic ideas, and Egyptian principles. This classical world was a clear case of interaction between North Africa, West Asia and Southern Europe.

But Bernal tells us that in the modern period Europe went racist and manipulated classical Greek history in order to deny the influence of Egypt and the Semites upon it. Bernal reminds us: 'Egypt had by far the greatest civilization in the East Mediterranean during the millennia in which Greece was formed.... Clearly there were very profound cultural inhibitors [among Europeans] against associating Egypt with Greece' (1987: xiv).

Bernal further argues that this rewriting of ancient Greek history was not done by ancient Greeks themselves. On the contrary, the ancients freely acknowledged their debt to Egypt. The revisionist historians emerged mainly in the eighteenth and nineteenth centuries in the wake of the growth of racism and anti-Semitism in Europe. There was a determined attempt to deny any cultural indebtedness to either a Semitic people (like the Phoenicians) or to an African people (like the Egyptians). European racism moved from bad to worse.

By the late nineteenth and throughout the twentieth century the influence which Africa had on Western languages sometimes became negative to Africa's image. African traditional religions were so widely misunderstood and despised that they inadvertently contributed to the English language such words as *voodoo* (from a Dahomey or Benin language) and *mumbo-jumbo* (vulgarized Bantu). North Africa also contributed the word 'barbarians' to English – there are alternative etymologies for this word – because of North African maritime activities against Westerners on the Barbary Coast.

The long sad story of the association of Africa with disease quite early left the Ghanaian concept of *kwashiorkor* embedded in the English language – the disease of small children with protruding bellies. More recently we had the outbreak of *Ebola* in Zaire (now the Democratic Republic of the Congo). AIDS would probably have been given a distinctly African name but for the fact that it was diagnosed in the West before it was discovered in Africa.

Twentieth-century Africa has also sometimes been a *tourist* attraction, with linguistic repercussions. By far the most familiar Kiswahili tourist word which has found its way into the English language is *safari*. Although in Kiswahili *safari* means any trip whatsoever, in English the word has come to mean more narrowly a trip in search of wild animals in Africa, either to hunt them or to photograph them.

And yet the word *safari* reconnects us with one of the older and more wide-ranging impacts of Africa upon the world – the Hamito-Semitic or Afro-Asiatic impact. Although among white hunters the word *safari* is a Kiswahili word, its origins are in fact Semitic. It is one of Kiswahili's loan words from Arabic.

The dialectic of Africa's linguistic history is still at work – from the origins of human speech in places like the Olduvai Gorge to the mutations of the ancient Egyptian language; from the Phoenicians in history to white hunters on *safari* in Kenya. Africa's influence on world languages has known both pinnacles of accomplishment and pits of frustration. The struggle continues, the *safari* proceeds.

But as the twentieth century got under way the direction of influence decisively changed. European languages – which had once been the recipients of African and Semitic influences – became hegemonic and exerted counter-power upon African languages and societies. Formal colonialism came and went; the old Cold War emerged and subsided; apartheid triumphed and retreated. But certain hegemonic realities persisted.

Anglicizing Africa versus Africanizing English?

Regardless of the end of apartheid or the end of the Cold War, European languages in Africa continue to play a chess game with African cultures. Will the African languages be Europeanized or will the European languages be Africanized?

Some of the measurements link language to wider cultural values. Where do the 'pronouns' come in? Languages betray the cultures from which they spring. Pronouns are part of that story. In referring to a third person English is gender-conscious – so the pronoun *he* refers to the male and the pronoun *she* refers to the female. In many African languages pronouns are gender-neutral. The words for 'he' or 'she' are fused into one. To the present day many Africans competent in the English language sometimes refer to a third person female as 'he' when speaking in English because of the linguistic influence of their own mother tongues.

Most African languages do not have separate words for 'nephews' and 'nieces' because your sister's children are supposed to be the equivalent of your own biological children. The same word which is used for your child (*mtoto* in Kiswahili) is used for your niece or nephew. Very few African languages have a word for 'cousin'. Your uncle's daughter or son is the equivalent of your sister or brother, so cousins are counted almost as siblings. Once again language betrays the tightness of kinship ties in the African extended family.

More intriguing is why the first person singular in English is capitalized I, with a higher case 'I' for number one! Does the English language betray a higher level of individualism in its culture, and a greater legitimation of the pursuit of personal goals?

Then there is the tale of two Englishes: British and American. George Bernard Shaw used to say that the Americans and the British were a people divided by the same language. Only Liberia in Africa got its English from the Americans. Everywhere else in Africa got its English from the British. But idiomatically Africans are becoming Americanized in their usage. Americans are people in a hurry; the British are more sedate. So Americans *run* for elections; the British *stand* for elections. Africans are beginning to pick up the American idiom of 'running' for elections. The British greet each other by asking 'How are you?' which is a static condition. The Americans ask 'How are you doing?' which is an active condition. Africa is caught in between.

Then there is the inevitable link between literature, language and politics in both Africa and Europe. We have noted elsewhere that one African president has translated two of Shakespeare's plays into an African language – Kiswahili. The plays he translated were *Julius Caesar* and *The Merchant of Venice*. The President was of course Julius K. Nyerere. His compatriot, S. Mushi, has translated a third play by Shakespeare – *Macbeth*.

Another African president Apollo Obote, admired the author of *Paradise Lost*, John Milton, so much that the African adopted the name Milton as his own *de facto* first name. He is going down in history as Milton Obote. The poet John Milton is widely regarded as the second greatest poet in the English language after William Shakespeare. Obote admired especially Milton's portrayal of Lucifer before he fell and deteriorated into Satan. It was Lucifer who proclaimed, 'Better to reign in hell than serve in heaven' – which nationalists interpreted as better to reign in post-colonial hell than serve in a colonial heaven. Freedom in poverty was better than slavery in luxury.

A third African president – Léopold Sédar Senghor – was actually nominated for the Nobel Prize for literature in his own right more than once. This was the poet president of Senegal, who wrote poetry and philosophy for half a century. He was President of Senegal from 1960 to 1980. In Senghor's case the European language he had mastered so eloquently was not English, but French. He was elected to the French Academy. He was consulted by President Charles de Gaulle on the drafting of the Constitution of the Fifth Republic of France. So widely admired by the French people was Senghor's command of 'their' language that nominations for the Nobel Prize came his way regularly. When the Nobel Prize went to an African, however, it was to Wole Soyinka, the Nigerian.

These are some of the chess games which Africa has played with major aspects of Western culture. In this chapter we have looked at Africa in a global context. How does its experience compare with Asia's? How does Africa relate to the American social experience? What is Africa's own impact on world languages? We have touched upon some of the linguistic repercussions of the collapse of the Warsaw Pact for Africa. We have also taken a glimpse at the linguistic trends in the Arab world and their relevance for Africa. Some of the forces at work may now have become perennial. Market ideologies have competed with statism. An apartheid era bared its ugly teeth and then whimpered away; a Cold War erupted and subsided. Structural adjustment is just the latest of the agendas of the World Bank and the International Monetary Fund. But the struggle continues between the forces of dependence and the tides of authenticity. And language is one of the grand arenas of that struggle, one of the theatres of cultural combat.

REFERENCES

Sources
Most of the chapters in this book have appeared elsewhere before in slightly different versions. The sources are as follows:

'Language and Race in the Black Experience: An African Perspective'. *Dalhousie Review*, 68.1 and 2, Spring/Summer 1989: 87–110.

'African Languages in the African American Experience'. Carol Aisha Blackshire-Belay (ed.), *Language and Literature in the African American Imagination*. Westport (CT): Greenwood Press, 1992:75–90.

'Linguistic Eurocentrism and African Counter-Penetration: Ali Mazrui and the Global Frontiers of Language'. Previously published as 'Mazruiana and Global Language.' Omari H. Kokole (ed.), *The Global African: A Portrait of Ali A. Mazrui*. Trenton (NJ): Africa World Press, 1995: 275–304.

'Language and the Quest for Liberation: The Legacy of Frantz Fanon'. *Third World Quarterly*, 14.2, 1993: 351–64.

'Language in a Multicultural Context: The African Experience'. Michael C. Beveridge and Gordon Reddiford, *Language, Culture and Education*. Clevedon: Multilingual Matters, 1993: 3–18.

'Language Planning and Gender Planning: An African Perspective'. *International Journal of the Sociology of Language*, 118, 1996: 125–34.

'Language Policy and the Foundations of Democracy: An African Perspective'. *International Journal of the Sociology of Language*, 115, 1993: 107–24.

'Dominant Languages in a Plural Society: English and Kiswahili in Post-Colonial East Africa'. *International Political Science Review*, 14.3, July 1993: 275–92.

'A Tale of Two Englishes: The Imperial Language in Post-Colonial Kenya and Uganda'. Joshua A. Fishman, Andrew W. Conrad and Alma Rubal-Lopez (eds), *Post-Imperial English: Status Change in Former British and American Colonies, 1940-1990*. Berlin: Mouton de Gruyter, 1996: 271–302.

'Roots of Kiswahili: Colonialism, Nationalism, and the Dual Heritage'. *Ufahamu*, 20.3, Fall 1992: 88–100.

'The Secularization of an Afro-Islamic Language: Church, State and the Market Place in the Spread of Kiswahili'. *Journal of Islamic Studies*, 2, 1990:25–53.

References

Abdulaziz, Mohamed H. 'East Africa (Tanzania and Kenya)'. Jenny Chesire (ed.), *English Around the World: The Social Contexts.* Cambridge: Cambridge University Press, 1991: 391–401.

Adhiambo-Oduol, Jacqueline. 'Gender and Ideology: The Role of Language'. Wanjiku M. Kabira, Jacqueline A. Oduol and Maria Nzomo (eds), *Democratic Change in Africa: A Woman's Perspective.* Nairobi: Association of African Women for Research Development (AAWORD), 1993: 35–46.

Alexander, Pierre. *Languages and Language Policy in Black Africa.* Evanston (IL): Northwestern University Press, 1972.

Al-Rahim, Abd. 'Arabism, Africanism, and Self-Identification in the Sudan'. *The Journal of Modern African Studies.* 8.2, July 1970.

Amin, Samir. 'Eurocentrism'. New York: *Monthly Review Press*, 1989.

Andereggen, André. *France's Relationship with Sub-Saharan Africa.* Westport (CT): Praeger, 1994.

Asante, Molefi Kete. *Afrocentricity.* Trenton (NJ): Africa World Press, 1988.

—'The African Essence in African American Language'. M.K.Asante and K. W.Asante (eds), *African Culture: The Rhythms of Unity.* Trenton (NJ): Africa World Press, 1990: 47–81.

Baldwin, James. 'Why I Stopped Hating Shakespeare'. *Insight.* 11. Ibadan: British High Commission, 1964.

Baraka, Imamu Amiri. *Blues People: Negro Music in White America.* New York: W. Morrow Press, 1963.

Bender, Marvin L. *Language in Ethiopia.* London: Oxford University Press, 1976.

Bernal, Martin. *Black Athena: The Afroasiatic Roots of Classical Civilization* (Vol. I). New Brunswick (NJ): Rutgers University Press, 1987.

Berk-Seligson, Susan. 'Bilingual Court Proceedings: The Role of the Court Interpreter'. Judith N. Levi (ed.), *Language in the Judicial Process.* New York: Plenum Press, 1992.

Bernstein, Basil. 'Education Cannot Compensate for Society'. *New Society.* 387, 1971: 36–55.

—'Social Class, Language and Socialization'. P. Gilgioli (ed.), *Language and Society.* Harmondsworth: Penguin, 1972.

Bhola, H. S. 'A Review of Literacy in Sub-Saharan Africa: Images in the Making'. *African Studies Review.* 33.3, 1990: 5–20.

Bickerton, Derek. *Language and Species.* Chicago: The University of Chicago Press, 1990.

Bohannan, Paul. *African Outline.* Harmondsworth: Penguin, 1966.

Borishade, Adetokunbo K. 'The Niger-Kordofanian Linguistic Bases of African American Ebonics: a Creole Language'. *The Western Journal of Black Studies,* 18, 1, Spring 1992: 1–9.

Boutros-Ghali, Boutros. 'The Foreign Policy of Egypt'. Black and Thompson (eds), *Foreign Policy in the World of Change.* New York: Harper and Row, 1963.

Bruhn, Thea. *African Lingua Francas.* Washington DC: Center for Applied Linguistics, 1984.

Caffentzis, George. 'It is Not With You but Against You that we Learn Your Language: Sankara and Derrida as African Intellectuals'. unpublished manuscript, 1990.

Childers, Erskine. *Common Sense About the Arab World.* London: Victor Gollancz Ltd., 1960.

References

Chiraghdin, Shihabuddin. 'Kiswahili na Wenyewe'. *Kiswahili*. 44.1, 1974: 48–53.

Chomsky, Noam. *Language and Mind*. New York: Harcourt, 1986.

Coleman, James S. *Nigeria: Background to Nationalism*. Berkeley and Los Angeles: University of California Press, 1958.

Comrie, Bernard (ed.) *The Major Languages of South Asia, the Middle East and Africa*. London: Routledge, 1990.

Curtin, Philip, Steven Fierman, Leonard Thompson and Jan Vansina. *African History*. Boston (MA): Little, Brown and Company, 1978.

Curtis, H. A. 'The New Primary Approach'. *Kenya Educational Journal*. October 1965: 30–37.

Davis, Ossie. 'The English Language is my Enemy'. Robert H. Bentley and Samuel D. Crawford (eds), *Black Language Reader*. Glenview (IN): Scott, Foresenan and Company, 1973.

Deane, Seamus. 'Introduction'. Terry Eagleton, Fredric Jameson and Edward Said (eds), *Nationalism, Colonialism and Literature*. Minneapolis: University of Minnesota Press, 1990: 3–19.

Duke, Lynne and James Rupert, 'Power Behind Kabila Reflects Congo War's Tutsi Roots', *International Herald Tribune*, 29 May 1997.

Eagleton, Terry. 'Nationalism: Irony and Commitment'. Terry Eagleton, Fredric Jameson and Edward Said (eds), *Nationalism, Colonialism and Literature*. Minneapolis: University of Minnesota Press, 1990: 25–39.

Egejuru, P. A. *Towards African Literary Independence: A Dialogue with Contemporary African Writers*. Westport (CT): Greenwood Press, 1980.

Fanon, Frantz. *The Wretched of the Earth*. Harmondsworth: Penguin, 1967a.

— *Black Skin, White Masks*. New York: Grove Press, 1967b.

— *A Dying Colonialism*. New York: Grove Press, 1967c.

— *Towards a Dying Colonialism*. New York: Grove Press, 1969.

Faraclas, Nicholas. 'They Came Before the Egyptians: Linguistic Evidence for the African Roots of Semitic Languages'. Silvia Federici (ed.), *Enduring Western Civilization:The Construction of the Concept of Western Civilization and its Others*. Westport (CT): Praeger, 1995.

Fardon, Richard and Graham Furniss. 'Language and Languages: Frontiers and Boundaries'. Paper presented at the Conference on African Languages, Development and the State. Centre for African Studies, University of London, 25–26 April 1991.

Ferreira, Eduardo de Sousa. *Portuguese Colonization in Africa: The End of an Era*. Paris: UNESCO, 1974.

Fishman, Joshua. 'A Systemization of the Whorfian Hypothesis'. *Behavioral Sciences*. 5, 1960: 323–39.

Forster, Peter, G. *The Esperanto Movement*. The Hague: Mouton, 1982.

Freeman-Grenville, G.S.P. 'The Coast: 1498–1940'. Roland Oliver and G. Matthew (eds), *History of East Africa*. Oxford: Clarendon Press, 1963.

Ghai, Yash. 'The Theory of the State in the Third World and the Problematique of Constitutionalism'. Kibutha Kibwana (ed.), *Law and the Administration of Justice*. Nairobi: The International Commission of Jurists, 1992: 3–15.

Gitonga, Afrifa K. 'The Meaning and Foundations of Democracy'. Walter O. Oyugi and Afrifa Gitonga (eds), *Democratic Theory and Practice in Africa*. Nairobi: Heinemann Kenya Ltd., 1987: 4–23.

Godfrey, Martin. 'The Outflow of Trained Personnel from Developing

References

Countries, Brain Drain: The Disengagement Alternative'. UN doc., ECOSOC, No. t/CN.5/L.421. Paris: United Nations, 1976.

Goke-Pariola, Abiodun. *The Role of Language in the Struggle for Power and Legitimacy in Africa*. Lewiston (UK): The Edwin Mellon Press, 1993.

Gordon, J.C. *Verbal Deficit*. London: Croom Helm, 1981.

Gorman, Thomas P. 'The Development of Language Policy in Kenya With Particular Reference to the Educational System'. W.H. Whiteley (ed.), *Language in Kenya*. Nairobi: Oxford University Press, 1974a: 397–454.

Gorman, Thomas P. 'Patterns of Language Use Among School Children and Their Parents'. W.H.Whiteley (ed.), *Language in Kenya*. Nairobi: Oxford University Press, 1974b: 351–95.

Gowers, W. F. 'Development of Kiswahili as an Educational and Administrative Language in the Uganda Protectorate'. Memorandum, 25 November 1927.

Gramsci, Antonio. *Selections from Cultural Writings*. David Forgacs and Geoffrey Nowell-Smith (eds). Cambridge (MA): Harvard University Press, 1985.

Greenberg, Joseph. *The Languages of Africa.* The Hague: Mouton, 1963.

— 'Concerning Inferences from Linguistic to Non-linguistic Data'. Harry Hoijer (ed.), *Language and Culture*. Chicago: University of Chicago Press, 1979: 3–19.

Hartford, E. F. *Pilkington of Uganda*. 1899.

Haugen, Einer. 'Linguistic Relativity: Myths and Methods'. W.C. McCormick and S.A.Wurm (eds), *Language and Thought: Anthropological Issues*. The Hague: Mouton, 1977: 1–8.

Hay, Margaret Jean. 'Luo Women and Economic Change During the Colonial Period'. Nancy J. Halfkin and Edna G. Bay (eds), *Women in Africa: Studies in Social and Economic Change*. Stanford (CA): Stanford University Press, 1976.

Heine, Bernd. 'Language and Society'. B. Heine and W.J.G.Mohlig (eds), *Language and Dialect Atlas of Kenya*. Berlin: Dietrick and Reimer Verlag, 1980: 59–78.

Henson, Hilary. *British Social Anthropologists and Language: A History of Separate Development*. Oxford: Clarendon Press, 1974.

Herbstein, Denis. 'The Alphabet War'. *Africa Report*, 36 May/June 1991: 67–9.

Hinnebusch, Thomas, 'What Kind of Language is Swahili?' *Afrikanistische Arbeitspapiere*, 47, 1996: 73–95.

Holloway, Joseph E. and Winifred D. Vass. *The African Heritage of American English*. Bloomington: Indiana University Press, 1994.

Hyder, Mohamed. 'Swahili in a Technical Age'. *Contemporary African Monograph Series, Number 4: East Africa's Cultural Heritage*. Nairobi: The East African Institute of Social and Cultural Affairs. 1966: 78–87.

Jones, Thomas Jesse. *Education in East Africa: A Study of East, South and Equatorial Africa by the African Education Commission*. New York: Phelps-Stokes Fund, 1925.

Kabwegyere, Tarsis B. *The Politics of State Formation: The Nature and Effects of Colonisation in Uganda*. Nairobi: East African Literature Bureau, 1974.

Karenga, Maulana. *Essays in Struggle*. San Diego: Kawaida Publications, 1978.

Kasfir, Nelson. *The Shrinking Political Arena*. Los Angeles: University of California Press, 1976.

Kioga, M.M. 'Administration of Justice in the Rural Areas of Kenya'. *Law and Society*. Nairobi: The International Commission of Jurists, 1989: 74–82.

References

Ladefoged, P., R. Glick and C. Criper. *Language in Uganda*. London: Oxford University Press, 1972.

Laitin, David D. *Politics, Language and Thought: The Somali Experience*. Chicago: University of Chicago Press, 1977.

— 'Linguistic Dissociation: A Strategy for Africa'. J. G. Ruggie (ed.), *The Antinomies of Independence*. New York: Columbia University Press, 1983: 367–86.

— 'Language Policy and Political Strategy in India'. *Policy Sciences*. 22, 1989: 415–36.

— *Language Repertoires and State Construction in Africa*. New York: Cambridge University Press, 1992.

Lambert, Wallace. 'Language as a Factor in Intergroup Relations'. Howard Giles and Robert N. Clair (eds), *Language and Social Psychology*. Oxford: Basil Blackwell, 1979.

Laponce, J. 'Les Langages comme acteures internationaux: Phénomènes de contagion et phénomènes d'irradiation'. B. Badie (ed.), *Mélanges en l'honneur de Marcle*. Paris: Economica, 1993: 247–64.

Lee, Stephen J. *The Thirty Years War*. London: Routledge, 1991.

Lenninnberg, Eric. 'Cognition in Ethnolinguistics'. *Language*. 29, 1953: 463–71.

Licklider, Roy (ed.), *Stopping the Killing: How Civil Wars End*. New York: New York University Press, 1993.

Livingston, George J. 'Foreword'. Newbell Niles Puckett, *Black Names in America: Origins and Usage*. Boston (MA): G. K. Hall and Company, 1975: 74–93.

Lumpkin, Beatrice. 'Mathematics and Engineering in the Nile Valley'. Ivan van Sertima (ed.), *Nile Valley Civilizations*. Atlanta (GA): *Journal of African Civilizations*, 1985: 101–15.

Mackay, Bishop A. *Mackay of Uganda* (8th Edition). 1989.

— *Fifteen Years in Uganda and East Africa*. 1908.

Mair, Lucy Phillip. *An African People in the Twentieth Century*. New York: Russell and Russell, 1934.

Mann, Michael and David Dalby. *A Thesaurus of African Languages: A Classified and Annotated Inventory of the Spoken Languages of Africa*. London: Hans Zell Publishers, 1987.

Marshad, Hassan. 'An Approach to Code Elaboration and Its Application to Swahili'. Unpublished PhD Thesis, University of Illinois, Urbana-Champaign, 1984.

Massamba, David P. B. 'An Assessment of the Development and Modernization of the Kiswahili Language in Tanzania'. F. Coulmas (ed.), *Language Adaptation*. Cambridge: Cambridge University Press, 1989.

Mauny, Raymond. 'Eléments de vocabulaire Africain dans la langue Française'. *France-Eurafrique: La Tribune Libre des deux Continents*, February 1975: 16–20.

Mazrui, Alamin. 'Acceptability in a Planned Standard: The Case of Kiswahili in Kenya'. PhD Dissertation, Stanford University (Stanford, CA), 1981.

— 'Language and Community Formation Among the Urban Poor: A Case Study of Nairobi's Kibera Slum'. Unpublished MS, 1988.

— 'Relativism, Universalism and the Language of African Literature'. *Research in African Literatures*. 23.2, Spring 1992: 65–72.

Mazrui, Alamin and Ali A. Mazrui. 'Language in a Multicultural Context: The

References

African Experience'. *Language and Education: An International Journal.*
6.2,3 and 4, 1992; 83–98.

Mazrui, Alamin and Ali A. Mazrui. 'Dominant Languages in a Plural Society:
English and Kiswahili in Post-Colonial East Africa'. *International Political
Science Review.* 14.3, 1993: 275–92.

Mazrui, Alamin and Ibrahim Shariff. *The Swahili: Idiom and Identity of an
African People.* Trenton (NJ): Africa World Press, 1994.

Mazrui, Ali A. 'Political Sex'. *Transition.* 4.17, 1964: 19–23.

— *World Culture and the Black Experience.* Seattle:The University of Washington Press, 1974.

— *The Political Sociology of the English Language: An African Perspective.* The
Hague: Mouton, 1975.

— *Africa's International Relations: The Diplomacy of Dependency and Change.*
London: Heinemann, 1977.

— *The Africans: A Triple Heritage.* Boston (MA): Little Brown and Company,
1986.

— 'Language and Race in the Black Experience: An African Perspective'.
Dalhousie Review. 68.1&2, 1989: 87–110.

— 'Viewing the World Through African Eyes'. *The Woodward Review.*
March/April 1993: 15–17

— 'Three Schools of African Political Philosophy: Cultural, Ideological and
Critical'. Paper presented at the Conference on Ancient, Medieval and
Modern Philosophy and Thought, Binghamton University (SUNY), 24–31
October 1993.

Mazrui, Ali A. and Alamin Mazrui. *Swahili, State and Society: The Political
Economy of an African Language.* Nairobi: East African Educational Publishers, and London: James Currey, 1995.

Mazrui, Ali A. and Michael Tidy. *Nationalism and New States in Africa.* Nairobi:
Heinemann Educational Books, 1984.

Mazrui, Ali A. and Pio Zirimu. 'The Secularization of an Afro-Islamic Language:
Church, State and the Market-Place in the Spread of Kiswahili'. *Journal of
Islamic Studies.* 1, 1990: 2–53.

Miller, Robert L. *The Linguistic Relativity Principle and Humboldtian Ethnolinguistics.* The Hague: Mouton, 1968.

Moore, Robert. *Racism in the English Language: A Lesson Plan and Study Essay.*
New York: The Racism and Sexism Research Center for Educators, 1976.

Mukama, Ruth. 'Getting Ugandans to Speak a Common Language: Recent
Developments in the Language Situation and Prospects for the Future'. H. B.
Hansen and M. Twaddle (eds), *Changing Uganda: The Dilemma of Structural
Adjustment and Revolutionary Change.* London: James Currey, 1991: 334–50.

Mukiibi, Catherine N. 'Is There a Need for a Communication Skills Course at
Makerere University?' *Proceedings of the Conference on Academic Communication Skills in African Universities.* Nairobi: The British Council, 1991:
40–5.

Mulokozi, M. M. 'English Versus Kiswahili in Tanzania's Secondary Education'.
J. Blommaert (ed.), *Swahili Studies.* Ghent: Academic Press, 1991: 23–38.

Mutunga, Willy. *The Rights of an Arrested Person.* Nairobi: Oxford University
Press, 1991.

Mwaura, Peter. *Communication Policies in Kenya.* Paris: UNESCO, 1980.

Mzala, Nxumalo and John Hoffman. 'Non-Historic Nations and the National

References

Question: A South African Perspective'. *Science and Society* 54, Winter 1990/91: 408–26.

Ngugi wa Thiong'o. *Decolonizing the Mind: The Politics of Language in African Literature*. London: James Currey, 1986.

Nicholls, C.S. *The Swahili Coast*. London: George Allen and Unwin Ltd, 1971.

Nurse, Derek and Thomas Spear. *The Swahili: Reconstructing the History and Language of an African Society, 800–1500*. Philadelphia: University of Pennsylvania Press, 1985.

Obote, Milton. 'Language and National Identification'. *East Africa Journal*. April 1967: 1–11.

Offiong, Daniel A. *Imperialism and Dependency*. Washington, DC: Howard University Press, 1982.

Ohly, Rajmund. 'Dating the Swahili Language'. *Kiswahili: Journal of the Institute of Swahili Research*. 42.2 and 43.1, 1973: 15–23.

Oliver, Roland. *The Missionary Factor in East Africa*. London: Longmans, 1965.

Ottaway, Marina, *Soviet and American Influence in the Horn of Africa*. New York: Praeger, 1982.

Oxfam. *Partnership for Economic Growth and Opportunity in Africa: An Oxfam Response to the US Initiative*. Washington, DC: Oxfam International Advocacy Office, 1997.

p'Bitek, Okot. *African Religions in Western Scholarship*. Nairobi: East African Literature Bureau, 1971.

Phillipson, Robert. *Linguistic Imperialism*. Oxford: Oxford University Press, 1992.

Piamenta, Moshe. *Islan in Everyday Arabic Speech*. Leiden: E.J. Brill, 1979.

Polome, Edgar C. 'Tanzania: A Socio-linguistic Profile'. E. C.Polome and C.P. Hill (eds), *Language in Tanzania*. London: Oxford University Press, 1980: 130–8.

Polome, Edgar C. and C. P. Hill (eds). *Language in Tanzania*. London: Oxford University Press, 1980.

Puckett, Newbell Niles. *Black Names in America: Origins and Usage*. Boston (MA): G. K. Hall and Company, 1975.

Rao, K.R.V. *Many Languages and One Nation: The Problem of Integration*. Bombay: Hindustan Prachar Sabha, 1979.

Republic of Kenya. *Kenya Education Commission Report: Part I*. Nairobi: Government Printers, 1964.

— *The National Assembly, House of Representatives Official Report*. Vol. IV, 14 December 1964–12 May 1965. Nairobi: Government Printers, 1965.

— *Education Department Triennial Report, 1964–1966*. Nairobi Government Printers, 1967.

— *The National Assembly, House of Representatives Official Report*. Vol. XVII, 27 June–27 August 1969. Nairobi: Government Printers, 1969.

— *The National Assembly, House of Representatives Official Report*. Vol. XXXVIII, 5 July–7August 1974. Nairobi: Government Printers, 1974.

— *The National Assembly, House of Representatives Official Report*. Vol. LXXI, 3 March–30 April 1987. Nairobi: Government Printers, 1987.

— 'An Evaluation of the Secondary English Language Project'. An Unpublished Report by Hirani Ratcliffe Development Consultants, Nairobi, 1992.

Richards, Dona Marimba. *Yurugu: An Afrocentric Critique of European Thought and Behavior*. Trenton (NJ): Africa World Press, 1994.

Sapir, Edward. 'The Status of Linguistics as a Science'. *Language*. 5, 1929: 207–14.

References

Schmied, Joseph. *Recognizing and Accepting East African English Grammar. Proceedings of the International Conference on the Place of Grammar in the Teaching of English.* Nairobi: The British Council, 1988: 94–101.

Schmidt, Ronald J. 'Language Policy in the United States'. Crawford Young (ed.) *The Rising Tide of Cultural Pluralism: The Nation-State at Bay?* Madison (WI): The University of Wisconsin Press, 1993: 73–92.

Schwarz Jr., F. A. O. *Nigeria: The Tribes, The Nation and The Race.* Cambridge (MA): Massachusetts Institute of Technology Press, 1965.

Scotton, Carol Myres. *Choosing a Lingua Franca in an African Capital.* Edmonton: Linguistic Research Inc., 1972.

Seligman, L.G. *Races of Africa* (Third Edition). London: Oxford University Press, 1957.

Shakespeare, William. *Merchant of Venice.*

Shiner, Cindy. 'Kabila: A Study in Paradox'. *The Washington Post,* 19 May 1997.

Silverstein, Michael. 'Language Structure and Linguistic Ideology.' P. Clyre, W. Hanks and E. Haufbauer (eds). *The Elements: A Parasession on Linguistic Units and Levels.* Chicago: Chicago Linguistic Society, 1979: 193–247.

Steere, Edward. *A Handbook of the Swahili Language as Spoken in Zanzibar.* London: Sheldon Press, 1870.

Stigand, Captain C. H. *The Land of Zinj.* London: Frank Cass & Co., Ltd., 1913.

Sure, Kembo. 'Language Functions and Language Attitudes: A Case of Diglossia in Kenya'. *Proceedings of the Seminar on the Role of Language and Literature in the School Curriculum.* Nairobi: The British Council, 1991: 1–31.

Thris, Monique, 'La biennale de la langue Française demande un grand dictionnaire des termes Africains entre dans le Français'. *France Euroafrique: La Tribune Libre des deux Continents.* February 1975: 10–11.

Trevor–Roper, Hugh. Opening lecture in a television series, *The Rise of Christian Europe,* in *The Listener.* London: 28 November 1963: 87.

Turner, Lorenzo. *Africanisms in the Gullah Dialect.* Chicago: University of Chicago Press, 1949.

Twiggs, Robert D. *Pan-African Language in the Western Hemisphere.* North Quincy (MA): The Christopher Publishing House, 1975.

Ullendorf, E. *The Ethiopians: An Introduction to Country and People.* London: Oxford University Press, 1960.

Van Dyken, J. R. 'The Role of Languages of Minority Groups for Literacy and Education in Africa'. *African Studies Review.* 33.3, 1990: 39–52.

Walusimbi, Livingstone. 'The Teaching of Vernacular Languages in Uganda'. P. Ladefoged, R. Glick and C. Criper, *Language in Uganda.* London: Oxford University Press, 1972: 143–51.

Weissbourd, Bernard and Elizabeth Mertz. 'Role-Centrism Versus Legal Creativity: The Skewing of Legal Ideology Through Language'. *Law and Society Review.* 19.1, 1985: 623–59.

Welsh-Asante, Kariamu (ed.). *The African Aesthetic: Keeper of the Tradition.* Westport (CT): Greenwood Press, 1993.

Wheeler, Harvey. *Democracy in a Revolutionary Era.* New York: Frederick A. Praeger, 1968.

Whitely, Steve. 'English as a Tool of British Neocolonialism'. *East Africa Journal.* 8.12, 1971: 4–6.

Whiteley, Wilfred. H. *Swahili: The Rise of a National Language.* London: Methuen, 1969.

References

— 'Patterns of Language Use in Rural Kenya'. W. H. Whiteley (ed.), *Language in Kenya*. Nairobi: Oxford University Press, 1974a: 319–59.

— 'The Classification and Distribution of Kenya's African Languages'. W. H. Whiteley (ed.), *Language in Kenya*. Nairobi: Oxford University Press, 1974b: 13–68.

Whorf, Benjamin Lee. 'Language, Mind and Reality'. John B. Carrol (ed.), *Language, Thought and Reality: Selected Writings of Benjamin Lee Whorf*. Cambridge (MA): MIT Press, 1959: 246–70.

Williams, Colin H. *Called Unto Liberty! On Language and Nationalism*. Clevedon and Philadelphia: Multilingual Matters Ltd., 1994.

Williams, Robert I. (ed.). *Ebonics: The True Language of Black Folk*. St.Louis (MO): Institute of Black Studies, 1975.

World Bank. *Higher Education: The Lessons of Experience*. Washington, DC: World Bank, 1994.

Zawawi, Sharifa M. *Loan Words and their Effect on the Classification of Swahili Nominals*. Leiden: E. J. Brill, 1979.

INDEX

Index

Index

Index

health *see* disease; medical services
Hebrew language, 140, 208
Hellier, Rev. Canon, 161
Hindi language, 5, 206
Hinnebusch, Thomas, 167
Holloway, Joseph, 36
Hong Kong, 206
Horn of Africa, 201
Houtondji, P. J., 41
human rights, 113-14; *see also* linguistic rights; (United States) civil rights movement
Hyder, Mohammed, 161

Ibadan, 180
Igbo language, 5, 81, 83
Imperial Joint Committee on Closer Union in East Africa, 177-8
India, 5, 19, 139, 188, 197, 206
Indo-China, French, 196-7; *see also* under country
Indo-European languages, 44
International Monetary Fund, 89, 195, 199, 203-4, 211
interpreters (legal), 116-20
Interterritorial Language Committee, 177
Iran, 206
Iraq, 19
Ireland, 34
Islam, 1, 5, 29, 45, 69-70, 72, 83, 125, 127-8, 138, 163-5, 174-5, 188, 191; Algeria, 196; Ghana, 2; Iran, 206; Kenya, 108, 182-3; law, 108, 111; Lebanon, 164; Mali, 2; Nigeria, 108, 180; Oman, 82; poetry, 74, 126, 169, 171, 173, 189; Sierra Leone, 82; Songhay, 2; Sudan, 16; Tanzania, 182; Uganda, 82, 190; Zanzibar, 170; *see also* (languages) Afro-Islamic
Israel, 140, 207
Italian language, 13, 28, 96
Italy, 14

Japan, 64, 78, 101-2
Japanese language, 65
Jews, 140
Jinja, 180
Journal of Criticism, 50
journals *see* magazines
judiciary, 112-13, 116-20, 134
juries, 118-19

Kabila, Laurent, 183-4, 197
Kabwegyere, Tarsis B., 144, 178
Kamba people, 173
Kampala, 146, 158, 182-3
Kanuri language, 164
Karenga, Maulana, 39
Kawaida, 39

Kenya, 82, 108, 113, 180-1, 186; Advisory Council on African Education, 144; Department of Education, 143; Egerton University, 204; English language, 14-15, 21-2, 55, 99-100, 103, 116, 125-59, 171, 178, 183, 185, 187-8, 190; Gikuyu language, 156-7, 182-3; Kiswahili language, 14-15, 21, 35, 56, 76, 80, 95-6, 100, 103, 106, 110-12, 125-40, 144, 147-8, 151-4, 156, 159-60, 170-2, 177-8, 182, 186-8, 190; Ministry of Education, 146; Moi University, 204; Special Centre, 146; women, 87, 90, 104-5, 151
Kenya African National Union, 154, 187
Kenya Broadcasting Corporation, 152
Kenya Institute of Education, 147
Kenya Leo, 151
Kenya National Examination Council, 148
Kenya Television Network, 152
Kenya Times, 151
Kenyatta, Jomo, 27, 111, 154, 156, 159, 187
Kenyatta, Margaret, 87
Kidigo language, 64
Kiganda culture, 182
Kinigi, Mrs Sylvie, 88
kinship, 210
Kinyarwanda language, 184, 188
Kioga, M. M., 117
Kiptoon, Professor J., 148
Kirundi language, 188
Kiswahili language, 18, 26, 31, 34, 36-7, 39-40, 43, 45, 47, 49-51, 64, 69, 73, 109, 116, 161-70, 209; alphabet, 170; Democratic Republic of Congo, 81, 184, 190-1; dialects, 42, 170, 189; East Africa, 6, 15-17, 21, 35, 55-6, 76, 80, 83, 86, 95-6, 99-101, 103, 106, 110-12, 114, 125-60, 171-91, 203, 206; economic role, 172-3; ecumenicalization, 171, 175, 177-8, 188-91; integrative role, 178-88, 190; politicization, 178; secularization, 171, 178, 181, 183-5, 188-91; universalization, 171-84, 188-9, 191
Kiwanuka, Chief Justice Benedicto, 113
Koran *see* Qur'an
Korea, 18
Krapf, Reverend, 175
Krio language, 33, 71, 75, 77
Kriyol language, 71
kuitegemea, 95
Kwanzaa ceremony, 38-41

labour, 56, 101, 103; migrant, 17, 49, 90-1, 129, 138, 179-81, 183; unions *see* trade unions
Ladefoged, P., 147, 150-1, 181
Laitin, David, 100-2, 139

224

Index

Index

Milton, John, 26-7, 210-11
mining industries, 16, 90-1, 183
missionaries, 16, 55-6, 58, 115, 127, 164-5, 171, 174-9, 181, 189-90
Mobutu Sese Seko, 183-4, 188, 197
Mohammed Siad Barre, 7, 96
Moi, Daniel Arap, 111, 113, 159
Mombasa, 170, 180, 182-3, 189
Mondlane, Eduardo, 41
Monthly Review, 151
Monitor, The, 152
Moore, Robert, 31
Morocco, 80
Mozambique, 56, 78, 91, 170, 191
Mozambique National Resistance, 91
Mphalele, Ezekiel, 137
Mtembezi, John Innis, 50
Muddathir Abd Al-Rahim, 20
Mugabe, Robert, 91
Mugabe, Mrs Sally, 87
Muhammad (Prophet), 72, 163
Mukama, Ruth, 153
Mukiibi, Catherine, 148
multiculturalism, 51, 202-5, 207
multilingualism, 54-5, 81, 117, 136, 180; India, 19, 139; Kenya, 99-100, 111, 134, 137, 146, 149-50, 153, 187-8; Nigeria, 5, 19; Tanzania, 134; Uganda, 134, 137, 149; women, 17, 86-7, 89
Museveni, Yoweri, 131, 150, 152, 155, 158, 187, 190
Mushega, Amanya, 155
Mushi, S., 27, 210
Mutesa II, Kabaka of Buganda, 141, 157
Mutiiri, 50, 114-15
Mutunga, Willy, 116
Mwaura, Peter, 53
Mwyinyi, Ali Hassan, 134
Myanmar, 197

Nairobi, 146, 150-1, 158, 182-3
Nairobi Law Monthly, 151
Nairobi Weekly, 151
Nakawa, 146
names, 37-8
Namibia, 13-14, 197
nationalism, 34, 39-40, 49, 128, 144-5, 195, 207; cultural, 185-6, 188; ethnic, 205; linguistic, 4-9, 51, 135, 140, 154-7, 160-1, 165-6, 168, 197; neonationalism, 53, 55-6, 65n, racial, 8
nationhood, 3-4
Native American languages, 47
Negritic languages, 44, 163
Negritude, 205
New Vision, 152
newspapers, 151-2, 159

Ngabo, 152
Ngugi wa Thiong'o, 37, 50, 54, 114-15, 152, 156-7, 160
Nigeria, 4-5, 18-19, 36, 73, 75, 77-8, 81-3, 92, 108, 112, 131, 133, 137, 160, 167, 180
Nile, River, 1, 15-16
Nilotic languages, 17, 132
Nilotic peoples, 17, 131-2, 190
Njonjo, Charles, 130, 154
Njoya the Great, Sultan, 72
Nkrumah, Kwame, 32
Nobel Prize, 211
North Atlantic Treaty Organization, 195
Nubi language, 164
numeracy, 1-2, 206
Nurse, Derek, 166-7
Nyerere, Julius K., 25-7, 31, 95, 134, 187, 210

Obote, Milton, 26-7, 82, 96, 99, 131, 155, 158-9, 180, 210-11
O'Flaherty (missionary), 175
Ogaden, 4, 76
Ogot, Grace, 87
Ohly, Rajmund, 166
Okigbo, Christopher, 75
Olowo, Bernadette, 87
Oman, 82, 133
Ominde Commission, 146-7
OPEAC, 207
OPEC, 207
oral tradition, 2-3, 5, 7, 69, 72-5, 79, 121; *see also* courts of law
Organization of African Unity, 88, 206
Organization of Economic Co-operation and Development, 199
Organization of the Islamic Conference, 207
Orominya language, 161
Osman, Dan Fodio, 74

Padmore, George, 32
Pakistan, 197
Pan-African Congress (Sixth), 35
pan-Africanism, 32-6, 38, 40, 48, 88, 112, 158, 160, 185-6, 205
parliaments, 85-6, 95-6, 99-100, 110-12, 122, 129-30, 134, 154, 185, 187
p'Bitek, Okot, 75, 94n
Peace of Westphalia (1648), 4
peasants *see* agriculture
People, The, 151
periodicals *see* magazines
Periplus of the Erythraean Sea, 166-7
Phelps-Stokes Commission, 143
Philippines, 199
philosophy, 41
Phoenicians, 169, 209
Pidgin languages, 23, 33, 71, 75, 77, 165-7, 206

226